Nasty Women

Nasty Women: Transgressive Womanhood in American History is part of the Virginia Tech Student Publications series. This series contains book-length works authored and edited by Virginia Tech undergraduate and graduate students and published in collaboration with Virginia Tech Publishing. Often these books are the culmination of class projects for advanced or capstone courses. The series provides the opportunity for students to write, edit, and ultimately publish their own books for the world to learn from and enjoy.

Nasty Women

Transgressive Womanhood
in American History

A class project by the students in the Department
of History at Virginia Tech

Edited by
Marian Mollin

With the Students of
HIST 4914 - Spring 2020

VIRGINIA TECH DEPARTMENT OF HISTORY
IN ASSOCIATION WITH

BLACKSBURG ♦ VIRGINIA

First published 2021 by the Virginia Tech Department of History in
association with Virginia Tech Publishing.

Virginia Tech Department of History
431 Major Williams Hall
220 Stanger Street
Blacksburg, VA 24061

Virginia Tech Publishing
University Libraries at Virginia Tech
560 Drillfield Dr.
Blacksburg, VA 24061

Nasty women: transgressive womanhood in American history / edited by
Marian Mollin, with the spring 2020 students of HIST 4914. Blacksburg,
Virginia : Virginia Tech Department of History, in association with Virginia
Tech Publishing, 2021 | Includes bibliographical references. | This collection
of essays began as a class project for a Virginia Tech Department of History
undergraduate capstone research seminar (HIST 4914), focussing on the
history of American women who transgressed cultural bounds and societal
constraints.

ISBN: 978-1-949373-51-6 (pbk) | ISBN: 978-1-949373-52-3 (PDF) | ISBN: 978-1-
949373-53-0 (epub) | DOI: https://doi.org/10.21061/nasty-women

Women—United States—Social conditions. 2. Women slaves—United States—
Social conditions. 3. Women in public life—United States. 4. Women in
popular culture—United States. 5. Feminism—United States. I. Mollin, Marian

Cover design by Liv Wisnewski. See cover image credits on p. 249.

Contents

Acknowledgments vii

Introduction 1
#TeamNastyWomen

Part I. Making the Move from Private to Public

1. Resistance: Strength of the Enslaved Women's Spirit 7
Alyssa Thompson

2. "I feel O so lonely and desolate": White Northern and 23
Southern Women's Feelings of Loneliness and Sadness
during the Civil War
Gillian Barth

3. The American Plan: How Women Came to Be Viewed as 41
Dangerous
Caroline McLean

4. Alice Roosevelt and the Rise of the Infamous American 59
Woman
Liv Wisnewski

5. Paving Her Own Best Way: Lillian Gilbreth's Journey From 75
Housewife to Career Woman
Helen Hickman

Part II. Wartime Opportunities

6. Fighting Nazis: A Collective of Trailblazing American 95
Women in the 1930s and 1940s
Savannah Lawhorne

7. The All-American Girls Professional Baseball League: The New Women of World War II   109

Madison Sheehan

8. Seeing Eleanor: The First Lady of the World   127

Olivia Wood

Part III. Popular Culture and Modern Women

9. "Funny Like A Guy": Women in American Standup Comedy   145

Elizabeth Sholtis

10. A Different Kind of Feminine: How Marilyn Monroe Challenged Expectations of Womanhood   161

Alicia Aucoin

11. Mary Tyler Moore: The Unlikely Feminist   177

Grace Barth

12. A Tight White Super Suit: How Women's Underground Comics Came to Be   191

Trenton Spilman

13. Dolly Parton: The Appalachian Advocate, Wild Wife, and Sexualized Singer   203

Bethany Stewart

14. Keepin' It Movin': Appalachian Women's Resistance Through Music   223

Kat McGowan

Notes on Contributors   245

Photo Credits   249

Acknowledgments

The chapter authors of this book are particularly grateful for the assistance given by Dr. Marian Mollin, who guided each of us in our own unique writing and revision path and dedicated extensive time to teach us how to become historical writers. Dr. Mollin also taught us the importance of teamwork and friendship, and that they hold just as much value as the words written in these chapters. We would like to express our deepest gratitude for her patience, understanding, and hard work in taking this book to publication.

Additionally, our research would not have been possible without the support of the University Libraries at Virginia Tech. Research librarians and Interlibrary Loan support staff helped us to locate and obtain necessary primary and secondary sources. The Virginia Tech Publishing team—especially Robert Browder, Lauren Holt, and Grace Baggett—played an instrumental role in turning our writing into a polished publication. We could not have completed this book without them.

We would like to dedicate this book to all the "Nasty Women" who came before our time. Without them, women would not enjoy the freedoms we have today. This book is also dedicated to "Nasty Women," now and in the future, that continue the fight for women's rights. We hope that these women will follow their predecessors to reach new heights of equality.

Introduction

#TEAMNASTYWOMEN

This collection of essays began as a class project for a Virginia Tech Department of History capstone research seminar and was transformed into an act of resilient defiance to the many disruptions caused by the spring 2020 COVID-19 pandemic. Our class topic, a shared exploration into the history of American women who transgressed cultural bounds and societal constraints, brought us deep into the experiences of women who dared to resist the odds of their times and who worked to live their lives on their own terms. In response to the pandemic, the students of this class decided to resist the odds and complete their semester and the research projects that comprise this book on their own terms as well. The result is a volume that reflects the determination and will to persist of both the student authors and the women they chose to study.

This volume is very much a collaborative endeavor. Under the broad framework of *Nasty Women in American History*, each student author selected a topic of their choice, engaged in original primary source research, and developed their research and analysis into a chapter-length essay. In addition to writing each chapter, class members also chose the book's organizational structure, crafted a title, designed the cover, and engaged in extensive editing and copyediting. While the class professor, Dr. Marian Mollin, served as "head coach," sounding board, and developmental editor, this book is primarily the product of an intentionally collective student-centered effort that drew on everyone's interests and skills. The students' nickname for themselves–#TeamNastyWomen–quite accurately highlights their shared commitment to making this book a reality.

Part I: Making the Move from Private to Public

The first five chapters examine the way women pushed the boundaries of the private sphere and increased their interaction with the public world. From the early nineteenth century through the mid-twentieth century, women in all social classes were expected to remain in the private sphere, sheltered from the more masculine public arena. Despite societal prescriptions, there have always been women who transgressed the limitations of their time. The first chapter, "Resistance: Strength of the Enslaved Women's Spirit in Virginia in the Last Decades of Slavery," focuses on enslaved women that rebelled against the institution of slavery in an era where they were expected to be obedient to their masters. These women completely disregarded societal hierarchies in an effort to maintain a sense of self and dignity, while also breaking out of the private realm. The second chapter, "'I feel O so lonely and desolate': White Northern and Southern Women's Feelings of Loneliness and Sadness during the Civil War," examines the diaries and letters of Sarah Morgan Dawson, Kate Stone, Catharine Peirce, and Rachel Cormany. Each of these women, from different regions and different social classes, expressed similar sentiments of apprehension, loneliness, and sadness as they navigated new domestic lives when their husbands, fathers, and brothers left their homes to fight in the Civil War.

Chapter three, titled, "The American Plan: How Women Came to Be Viewed as Dangerous," analyzes women's promiscuity in relation to the Chamberlain-Kahn Act, also called the American Plan. This act attempted to control the spread of venereal disease in the United States and allowed officials to arrest and quarantine any woman that appeared promiscuous. The study of the types of women arrested under the American Plan and the specific goals of the American Plan revealed a shift in the public's perception of so-called promiscuous women during the early twentieth century. The chapter "Alice Roosevelt and the Rise of the American Infamous Woman" takes a long view of Alice's life, examining how she flouted standards of femininity and ignored societal norms across several decades. Alice's staunch refusal to bend to anyone's will but her own earned her a place in the emerging celebrity culture of the early twentieth century, and her continued insistence to play by her own rules canonized her as America's original "Infamous Woman." The last chapter in this section, "Paving Her Own Best Way: Lillian Gilbreth and Working Women in the Early Twentieth Century," explores how Lillian Gilbreth transformed herself from a housewife and mother into a successful engineer. Gilbreth balanced both her family and a career while proving herself in the male-dominated field of engineering and advocating for other women in their endeavors. The women discussed in these chapters placed themselves into public society in a time where they were expected to remain within their prescribed gender roles. They broke down barriers against opportunities for women and fought for what they believed in, whether that was resistance to slavery, recognition for their accomplishments, or simply the ability to go out and have a good time.

Part II: Wartime Opportunities

The next three chapters describe the more active public role of women in the World War II era. While these women answered the call to action during the 1930s and 1940s, they still faced gender discrimination. Nevertheless, these women continued their efforts to assert themselves in positions where women were not typically found. By asserting themselves, these women inspired young girls of the next generation who were interested in roles such as journalist, soldier, athlete, and political activist.

In the first chapter of this section, the researcher focuses heavily on women taking a frontline role in World War II. These women left their homes and broke traditional gender roles to help win the war just as men risked their lives for freedom, liberty, and peace. These women armed themselves with a house for refugees, a voice, or a pen. While this first chapter speaks of a more frontline approach, the women of the second chapter continued to break traditional gender norms by playing a male-only sport. Even though they were required to fit a mold acceptable for the public, they represented the change in how women were viewed as working mothers and wives. They continued the effort of women moving into the workforce during World War II by separating themselves from their role as homemakers and creating their own identity, as in the section's final chapter when one woman used her position to forever change the role of America's First Lady and the political potential that position holds. This woman used her position to break through the barrier of the home to speak to the women of America about politics and issues both domestic and abroad.

Part III: Popular Culture and Modern Women

Even with the advancement of women in politics and in the workplace, younger women coming of age in the second half of the twentieth century looked to the media and popular culture to build their sense of self. This section explores the ways women of popular culture used their platform to transgress the status quo during the second wave of feminism. While the chapters in this section span across region and class status, they all discuss performance as a means of resistance and expression.

The first chapter in this section, "'Funny Like a Guy': Women in American Standup Comedy" outlines the careers of four of America's first female standup comedians and explores the impact of their careers on ideas about American womanhood. "A Different Kind of Feminine: How Marilyn Monroe Challenged Expectations of Womanhood," offers a narrative of the actress and American icon, Marilyn Monroe, as a strong, confident woman who challenged the societal expectations of women to be maternal and domesticated housewives through her personal life, career, and sexuality. "Mary Tyler Moore: The Unlikely Feminist" analyzes how *The Mary Tyler Moore Show* supported feminist ideals and beliefs such as equal pay, independence, and reproductive rights through television. "A Tight White Super Suit: How Women's Underground Comics Came To Be," discusses how inequality and marginalization of the comic book industry forced women to write comics underground. "Dolly Parton: The Appalachian Advocate, Wild Wife, and Sexualized Singer" explores how Parton, the infamous country singer, reinforced and rejected traditional aspects of Southern womanhood throughout the 1970s and 1980s. The final chapter, "Keepin' It Movin': Appalachian Women's Resistance through Music" delves into the music of the Appalachian region and examines how this music genre was used to both resist women's unique oppression and acted as a cathartic release from the trying experiences both in and out of the home.

While each of these chapters examines a different medium from television, music, and comic books, the women detailed in these chapters all use media to challenge traditional ideas about womanhood and display new ideas about performing femininity. Ultimately, these chapters demonstrate how women during the second half of the twentieth century used popular media and media culture as a means to express and create power within themselves and their communities.

PART I

MAKING THE MOVE FROM PRIVATE TO PUBLIC

1. Resistance: Strength of the Enslaved Women's Spirit

ALYSSA THOMPSON

...muma had sed don't let no body bother yo' principle cause dat wuz all yo' had.
–Mrs. Minnie Fulkes[1]

Mrs. Minnie Fulkes, enslaved in Chesterfield County, Virginia, was roughly five years old when she obtained her freedom.[2] As a young girl, she gained devastating knowledge of her condition during her years of slavery and learned resilience and strength from her mother. Enslaved women in the Antebellum South, such as Fulkes and her mother, strongly held on to their belief that the horrid conditions of slavery were morally corrupt. They resisted their oppressors until emancipation in 1865; in some cases, women resisted slavery even after the war when their masters refused to relinquish them. Against unimaginable opposition, enslaved women sustained their efforts to fight back against their captors with a multitude of tactics. Women banded together and resisted their masters in an effort to maintain a sense of pride and agency.

The historical conversation about American slavery is as old as the peculiar institution itself. The shift towards focusing on the specific plight of enslaved women is relatively recent. However, in the late 1990s, historian Deborah Gray White began the discussion of the double-edged sword faced by enslaved women. Not only was there a racial hierarchy in the slaveholding South, but there was a gendered hierarchy in place as well. The racial hierarchy placed whites above people of color, while the gendered hierarchy placed men above their female counterparts. Enslaved women were placed at the bottom of both these hierarchies and thus felt the blunt ends of being both African American and women.

Other historians, such as Stephanie Camp, delve further into the lives of enslaved women by researching different aspects of resistance such as secret gatherings at night and temporary truancy.[3] Many historians, such as Richard Dunn, Mary Frederickson, and Delores Walters, focused on case studies of specific women in the early 2010s. Dunn wrote of Winney

Grimshaw, a Virginian slave, and focused on tragedies such as the sexual coercion women endured as well as the aspect of familial separation.[4] Frederickson and Walters wrote of the infamous Margaret Garner, a fugitive slave that killed her young infant and intended to kill her other children upon being captured in 1856 in an effort to avoid seeing them returned to a life of slavery.[5] Enslaved women proved their undying resilience and spirit by their continuous efforts to resist the perils of slavery in its final years. The topic of gendered resistance to slavery in the American South is of great significance because it proves the sheer strength of the human spirit.

In this chapter, I will explore several different forms of resistance demonstrated by enslaved women in Virginia in the last few decades of slavery (roughly 1845–1865). I organized the various acts of resistance into three categories: truancy, unity, and overt resistance. Truancy came in two forms: short duration and the attempt to permanently flee towards freedom. Unity among enslaved women undoubtedly existed in many forms. I highlight the unity illustrated by mainly focusing on illegal gatherings held by the enslaved under the darkness of night. I discuss the various forms of overt resistance carried out by enslaved women. I aim to prove how their acts of courage were not only a stand against human bondage but a testament to the nerve and strength of these brave women. Furthermore, this chapter illustrates that enslaved women sensed the changing tides in the United States and became even more defiant of their masters in the final years of institutionalized slavery.

In the last couple of decades that slavery thrived within the United States, enslaved black women and men sensed that they had potential to force change in their circumstances. Virginia's plantations were not as large or labor-intensive as cotton plantations further South. Located in the Upper South, enslaved people in Virginia did not have to travel as far as those in the Lower South to reach freedom. The abolition movement gained significant strength in the nineteenth century, yet southern slaveholders were not willing to relinquish their labor force. Slavery held strong in the South, especially in Virginia as the Civil War drew close. Two slave rebellions, Gabriel's Rebellion of 1800 and Nat Turner's Rebellion of 1831, proved that enslaved people were willing to lend efforts to help abolition succeed. Women enslaved in the South fought against their captors in a variety of ways as a means to control their own lives and find a sense of agency in a society that depicted them as mere property.

Enslaved women found themselves in a particularly vulnerable position in Virginia. The slave trade was Virginia's largest industry in the nineteenth century, with Richmond as the largest slave auction center in the Upper South.[6] When women resisted against their masters, they were threatened with the auction block. Because women were not only enslaved but victims of sexual assault, women frequently had good reason to fight back in an effort to protect themselves, resulting in their sale down South. Enslaved women in Virginia were not willing to sit idly by under the cruelties of slavery.

A well-known form of resistance to slavery is runaways. However, not all runaways departed the plantation with the same goal in mind. Some slaves escaped slavery to hide out in the nearby woods or swamps. Historians have dubbed this type of runaway slave "truants" or "absentees."[7] Women were more drawn to flee for short durations instead of permanent attempts at freedom due to their maternal and familial duties.[8] During the years in which a female slave was strong enough to make the treacherous journey north, she was also in her reproductive prime. This time period of an enslaved woman's life saw pregnancy, child-rearing, and care.[9] All of these factors made women less likely, as well as less able, to run away permanently and leave their families behind. Motherly obligations did not hinder enslaved women from escaping the conditions of captivity altogether, as women would frequently bolt temporarily from captivity.

One of the most common reasons enslaved women fled to the woods was to escape beatings from their masters. In a 1937 interview, Armaci Adams mentioned the time she hid from a beating. Adams, born in 1859, recalled giving food to her runaway uncle as a young child on her plantation near Norfolk, Virginia: "I slipped in de kitchen an' brung 'im all de 'llasses an' co'nbread I could carry."[10] Her master, Isaac Hunter, caught her and came after her with a whip even though she was just five years old. Adams escaped the beating by running and hiding in the bushes. Due to her young age, Adams likely did not run far and returned to her fellow slaves after a relatively short truancy. Some would stay in the woods for a much longer duration to escape the wretched conditions they faced on the plantation.

Slaves would often take to the woods and remain truant for weeks at a time. Reverend Ishrael Massie, a former slave, remarked in a 1937 interview, "aw Chile, woods stayed full of niggers."[11] Slaves survived in the woods nearby their plantations by relying on their enslaved community and seeking meals in the cover of night.[12] When feasible, truant slaves also stole hogs and other livestock from surrounding farms for sustenance.[13] Charles Crawley, a former slave from Lunenburg County, discussed this way of life in a 1937 interview: "some of 'em lived in de woods off of takin' things, sech as hogs, corn an' vegetables from other folks farm."[14] Many women stayed in the woods as long as they could. They feared that upon return, their master would beat them mercilessly. It was not uncommon for women to refuse to come back until they received word from fellow slaves that their master promised not to beat them. This was the case for Sallie Douchard.[15] Douchard's grandson, Lorenzo L. Ivy, recalled being told about the time his grandmother stayed in the woods for roughly a month to escape the constant beatings she received: "so she run 'way to de woods an' stayed in hidin' on de day time an' come out onlies' at night."[16] Douchard frequently visited the plantation to see her daughter and receive food. Her master told Douchard's daughter that if she decided to come back within a few days, he would not beat her for her truancy. Douchard eventually decided to come back and was not harmed for her absence. However, not all masters kept their word. Due to the fear of being beaten to death upon returning, some slaves left the plantation without planning to come back.

Knowing that the journey north to freedom was dangerous and not guaranteed to be successful, some women chose to live in the woods permanently. Interviews from emancipated slaves indicate that there were a great deal of families living in caves in the ground not too far from their plantation. Reverend Massie briefly mentioned a man that lived in the Virginia woods with his wife and kids.[17] A similar account surfaced in another freedman's interview. A similar account surfaced in an interview with Arthur Green, where he recalls a man he knew that took off for the woods with his wife and started a family in a cave:[18] "He lived in a cave in de groun' fer fifteen yeahs 'fo' Lee's surrender. He made himself a den under de de groun'; he an' his wife, an' raised fifteen chillum down dar."[19] They survived by stealing livestock from plantations within the area. Enslaved communities still kept in touch with these fugitives, supporting them with resources they could afford to give up. These families financially gained from their masters through theft, and old communities shared what they could with the fugitives. Fugitive families that lived in the woods disrupted the social hierarchy and institution of slavery in the South.

While fleeing was not always a viable option for enslaved women, they often helped those who made the difficult decision to run. Mrs. Jennie Patterson, a Chesterfield County native, recalls helping a woman that had run and sought refuge in her cabin.[20] Patterson awoke to a knock at her door in the middle of the night and a stranger asking to hide out until dawn. Without a second thought, Patterson welcomed the woman into her bed as the search party ran past. After the woman's departure the next morning, Patterson never saw her again. Patterson knew all too well of the danger of being caught harboring a runaway. In the same interview, she reminisced of the time her mistress had a man killed because he had plans of running away. Even so, she tangled with a runaway without hesitation. As she put it, "we never tole on each other."[21]

As the end of slavery approached the South, enslaved women continued to disrupt the lives of southern slave owners. As the Civil War ensued and Union lines encroached on more plantations, enslaved women had a better chance of running towards freedom without being killed. Slaves flocked to the Union Army as they passed their plantations. Men had the opportunity to join the army and fight against the Confederacy. Some women chose to go to Union camps with their loved ones and perform domestic duties such as cooking and washing for the troops.[22] Others took advantage of Union boats that traveled back and forth from the Confederacy to Union lines, using them as an opportunity to escape their captivity. A Virginian man by the name of Richard Slaughter recalled hiding out on a Union gunboat, the *Meritanza*, alongside his father and mother in the summer of 1862.[23] He detailed that his father and other men boarded the ship under the cover of night. The ship fired towards the towns and plantations to scare the white people off so that more slaves, such as his mother and other women, as well as children and the elderly, could board. With the Union Army pushing onward, enslaved women seized their opportunity to break towards freedom, thus hammering the final nails into the coffin of slavery.

Women resisted the foundations of slavery by choosing to be loyal to one another instead of their white owners. Under the institution of slavery, a woman's primary concern was meant to be of service to her master, not to her enslaved community.[24] This was the case when it came to an enslaved woman's own children versus the master's children, whom she was tasked with taking care of. While masters tasked black women with taking care of their white children, these women often simultaneously took care of the children of their enslaved community. Louise Jones, for example, recalled tying meat skin to a string and allowing the slave children to suckle on it while she watched over the white children of the plantation.[25] By taking care of enslaved children while they were supposed to be giving undivided attention to the white children, they pushed the boundaries of their enslavement. Enslaved women realized that they could break traditional roles by putting the needs of their loved ones before their captors' wishes and maintaining a sense of solidarity among fellow slaves.

Religion was one of the ways enslaved women were able to break the molds of the Antebellum South while also congregating and rejoicing with one another. Many slave owners across the South held a policy to not allow unsupervised religious gatherings among their slaves. This policy resulted out of fear that their slaves would become enlightened and be able to plan coordinated upheaval. Even so, the policies were often placed in vain as the enslaved would often worship at night despite the risk of patrollers finding them and physically retaliating for breaking traditional practices.[26] Mrs. Fulkes recalled putting a large iron pot upside down at the door where they were worshipping in an effort to capture the sound so that the patrollers would not hear their songs and prayers.[27] The saying "turn down the pots" signified that a secret meeting was going to be held.[28] In some cases, slaves filled the pots with water in an effort to drown out even more sound.[29] These gatherings were of great significance to enslaved men and women as they continued to transgress orders at the risk of vicious beatings.

Many women looked towards religion as a way to escape the pains of everyday life under the violence of slavery. Enslaved individuals passed down religious songs from generation to generation over the years of human bondage within the Antebellum South. Religion gave enslaved women hope of salvation and a day where the horrors of slavery were long gone. Mrs. Williams, a freedwoman from Norfolk, sang a song praising God in a recorded interview where she disclosed beatings and murders she witnessed on her plantation.[30] Religious songs were also an important way for enslaved communities to mark the Sabbath and holidays such as Easter and

Christmas.[31] Julia Frazier, born in 1854, recalled that "de slaves would get together an' would sing an' have a big time."[32] Music was an integral part of celebrations since enslaved women did not have abundant resources to offer one another on special occasions. Although this may not seem significant to resistance, these songs gave enslaved women a sense of faith and community. This sense of faith and community strengthened their spirits.

Not all secret gatherings and traditions had religious undertones. Enslaved men and women ran off at night to take "pleasure in their own bodies" as scholar Stephanie Camp claimed in her 2002 article, "The Pleasures of Resistance: Enslaved Women and Body Politics in the Plantation South, 1830-1861."[33] At these "outlaw dances" men and women drank alcohol, danced, and dated one another.[34] Freedwoman Nancy Williams, born 1847, reminisced on these secret gatherings fondly: "Whoops! Dem dances was somepin ... An' sech music!".[35] Dressed in her homemade clothes and shoes, Williams escaped to a cabin in the woods to gamble, dance, and court young men. Another freedwoman from Virginia, Sally Ashton, had similar gatherings in the final years of slavery.[36] When discussing these gatherings, she claimed, "Chile, when I was a girl guess I'd ruther dance den eat."[37] However, Ashton's experience was unique from Williams in that her master authorized his slaves to have festive gatherings on Saturdays.[38] Even so, this unity was resistive to the institution itself, albeit not to her master specifically. Enslaved women broke through the barriers of slavery by leaving the plantation and partaking in festive activities with other enslaved communities.

Under the abuses of slavery, women found camaraderie as a way to collectively cope. Physical abuse did not always equate to whippings and beatings. Death was often a white man's final resort when it came to keeping order and obedience among his human chattel. In a late 1930s recorded interview with an unidentified freedwomen from Petersburg, Virginia, the women interviewed recalled the tragic hanging of two female runaways.[39] Before they were murdered, they stood as one and sang a song as their final act. In the face of death, these women chose not to submit to their master one last time, but to carry out an act of unity and bravery with one another. Enslaved women were tortured to horrifying ends, but by uniting together they were able to rebel against the pillars of slavery in the face of evil.

Perhaps the most obvious form of resistance that enslaved women partook in was overt verbal and physical resistance. As the Civil War progressed, more women began to assert their right to freedom and blatantly resist their masters.[40] After hundreds of years of oppression, enslaved women were not prepared to passively wait for freedom to reach them. In the final decades of institutionalized slavery, enslaved women's spirit of resistance was stronger than ever.

Verbal resistance put enslaved women in direct opposition to their oppressors. Verbal resistance ranged from taunting to proclaiming freedom to begging for death. In all circumstances, these brave women wanted to be heard by the people who cared to listen to them the least.

Some women took their chances by heckling their abusers. Mrs. Eliza Robinson, a freedwoman from Richmond, recollected about one of these "unruly and mean" women, her cousin Jane Minor.[41] Minor, who was allegedly "always up to some mischief," waited one night until her master had company visiting in the parlor and lifted up her clothing over her head and taunted, "Marse, is you gwine whip me? Here I is."[42] Her master was so dumbfounded by Minor that he apparently never beat her. By completely disregarding the racial and gender hierarchy that dominated the Antebellum South, Minor proved that she did not fear or respect her master or slavery itself. Enslaved women found that they could push the boundaries of slavery, sometimes without punishment.

After years of obeying instruction for their every move, some women stood their ground in a verbal manner despite the threat of physical consequences. Throughout the last decades of slavery, the enslaved population did complete an intense workload, yet it is evident that everyone had their breaking point. Mrs. Virginia Hayes Shepherd, born roughly 11 years before the end of the Civil War, recalled the day her mother decided to stand her ground.[43] One day her mother had worked as fast as she could when an overseer threatened that she would be beaten if she did not increase her speed. She paused and said, "go a-head, kill me if you want. I'm working as fast as I can and I just can't do more."[44] Shepherd's mother had reached her limit that day, and as Shepherd noted, "they saw she was at the place where she didn't care whether she died or not: so they left her alone."[45] When the human spirit has reached the point where they are not afraid of death, it has no regard for the strongest and most vile of earthly forces, even slavery.

As the whispers of the Emancipation Proclamation spread through the plantations of the South, many women felt empowered enough by this news to proclaim their freedom before they were freed by Yankee forces. This was the case of Betty Jones' grandmother in Charlottesville, Virginia.[46] As she worked in the fields, another slave came and told her that "Marse Lincum done set all us slaves free."[47] Jones' grandmother immediately dropped her hoe and ran seven miles back to the home of her mistress and screamed: "I'se free! Yes, I'se free! Ain't got to work fo' you no mo'."[48] Her grandmother claimed that seeing the tears stream from her mistress's eyes proved that the rumor of emancipation was true. Even young children were aware of President Lincoln's proclamation. Another freedwoman from Charlottesville, Mrs. Margaret Terry, born in 1857, was aware of the Emancipation Proclamation as a young girl during the Civil War.[49] In a 1937 interview, she recalled the time she walked in on her mother being beaten by her mistress. At the young age of roughly six to eight, Terry had the courage to intervene by yelling at her mistress, "stop! Stop beating my mother! She is free!"[50] She pulled her mother apart from her abuser and stated, "let her alone; my mother is free!"[51] This statement infuriated her mistress who snapped back at Terry that she knew too much. After the proclamation was issued in September of 1862, it became clear to both slaveholders and enslaved people that the days of this institution were numbered and enslaved women saw to it that they aided the abolition of slavery within the South by resisting the very foundations of slavery.

Not only did enslaved women speak out against their abusers, but at times they would take measures to inflict emotional pain on their masters, as had been done to them. Fannie Berry, enslaved in Appomattox, Virginia, for over 20 years, inflicted pain on her mistress in a peculiar way.[52] Her mistress had a beloved pet dog that would entertain company by doing tricks and biting at Berry's younger brother's toes. One day, Berry strung up the dog and hung it from a tree. No one ever attributed this act of defiance to her. Although Berry generally spoke favorably of her mistress, it is clear she held her family above her owner. Acts such as these were symbolic of the hatred enslaved women held for their loved ones' pain being used as a source of amusement for the slaveholding class.

The final aspect of resistance in this chapter is that of overt physical resistance. Women physically fighting back against their captors was undoubtedly the most severe form of resistance. Not only did physical altercations carry the risk of grave physical retaliation, but it could also result in being ripped away from one's community to be sold further south. This was the case of Lizzie Stanfield, who frequently fought back against her master.[53] After beating her master, he had officers come down to the plantation to arrest her. In a 1937 interview, her brother Jess Stanfield recalled, "[d]ey tried to beat her an' couldn't, so dey sent for Big Jim, a slave, to hold her while dey beat her near to death."[54] Afterwards she was sent to the auction block. Not only were women breaking the molds of the racial hierarchy of slavery, but they often quarreled against men that were much larger and stronger than themselves. However, when enslaved women were pushed to the point of corporeal retribution, their spirit was more forceful than muscle.

At times, when patrollers discovered hidden gatherings, those caught would resort to overt physical measures to avoid capture. Mrs. Fulkes recalled how they retaliated against the patrollers for whipping the "poor souls [that] were praying to God to free 'em from dat awful bondage."[55] In order to delay patrollers from dispersing the congregation, the enslaved placed vines across the road to tangle up their horses and, on occasion, break their legs. She even claimed that one particular time, the vine got wrapped around a patroller's neck and choked him to death. Fulkes was unremorseful as she and her loved ones went through generations of blatant abuse at the hands of white people; the patroller's death was justified in their minds.

Another former enslaved woman from Fluvanna County remembered how her congregation would avoid being punished by the patrollers. Betty Jones, born circa 1845, recalled a night when they had a large gathering in a cabin.[56] As patrollers had come to the door, two slaves in attendance shoveled hot coals on them while Jones and others made a break for it. No one was captured that night. With the help of their fellow enslaved men, women rebelled against the white patriarchy at any cost.

Physical resistance was also resorted to while enslaved women fought off sexual advances from white men. The aforementioned Fannie Berry, born in 1841, spoke out about how she and fellow women rejected unwanted sexual encounters with their captors.[57] In a 1937 interview Berry described an assault from an overseer:

I wuz one slave dat de poor white man had his match… One tried to throw me, but he couldn't. We tusseled an' knocked over chairs an' when I got a grip I scratched his face all to pieces; an' dar wuz no more bothering Fannie from him.[58]

Berry knew that fighting back could have resulted in her death, but that knowledge did not stop her from maintaining control of her own body. She disclosed instances where other women were not as fortunate as her to an interviewer, Susie Byrd. At the end of recalling this courageous brawl, she remarked, "us Colored women had to go through plenty, I tell you."[59] Enslaved women truly had been treated terribly by their masters, yet their spiritual strength remained.

When backed into a corner, enslaved women used what little resources were available in an attempt to defend themselves. Mrs. Fannie Berry also recalled a time when a fellow enslaved woman fought against a predatory advance from their master.[60] Berry described the woman, Sukie, as a large woman who was not particularly vocal. One day Sukie was boiling soap when her master told her to undress. After Sukie refused, a physical altercation broke out. A fire ignited in Sukie and she pushed her master backward into a pot of soap, burning "him near to death."[61] Although Berry claims that their master did not bother his enslaved women any longer, Sukie's master still sold her off for her retaliation. In any case, Sukie was able to use her surroundings to defend herself while completely disregarding the complete control slave owners were meant to have over their slaves.

When enslaved women made the decision to leave their plantations, they resorted to physical retaliation when their masters tried to apprehend them. As previously discussed, it was not uncommon for runaways to rely on their community for food and sustenance while they resided in the woods. This was this case with West Turner's aunt Sallie.[62] Turner, born circa 1842, recalled hearing his master bang on his father's cabin at night when he knew his aunt Sallie was inside eating. Instead of giving up and returning to her captor, Aunt Sallie grabbed a scythe and bolted out of the cabin door, swinging it towards her master. "She cut her way out, den turned roun' and backed off into de woods, an' ole Marsa was just screamin' and cussin' … Didn't no one foller her neither."[63] She successfully made her escape and that was the last Turner ever saw of his aunt. Women were willing to risk everything to resist the conditions under slavery even if it meant leaving their earthly possessions and loved ones behind.

As it became clear that slavery was dead and the Union triumphed, some women chose to show one last sign of resistance towards their old masters. Mrs. Katie Blackwell Johnson's master beat Johnson up until the very moment he heard of the Union lines approaching his land.[64] At the time Johnson was just five years old. As the Yankees approached, Johnson's master grabbed her and trapped her head between his legs as he whipped her. Just as he had heard the news about approaching Union troops, her master attempted to get up to run, and Johnson conducted one last act of defiance by biting him on the leg. Armaci Adams was also young when the Civil War ended and did not realize she was free.[65] She remained enslaved for roughly seven years after the war until an old man told her not to take any more beatings because she was free. In an interview she recalled how she gained her freedom after receiving a beating from her master's son: "I drew back an' hit him as hard as I could an' ran 'way cross de fiel. I never did come back."[66] Even after the war, some Southerners tried to hold on to the Antebellum South; as long as there was bondage, enslaved women rebelled against it.

In the concluding decades of slavery, enslaved women were involved in several forms of resistance. Through truancy they undermined the notion that they were property that could not be removed from the hands of their masters. Short truancies were exceedingly disruptive in that they were frequent, and the slave community took part in supporting absentees living in the woods at night. Permanent runaways were an ultimate betrayal of the structure of slavery because they removed portions of the South's labor force and the slaveholding class's financial investments. Through maintaining a sense of unity among enslaved women, loyalty was placed within their faith and community instead of towards the masters. Women held one another higher than they held whites. This in itself breached the pillars that kept slavery stable. Lastly, overt resistance was the most forceful and dangerous way enslaved women resisted the perils of slavery.

Regardless of the physical beatings they received for blatantly disrespecting and physically resisting their captors, enslaved women continued to defend themselves and their principle, especially in the dying moments of their servitude. Enslaved women did not passively await their freedom, but proved their undying strength by their continuous efforts to rebel in the last decades of the most despicable American institution.

Notes

1. Interview with Minnie Fulkes, March 5, 1937, in *Federal Writers' Project: Slave Narrative Project*, Vol. 17, Virginia, Berry-Wilson, Library of Congress, 18, https://www.loc.gov/item/mesn170/.

2. Fulkes, interview, 18.

3. Stephanie M. H. Camp, "The Pleasures of Resistance: Enslaved Women and Body Politics in the Plantation South, 1830–1861," *Journal of Southern History* 68, no. 3 (August 2002): 533; Stephanie M. H. Camp, "I Could Not Stay There": Enslaved Women, Truancy and the Geography of Everyday Forms of Resistance in the Antebellum Plantation South," *Slavery & Abolition* 23, no. 3 (2002): 1–20.

4. Richard S. Dunn, "Winney Grimshaw, a Virginia Slave, and Her Family," *Early American Studies* 9, no. 3 (2011): 493–521.

5. Mary E. Frederickson and Delores M. Walters, eds., *Gendered Resistance: Women, Slavery, and the Legacy of Margaret Garner* (Baltimore: University of Illinois Press, 2013).

6. "Slavery," Virginia Museum of History & Culture, January 17, 2020, https://www.virginiahistory.org/what-you-can-see/story-virginia/explore-story-virginia/1825-1861/slavery.

7. Camp, "I Could Not Stay There," 1.

8. Amrita Myers, "'Sisters in Arms': Slave Women's Resistance to Slavery in the United States," *Past Imperfect* 5, (December 1996): 144.

9. Myers, "Sisters in Arms," 144.

10. Interview with Armaci Adams, June 25, 1937, "Lewis Papers," in *Weevils in the Wheat: Interviews with Virginia Ex-Slaves*, eds. Charles L. Purdue, Thomas E. Barden, and Robert K. Phillips (Indiana University Press, 1980), 2–3.

11. Interview with Rev. Ishrael Massie, April 23, 1937, "Lewis Papers," in *Weevils in the Wheat: Interviews with Virginia Ex-Slaves*, eds. Charles L. Purdue, Thomas E. Barden, and Robert K. Phillips (Indiana University Press, 1980), 209.

12. Interview with West Turner, n.d., "Negro in Virginia," in *Weevils in the Wheat: Interviews with Virginia Ex-Slaves*, eds. Charles L. Purdue, Thomas E. Barden, and Robert K. Phillips (Indiana University Press, 1980), 289.

13. Interview with Charles Crawley, February 20, 1937, in *Federal Writers' Project: Slave Narrative Project*, Vol. 17, Virginia, Berry-Wilson, Library of Congress, 11, https://www.loc.gov/item/mesn170/.

14. Crawley, interview.

15. Interview with Lorenzo L. Ivy, April 28, 1937, in *Weevils in the Wheat: Interviews with Virginia Ex-Slaves*, eds. Charles L. Purdue, Thomas E. Barden, and Robert K. Phillips (Indiana University Press, 1980), 154.

16. Ivy, interview.

17. Massie, interview.

18. Interview with Arthur Greene, April 16, 1939, in *Weevils in the Wheat: Interviews with Virginia Ex-Slaves*, eds. Charles L. Purdue, Thomas E. Barden, and Robert K. Phillips (Indiana University Press, 1980), 125.

19. Greene, interview.

20. Interview with Jennie Patterson, May 14, 1939, in *Weevils in the Wheat: Interviews with Virginia Ex-Slaves*, eds. Charles L. Purdue, Thomas E. Barden, and Robert K. Phillips (Indiana University Press, 1980), 220.

21. Patterson, interview.

22. Interview with Albert Jones, December 27, 1936, in *Federal Writers' Project: Slave Narrative Project*, Vol. 17, *Virginia, Berry-Wilson*, Library of Congress, 47, https://www.loc.gov/item/mesn170/.

23. Interview with Richard Slaughter, January 13, 1937, in *Federal Writers' Project: Slave Narrative Project*, Vol. 17, *Virginia, Berry-Wilson*, Library of Congress, 50, https://www.loc.gov/item/mesn170/.

24. Brenda E. Stevenson, *Life in Black and White: Family and Community in the Slave South* (New York: Oxford University Press, 1997), 161.

25. Interview with Louise Jones, February 12, 1937, in *Weevils in the Wheat: Interviews with Virginia Ex-Slaves*, eds. Charles L. Purdue, Thomas E. Barden, and Robert K. Phillips (Indiana University Press, 1980), 185.

26. Fulkes, interview, 15.

27. Fulkes, interview, 15.

28. Katie Blackwell Johnson, "File 1447," in *Weevils in the Wheat: Interviews with Virginia Ex-Slaves*, eds. Charles L. Purdue, Thomas E. Barden, and Robert K. Phillips (Indiana University Press, 1980), 161.

29. Interview with Fannie Nicholson, January 8, 1937, in *Weevils in the Wheat: Interviews with Virginia Ex-Slaves*, eds. Charles L. Purdue, Thomas E. Barden, and Robert K. Phillips (Indiana University Press, 1980), 217.

30. Interview with Mrs. Williams, ca. 1937–1940, in *Voices Remembering Slavery: Freed People Tell Their Stories*, Library of Congress, https://www.loc.gov/collections/voices-remembering-slavery/about-this-collection/.

31. Interview with Julia Frazier, April 20, 1937, in *Weevils in the Wheat: Interviews with Virginia Ex-Slaves*, eds. Charles L. Purdue, Thomas E. Barden, and Robert K. Phillips (Indiana University Press, 1980), 97.

32. Frazier, interview.

33. Stephanie M. H. Camp, "The Pleasures of Resistance," 534.

34. Stephanie M. H. Camp, "The Pleasures of Resistance," 533.

35. Interview with Nancy Williams, May 18, 1937, in *Weevils in the Wheat: Interviews with Virginia Ex-Slaves*, eds. Charles L. Purdue, Thomas E. Barden, and Robert K. Phillips (Indiana University Press, 1980), 316.

36. Interview with Sally Ashton, n.d., "Negro in Virginia," in *Weevils in the Wheat: Interviews with Virginia Ex-Slaves*, eds. Charles L. Purdue, Thomas E. Barden, and Robert K. Phillips (Indiana University Press, 1980), 14.

37. Ashton, interview.

38. Ashton, interview.

39. Interview with unidentified former slaves from Petersburg, Virginia, ca. 1937–1940, in *Voices Remembering Slavery: Freed People Tell Their Stories*, Library of Congress, https://www.loc.gov/collections/voices-remembering-slavery/

about-this-collection/.

40. Thavolia Glymph, "Du Bois's Black Reconstruction and Slave Women's War for Freedom," *South Atlantic Quarterly* 112, (2013): 491.

41. Interview with Eliza Robinson, n.d., "Lewis Papers," in *Weevils in the Wheat: Interviews with Virginia Ex-Slaves*, eds. Charles L. Purdue, Thomas E. Barden, and Robert K. Phillips (Indiana University Press, 1980), 238.

42. Robinson, interview.

43. Interview with Virginia Hayes Shepherd, May 18, 1937, in *Weevils in the Wheat: Interviews with Virginia Ex-Slaves*, eds. Charles L. Purdue, Thomas E. Barden, and Robert K. Phillips (Indiana University Press, 1980), 259.

44. Shepherd, interview.

45. Shepherd, interview.

46. Interview with Betty Jones, n.d., "Negro in Virginia," in *Weevils in the Wheat: Interviews with Virginia Ex-Slaves*, eds. Charles L. Purdue, Thomas E. Barden, and Robert K. Phillips (Indiana University Press, 1980), 180.

47. Jones, interview.

48. Jones, interview.

49. Interview with Margaret Terry, May 21, 1937, in *Weevils in the Wheat: Interviews with Virginia Ex-Slaves*, eds. Charles L. Purdue, Thomas E. Barden, and Robert K. Phillips (Indiana University Press, 1980), 285.

50. Terry, interview.

51. Terry, interview.

52. Interview with Fannie Berry, February 26 1937, "Lewis Papers," in *Weevils in the Wheat: Interviews with Virginia Ex-Slaves*, eds. Charles L. Purdue, Thomas E. Barden, and Robert K. Phillips (Indiana University Press, 1980), 46.

53. Interview with Jeff Stanfield, March 19, 1937, in *Weevils in the Wheat: Interviews with Virginia Ex-Slaves*, eds. Charles L. Purdue, Thomas E. Barden, and Robert K. Phillips (Indiana University Press, 1980), 280.

54. Stanfield, interview.

55. Fulkes, interview, 15.

56. Jones, interview.

57. Interview with Fannie Berry, February, 26, 1937, in *Federal Writers' Project: Slave Narrative Project*, Vol. 17, *Virginia, Berry-Wilson*, Library of Congress, 5, https://www.loc.gov/item/mesn170/.

58. Berry, interview.

59. Berry, interview.

60. Berry, interview.

61. Berry, interview.

62. Turner, interview.

63. Turner, interview.

64. Katie Blackwell Johnson, n.d., "File 1547," in *Weevils in the Wheat: Interviews with Virginia Ex-Slaves*, eds. Charles L. Purdue, Thomas E. Barden, and Robert K. Phillips (Indiana University Press, 1980), 162.

65. Interview with Armaci Adams, June 25, 1937, "Lewis Papers," in *Weevils in the Wheat: Interviews with Virginia Ex-Slaves*, eds. Charles L. Purdue, Thomas E.

Barden, and Robert K. Phillips (Indiana University Press, 1980), 4.

66.   Adams, interview.

2. "I feel O so lonely and desolate": White Northern and Southern Women's Feelings of Loneliness and Sadness during the Civil War

GILLIAN BARTH

"Still I get lonely—if only this cruel war were once over so my Dear Husband could be with us & we together at our own home."[1]

Rachel Bowman, born in Ontario, Canada, on April 12, 1836, moved to Ohio to receive a college education, where she met her future husband, Samuel Cormany.[2] In the summer of 1862, Rachel and Samuel settled in Chambersburg, Pennsylvania, and shortly after, Samuel enlisted in the United States Army.[3] When Samuel departed, Rachel recorded her experiences and emotions in her diary. In this way, Rachel acted comparably to many other Northern and Southern women of her age, who frequently wrote in their diaries in order to communicate difficult feelings during that time of war. The war forced these women to embark on a new life, one without the protection and comfort of their husbands. Rachel Cormany's diary clearly indicates that women ardently missed their loved ones and grew increasingly anxious and worried without them. Women on both sides waited for the return of their husbands, fathers, and brothers to resume their normal lives from before the war. However, the sense of normalcy changed, and these women never returned to their previous comfortable lives.

Before the Civil War broke out in the United States in 1861, society entrenched women in the "Cult of Domesticity," a patriarchal ideology that forced women to uphold characteristics of purity, piety, domesticity, and submissiveness.[4] Women must remain pure for their husbands, devoutly religious, happy in their private sphere, and obedient to men. When men went off to fight in the Civil War, women could not maintain these standards and new domestic roles emerged. Rather than viewing this wartime relaxation of gender norms as liberating, women felt feelings of anxiety, loneliness, and helplessness. The diary entries and letters kept by women revealed the uneasiness endured during a time when normalcy was thrown out the window and the image of the ideal woman in the mid-nineteenth century could not be upheld.

Since the 1980s, scholars of the Civil War-era women's history wrote about life on the home front and how women contributed to the war effort. Historians such as Sarah Evans and Drew Faust focus on how Southern women reacted to the Civil War by challenging gender norms and acting politically in the public sphere. Historians in the early twenty-first century, including E. F. Conklin, Judith Giesberg, and Nina Silber, shifted to include the examination of northern women during the Civil War era. These historians wrote on the beginnings of women who exercised their political voices, but noted the constrained political freedom within women's lives. Furthermore, these scholars started to analyze the diaries of Civil War women to better understand their experiences. This trend increased in the later 2010s when historians such as Paul Cimbala, Randall Miller, Stephanie McCurry, Maggi Morehouse, Zoe Trodd, and Susan Youhn highlighted Northern and Southern women's experiences from their diaries and letters.[5] Scholars focused on women's history during the Civil War era as a way to include narratives of women from both regions to gain an understanding of women's roles and responsibilities during the mid-nineteenth century.

Few historians examined Northern and Southern women's emotions. This chapter will examine the feelings of loneliness and vulnerability experienced by women during the Civil War. I will survey the diaries of two Southern women, Sarah Morgan Dawson and Kate Stone, and two Northern women, Catharine Peirce and Rachel Cormany. Their writings suggest that both Northern and Southern white women shared similar feelings during the Civil War when their husbands, fathers, and brothers left home to fight. Both groups of women believed in the patriarchal ideology that without a man by their side, their lives would not hold the same amount of meaning. Some women managed their grief and anxieties well, whereas other women became depressed and suicidal. These two groups of women, despite their differences, played a role in a changing society and carved out new roles for women in the nineteenth century.

Femininity in the Nineteenth Century and in Popular Magazines

Women in the nineteenth century were expected to live up to strict societal guidelines that instructed them on how to properly behave. In the North, women were pushed into the private realm of housekeeping, child-rearing, and wifely duties, while men ruled the public sphere of politics, industry, and business. Women were thought to have "indirect power of influence" in their public sphere which "nourished female community in the separate sphere of the home, religion, and female association."[6] Piety, purity, domesticity, and submissiveness were four characteristics grouped under the term "Cult of Domesticity" that instructed women on their proper role in society.[7] Attending church and reading the Bible regularly, engaging in sexual intercourse only with their husbands, performing domestic chores, and remaining obedient to their husbands governed how women were supposed to act under this patriarchal ideology. In the South, men were cast as akin to knights who operated with delicacy in addressing and handling women where "chivalric ideals required even greater delicacy on the part of women and gallantry on the part of men."[8] Women, in turn, believed men to be the superior sex, whereas they were inferior. Southern domesticity also included a racial component where "southern domestic ideology continued to be framed by the needs and anxieties of the planter class and permeated with racist assumptions."[9] African Americans were treated as subhuman in the South and white Southern men and women believed themselves superior. Women in the North and South operated within tight societal standards in order to be viewed as a proper lady, in the mid-nineteenth century, one of which was the dependency on men for their social, political, and economic well-being.

A major disruption in gender roles occurred when men left their homes to fight in the Civil War. Women were forced into lives filled with panic and anxiety. In the South, the departure of men meant the collapse of the plantation structure. The plantation "worked to institutionalize the subordination of white women, for the master was the designated head of what he frequently characterized as his 'family white and black.'"[10] Without men, women took on roles as breadwinners to bring in money for their families and performed manual labor. Women, who lived on farms, in the North also saw the departure of men as a crisis. Farm work now rested on the shoulders of "wives, children, extended family, and elderly parents."[11] Some women moved back home to be with family or relatives, and when all else failed, "women applied to local wartime relief societies for small sums of money offered to the wives and mothers of soldiers."[12] Women in the North and South responded to the crisis and anxieties of war by taking up men's work, applying for relief, or moving back home with relatives.

Popular magazines during the Civil War published illustrations and articles that accurately depicted the hardships endured by women. *Harper's Weekly* published an illustration titled *The Effect of the Rebellion on the Homes of Virginia* on December 24, 1864.[13] In this illustration, six miniature images revealed the destitution of women in their homes without much to eat, which led women to beg for money in order to feed their children. All of the women illustrated have grim, grave expressions on their faces as they endured the new realities of war. In 1889, *Harper's Weekly* published an illustration titled *Christmas Eve* that examined the separation of a husband and wife during the Civil War.[14] On one side of the illustration, a woman is kneeling by a window praying to God while her children sleep in the bed. On the other side of the illustration, the woman's husband is seen sitting down by a fire somberly reflecting on the Christmas holiday without his wife and children. The mood of the illustration is somber, and readers feel the anxiety and hope as the wives and husbands navigated the difficulties without one another.

Women in Northern and Southern societies were entrenched in a patriarchal ideology that affirmed men as protectors of women. When men left their homes to fight, women saw the departure of thousands of men as a "prompt ... to write in alarmed tones to their governor, reporting in circumstantial detail the transformations of their communities."[15] Confederate men upheld the moral characteristic of chivalry and fought "for the protection of hearth, home, and womanhood."[16] A periodical, written in 1903, demonstrated how women were left "utterly unprotected, for her natural protectors were dead or in prison."[17] The strong sense that women needed protection also extended throughout the Confederate government. Women in the South were enraged by the absence of their men and vented their frustrations to politicians. As a result, "ordinary white women ... gave the lie to their political exclusion by pressing on the official arenas of Confederate life for the means of protection, survival, redress, and justice."[18] Women did not stand idly by as their lives were upheaved and their government did nothing to protect them. Contrarily, Union soldiers did not place the protection of women at the forefront of their cause. Northerners "did, on occasion, stress the need to protect home and families, but generally only when there was an immediate threat to domestic stability."[19] Northern women recognized that their sacrifice "was not just for themselves and their homes but for the preservation of the nation."[20] Southern women recognized the importance of their own protection as a motivation for war; northern women knew that the preservation of the Union was the utmost importance. The withdrawal of men during the Civil War highlighted the patriarchal attitudes present in American culture.

Southern Perspectives: Sarah Morgan Dawson and Kate Stone

Sarah Morgan Dawson and Kate Stone were both young women who expressed their emotions in their diaries throughout the war. Their words highlight the sentiments of grief, anxiety, and hopelessness. Without the presence of their male loved ones, both women expressed anxiety and desperation about their lives. Dawson and Stone exhibited signs of worsening mental health, as they confronted grim realities of the downfall of the Confederacy and the realization that lives would not resume to their understanding of normalcy. For Stone, what would have been a summer of frivolity turned into a summer of danger. Dawson and Stone, two young women living in the deep South during the war, wrote similar feelings of grief, anxiety, and nervousness as the men in their lives disappeared—which led them to create new domestic lives.

Sarah Morgan Dawson, a twenty-year-old, middle-class Southern woman at the start of the war, felt hopeless without her father and brothers when they left to fight the war.[21] Dawson lived in Louisiana, near Baton Rouge, in a two-story farmhouse with her family, which owned less than ten enslaved people.[22] Dawson had seven siblings, three of whom went off to war.[23] Harry Morgan, her brother, died on April 30, 1861, from a duel, and Dawson's father died a few months later on November 14, 1861, from an asthma attack.[24] Dawson's other two brothers, George and Tom Morgan, died as prisoners of war only a few days apart on January 12, 1864, and January 21, 1864, respectively.[25] Dawson evoked somber and mournful imagery throughout her diary as she navigated life without her father and brothers. Dawson's diary began shortly after the new year in 1862, when she lamented the death of her brother Harry: "I was so heartbroken that even God seemed so far off that prayers could not reach him."[26] A few days later, when Dawson remarked the loss of her father the previous November, she made a startling comment about her family's situation: "and this is the simple story of how my poor mother was made a widow, and we were left orphans on that sad fourteenth of November, 1861."[27] Dawson was not left an orphan; her mother was still alive. The withdrawal of men "disrupted family tranquility," as women had to mold new home lives.[28] Dawson felt abandoned because her father and brother, who represented the top of the family structure, had died. Dawson's comment demonstrated how vital men were in Southern society, as they were expected to be the sole breadwinners and protectors of women.

Dawson believed women's lives had no purpose without men. Dawson observed that if her brothers died young, "we worthless women, of no value or importance to ourselves or the rest of the world, will live on, useless trash in creation."[29] This shocking statement from Dawson reflected the attitudes of many women whose loved ones had died. Women's lives centered around men, and without them, their purpose would be lost. Dawson even prayed to God that he spare her brother's lives for her own: "I cannot believe God will take any of our brothers from us yet. We are so helpless without them! He has been so merciful to us, that I am willing to leave this in His hands, satisfied that He will hear our prayers as He always does."[30] When news of Tom's death arrived in February of 1864, Dawson lamented, "how will the world seem to us now? What will life be without the boys?"[31] Dawson's desperation for a reunion with her brothers was palpable, as she worried about her family's future. Dawson placed value in her life with the presence of men and felt hopeless and scared of the withdrawal of men in Southern society.

As the war dragged on, Dawson's mental health worsened. In July of 1862, Dawson wrote about how tired she felt, and how "it is too great an exertion even to live … this life is killing me; I'll die in a month unless some brighter prospect opens."[32] A year later in July 1863, Dawson claimed, "I am glad that I was born to die! Death may be bitter; but I would rather endure its pain than forego the bliss of meeting father and Harry in the hereafter."[33] Dawson's comments on welcoming death revealed how grim home life was during the Civil War and for families, who had husbands or brothers fighting.

For Dawson, the war took three brothers and her father away from her, which resulted in a new domestic life. Dawson experienced emotions of sadness, mental instability, and depression. Dawson expressed fear about what life had in store for her, and her family and conveyed apprehension about her life without her brothers or father. Dawson could not envision a life without the stable presence of her father and her brothers, who were vital to her life and society. Dawson, like many women, adapted to a startlingly new life and questioned whether her life meant anything without her male loved ones.

Sarah Katherine "Kate" Stone wondered what shape her life would take during the war and feared the absence of men. Stone, an elite, twenty-year-old Southern belle, hoped to continue her summers of frivolity, style, and comfort during the war.[34] Stone lived on a cotton plantation in northeast Louisiana named Brokenburn that enslaved around one hundred fifty African Americans.[35] When Stone began her diary in 1861, she imparted an optimistic spirit about the war and had no doubts about continuing her Southern belle lifestyle and social engagements.[36] However, the war twisted Stone's vision of her summer when her brothers left to join the Confederate Army.[37] Stone shared a similar sentiment of worry about her familial stability when men left to fight. Women heavily depended on men in Southern society and the disruption of war changed the social structure of the South. This worry is evident through Stone's words: "Uncle Bo, Ashburn, and I walked back and forth … talking of soldier life and wondering what we who are left behind will do when both of our men folks are off and away."[38] However, Stone believed that her brothers and uncle "will return. The parting will be dreadful for Mamma. She so depends on My Brother, her oldest and best be loved."[39] Stone worried for the safety of her uncle and brothers, as they held the family structure together in Southern society.

Stone grew anxious for news of her loved ones and expressed sadness when news of their deaths arrived. Stone remarks in May of 1862 that "four of the dear familiar faces are absent. One sleeps the sleep that knows no waking. For him we have no fear or trouble, for we know he has passed from Death into Life—that 'all is well with the child.' But oh, the weary days of waiting and watching for the other three."[40] Stone's optimistic spirit turned grief-stricken when she received news that four members of her family died and grew uncertain about her life. In the South, "nostalgia for a romanticized version of the past would persist, but domestic life had been irrevocably altered."[41] What was hoped to be a short war, now reached well over a year and claimed one of Stone's brothers, which disrupted her carefree lifestyle. Women's domestic roles changed, and women had to face new realities without their men which fed to feelings of loneliness and vulnerability.

As with Dawson, Stone's mental health worsened as her new life took shape without her male family members. This caused Stone to reflect on death: "death does not seem half so terrible as it did long ago. We have grown used to it. Never a letter but brings news of the death of someone we knew."[42] As with Dawson, death became less scary and more real. Similar to Dawson, Stone believed her life did not hold the same meaning without men in her life. Stone could not imagine a life without men as they represented the key to family life. Without men, domesticity did not carry the same meaning. With the war and death constantly on women's minds, many women likely fell into depression as family members died and their previous lives of happiness and ease melted away.

As the war progressed into 1864, Stone reminisced about her past life. Stone noted that she "did not think two months ago I would ever dance or care to talk nonsense again. But one grows callous to suffering and death. We can live only in the present, only from day-to-day. We cannot bear to think of the past and so dread the future."[43] The typical Southern belle that existed prior to the war was a remnant of the past.[44] Women such as Dawson and Stone could not fulfill the Southern lifestyle that existed prior to the war as their lives shifted to include different definitions of womanhood. A summer of bliss turned into years of grief, hardship, and displacement for Stone. One of Stone's brothers eventually did return in 1865 after fighting, but life was not the same. Stone's diary symbolizes how even elite Southern families were not excluded from the ravages of war. Stone's former life of frivolity, courtships, dances, and social outings transformed into one replaced with war, suffering, and destitution.

Dawson and Stone were both young women who felt displaced in their own Southern societies as they were forced to create new domestic lives without the presence of men. Dawson and Stone lamented the deaths of their loved ones, and as a result, their mental health worsened to the point where each woman questioned the purpose of their lives and thought about death as welcoming. Even though both women belonged to two different economic backgrounds, Dawson and Stone were connected in their reactions, attitudes, and outlooks of the war articulated in their diaries.

Northern Perspectives: Catharine Peirce and Rachel Cormany

Catharine Peirce and Rachel Cormany, two women who lived in the North during the Civil War, shared alike characteristics of apprehension, sadness, and loneliness when their husbands left to fight the war. Peirce and Cormany were both young wives and mothers when they assumed new roles as heads of households in their families. Both women felt apprehensive about this unwelcomed burden placed on their shoulders. Both Peirce and Cormany navigated how to be a wife and a mother, without the quintessential component of their family structure: husbands. In their diaries and letters, both women continually expressed how lonely they were, and how they wished they could uphold the ideal vision of womanhood with their husbands back home. Both women struggled mentally and began to think of their life as meaningless if they could not fulfill the proper standards of being a wife. By the end of the war, Peirce and Cormany were overjoyed to welcome back their husbands and resume their lives from before the war. However, each woman knew internally that their normal lives from before the war could not be retrieved.

When Catharine Peirce, married Taylor Peirce on July 2, 1846, she envisioned a life full of marital bliss as she raised their children.[45] Instead, war tore that vision apart and Taylor Peirce enlisted in the 22nd Iowa Infantry Regiment in August of 1862, leaving behind his wife and two, about to be three, children.[46] In a letter written to Taylor in 1863, Catharine tells Taylor that she could not overcome feeling lonely: "I can be with out thee but I tell thee that I am not contented yet. I thought when thee first went that I would get over the lonesome feeling in a little time but it is better yet or I do not know wether I ever will satisfied on this or not."[47] Similar to Dawson and Stone, Catharine lived during an unsettling time as she tried to establish a life without Taylor. Catharine's apprehension turned to sadness as she faced a new reality without Taylor: "I do not think thee will be much pleased with this letter for I feel rather blue and of corse do not feel much like writing of any thing but the sturn realty."[48] Catharine's loneliness turned to resolve when in May, 1863, Catharine wished to "be down there with you boys if I had no young child that nead my care at home."[49] Catharine could not deal with the absence of her husband while she lived at home raising their children. Catharine's marital bliss abruptly changed as the war tore apart a life Catharine grew comfortable with and did not want to face the reality that she had to assume a new role for herself in order to raise her children.

In 1864, Catharine's anxieties and remorse for her new life flooded her correspondence with her husband Taylor. Catharine could not but envision what could have been their lives if the war had not interrupted it:

> It makes me begin to feel old and that I had all most spent my life in vain for I have nothing to show for all I have done and I begin to fear that this war is going last so long that thee will either be killed or worn out in the servise so that I will have no chance to make a mends in the time to come. For with out thee I can do nothing yet as I always have done.[50]

Catharine felt as though she had not achieved much in her life without Taylor. This sentiment linked Catharine to numerous other women, who believed their life had no purpose without their husbands, who represented the focal points of their lives. Many believed that they, their homes, and their families, were not interesting enough to the departed menfolk."[51] Dawson and Stone revealed the same belief that men added purpose to their lives and could not see the value in their lives without them. As Catharine settled into her new life, anxiety pervaded as she believed that her life had no purpose without her husband. Catharine did not believe she could achieve the life she intended without Taylor.

Even though Catharine endured emotional pain in raising her children without her husband, she gave Taylor permission to continue his service in the army. Catharine wrote to Taylor letting him know that he may continue serving his country until the war finished: "I have nothing to advise abut thee staying in the service another three years. That I will leave to thy will or circumstance to direct."[52] Catharine then described her melancholy but acknowledged that the decision was up to Taylor: "But I will say just do as thee thinks is for the best for all concerned. As for me I can get along some way or other."[53] Catharine's love for her husband transpired in her letters and she chose to sacrifice her happiness for Taylor's. Catharine understood Taylor's purpose by serving his country. Taylor eventually came home to Catharine who was joyous for the return of her beloved husband. Catharine's letters to Taylor demonstrated how apprehensive wives and mothers were about letting their husbands join the army to fight and raising their children during a time when their fathers were not present. Catharine, like Dawson and Stone, grew lonely and sad about her former life before the war interrupted it. Catharine could not envision her life without Taylor, who symbolized stability and purpose for Catharine. Catharine struggled to lead a life without her husband and the father to her children. After the war, however, Catharine was able to pick up the pieces and move on.

Rachel Cormany's vision of living happily with her husband and daughter in Chambersburg, Pennsylvania, shattered in the summer of 1862. Rachel, a middle-class mother similar to Catharine Peirce, settled with her husband, Samuel Cormany, in Chambersburg, and shortly after, Samuel enlisted in the U.S. Army.[54] Rachel wrote in her diary the day Samuel left: "it went hard to see him go. for he is more than life to me."[55] Rachel's diary chronicled her emotional highs and lows as she was left to take care of her infant daughter by herself while Samuel went to fight. Rachel wrote of longing for Samuel, suffered anxiety-driven days when she did not receive letters from Samuel, and confronted feelings of inadequacy. Rachel, along with Catharine Peirce, experienced a range of emotions without her husband, as she trudged through a new life during the mid-nineteenth century.

Rachel was anxiety-driven and lonely due to the lack of comfort and assurance from her husband. In January of 1863, Rachel wrote, "I feel anxious. I looked some for him home, tonight, still I hardly expected it. I feel a little sad and disappointed."[56] Rachel, similarly to Catharine Peirce, needed daily assurances from her husband in order to feel happy in her life. Without letters from their husbands, anxious thoughts and feelings crept into women's minds. In the coming months, Rachel exhibited signs of depression and longed to see Samuel: "I feel sad all day … I am fixing to go to see my Samuel in case he cannot come to see me"[57] and "O! My God—Haste the end of this war, & bring my dear dear Samuel back to again."[58] Rachel's apprehension about life without Samuel made her doubt his love for her:

I some times feel as if we had done wrong to bring such a little angel on earth to suffer—To have all this upon me, & Samuel away. O! I cannot help getting blue sometimes. I try to be happy. The question sometimes comes to my mind—Does he really love me?[59]

Rachel did not believe that her child was being properly raised during a time when its father was absent. Rachel doubted her domestic role as if she could not fulfill it without her husband. Women's lives were changing and "hardships abounded as these women tried to keep the family life intact as it was before. Even the simple tasks were difficult and frustrating."[60] Women felt lonely and some grew depressed and could not find comfort in their domestic roles and responsibilities.

These reservations also translate to feelings of inadequacy when these women could not uphold the pillars of the "Cult of Domesticity." Rachel was a unique woman in the mid-nineteenth century because she received a college education at Otterbein University.[61] Rachel was well-educated, yet she still hoped to attain the ideal married life with her husband. However, even the ideal vision of wife and motherhood lost its effects on Rachel:

I feel daily that I am so far below my ideal of what I should be or what I desire to be—both religiously & mentally. I do not accomplish what I wish to. My mind & soul are not in as elevated a state as I wish them to be…. My anxiety for my husband has in a measure diminished—I feel so confident that he will return.[62]

Rachel felt as though she could not accomplish what she wished to be without a return to normalcy and domesticity. Rachel's mental state prohibited her from contributing to a society that expected women to operate happily in their private spheres. She felt so discombobulated and depressed that "friends that come in ask me whether I am sick. I look so pale—but I wonder who would not look pale after parting with the dearest friend on earth. I am sure I do not look any worse than I feel."[63] The physical toll without Samuel became apparent with Rachel, as she tried to navigate a life where she felt inadequate as a domestic wife who envisioned more for herself. This led Rachel to feel displaced during a time when gender roles were constantly changing.

Rachel's increasing loneliness harbored feelings of depression. In May of

1863, Rachel notes that she again feels "blue—here I am all alone—cannot get out unless I carry my big baby & even when I do go I have to stay along like some lost sheep by myself. So many things combine to make me blue."[64] Rachel lost her appetite and found it arduous to find joy in life: "Mr. C is gone again. I can hardly stay in I feel so lonely. My room seems so empty—my eatable do not taste good, everything seems to have lost of its charms."[65] Rachel remarked that the war was breaking apart her marriage with Samuel. Rachel recounted how "a bright future was looming up before me" and now "clouds arose to overshaddow our bright skys."[66] If the Civil War did not occur, Rachel could have started her ideal domestic life with Samuel as a new wife and mother and raised their family in perfect marital bliss. In May 1865, Rachel's mental health significantly worsened and she wondered if "it would be a blessing to the world in general & myself in particular if Cora & I could just shut my (our) eyes never to open in this world—It is not right to feel thus. Hence I pray for Grace to live right & to overcome evil."[67] On June 10, 1865, Rachel wanted to creep "into a dark corner & weep that my tears might swell to a torrent."[68] Rachel did not know how to maintain a home life during the war without her husband there with her. This led to feelings of inadequacy and depression as she continued to live during the war without Samuel. The war hurt women economically, emotionally, and mentally in which they could not contribute to a patriarchal world if their men were off fighting a war and could not be with their families.

When Samuel returned home from the war, Rachel's spirits increased tenfold at the prospect of resuming her normal life before the war. Rachel's excitement to live a happy life with Samuel and her daughter and finally start their lives prevailed. As with Catharine Peirce, Rachel believed that she could recreate the world she and Samuel inhabited before the war. However, the war changed several aspects of society including gender roles in which the ideal vision of a woman vanished. Catharine Peirce and Rachel Cormany, two wives and mothers who lived in the North during the Civil War, could never resume their normal, domestic lives from before the war.

Conclusion

Prior to the outbreak of the Civil War, women were expected to uphold four pillars of the "Cult of Domesticity": piety, purity, domesticity, and submissiveness. These characteristics governed women's lives as they participated and engaged in a patriarchal world that shut women up in their private sphere whereas men ruled the public sphere. When war occurred in 1861, the ideal woman was thrust out the door. Men left to fight, and women recreated a new home life with different domestic roles. Women learned how to run a household and family without their husbands, fathers, or brothers who represented the key structural link in society. With the absence of men, women felt vulnerable and afraid. Before the Civil War, men represented the natural protectors of women. Now, these women were left alone.

These feelings of vulnerability also collided with emotions of sadness, loneliness, depression, and anxiety. Women wrote in personal diaries and wrote letters to their husbands and loved ones when they were gone. Southern belles, such as Sarah Morgan Dawson and Kate Stone, wrote on their war experiences in their diaries. Dawson was constantly worried about her brothers and was devastated when they died, and she knew their family would never meet again until heaven. Kate Stone felt the withdrawal of men as a time of loneliness and disruption to her social life before the war. Both Dawson and Stone worried about their new lives and believed that women could not perform their domestic duties without men. Northern women testified to those feelings, as well. Catharine Pierce felt burdened and worried without her husband, which led to her worsening mental health. Rachel Cormany felt sad and increasingly depressed and suicidal without her husband. Cormany, who was well-educated, found it difficult to adhere to the domestic vision of women if she could not achieve what she wanted. Peirce and Cormany struggled to uphold the image of the ideal woman when their husbands were absent. All four women from the North and South wrestled with the concept of running a household, performing domestic roles, and serving as ideal women in a society that was grounded in a reliance on men.

My examination of Northern and Southern women illustrates how despite the emergence of new domestic and gender roles for women during the Civil War, women fought these new responsibilities and hoped for a return to their previous lives. Dawson, Stone, Peirce, and Cormany rejected their lives without their men and wished for a return to normalcy. The war made these women realize how much value they placed in men in their society. The emotions of sadness, loneliness, vulnerability, and anxiety from women who lived without their husbands, fathers, and brothers demonstrated how deep the roots of the patriarchy go. This turbulent time in American history did not present itself favorably to women, who very much relied on men for support. As much as we would like to acknowledge the changed gender and domestic roles women were positioned into, these "nasty women" were not so nasty after all.

Notes

1. Richard Elliott and James C. Mohr, *The Cormany Diaries: A Northern Family in the Civil War* (Pittsburg, PA: University of Pittsburgh Press, 1982), 500–501.

2. Elliott and Mohr, *The Cormany Diaries*, ix.

3. Elliott and Mohr, *The Cormany Diaries*, 253.

4. Sara M. Evans, *Born for Liberty: A History of Women in America* (New York: Free Press, 1989), 96.

5. Sara M. Evans, *Born for Liberty: A History of Women in America* (New York: Free Press, 1989); Drew Gilpin Faust, *Mothers of Invention: Women of the Slaveholding South in the American Civil War* (Chapel Hill: University of North Carolina Press, 1996); Susan Youhn, "'You Have No Idea What I Have Gone Through': Letters from Behind the Lines to Prisoners at Point Lookout, Maryland," in *The Journal of Women's Civil War History: From the Home Front to the Front Lines: Accounts of the Sacrifice, Achievement, and Service of American Women 1861-1865*, ed. C. F. Conklin (Gettysburg, PA: Thomas Publications, 2001); Nina Silber, *Daughters of the Union: Northern Women Fight the Civil War* (Cambridge, MA: Harvard University Press, 2005); Judith Ann Giesberg, *Army at Home: Women and the Civil War on the Northern Home Front* (Chapel Hill: University of North Carolina Press, 2009); Stephanie McCurry, *Confederate Reckoning: Power and Politics in the Civil War South* (Cambridge, MA: Harvard University Press, 2010); Maggi M. Morehouse and Zoe Trodd, *Civil War America: A Social and Cultural History with Primary Sources* (London, UK: Routledge, 2012); Paul A. Cimbala and Randall M. Miller, *The Northern Home Front During the Civil War* (Santa Barbara, CA: Praeger, 2017).

6. Evans, *Born for Liberty*, 96.

7. Morehouse and Trodd, *Civil War America*, 33.

8. Morehouse and Trodd, *Civil War America*, 34.

9. Evans, *Born for Liberty*, 108.

10. Faust, *Mothers of Invention*, 32.

11. Giesberg, *Army at Home*, 21.

12. Giesberg, *Army at Home*, 30.

13. Anonymous, *The Effect of the Rebellion on the Homes of Virginia*, drawing, *Harper's Weekly*, December 24, 1864.

14. Thomas Nast, *Christmas Eve*, 1889, wood engraving, Library of Congress Prints and Photographs Division, https://www.loc.gov/pictures/resource/cph.3c26254/.

15. Faust, *Mothers of Invention*, 31.

16. Stephanie McCurry, *Confederate Reckoning: Power and Politics in the Civil War South* (Cambridge, MA: Harvard University Press, 2010), 94.

17. Elizabeth McCracken, "The Women of America: Third Paper—The Southern Woman and Reconstruction," *Outlook* (1893–1924), November 21, 1903, 699.

18. McCurry, *Confederate Reckoning*, 88.

19. Nina Silber, *Daughters of the Union: Northern Women Fight the Civil War* (Cambridge, MA: Harvard University Press, 2005), 25.

20. Silber, *Daughters of the Union*, 28.

21. Sarah Morgan Dawson, *A Confederate Girl's Diary* (Bloomington: Indiana University Press, 1960), xix.

22. Dawson, *A Confederate Girl's Diary*, xix.

23. Dawson, *A Confederate Girl's Diary*, xix.

24. Dawson, *A Confederate Girl's Diary*, xv.

25. Dawson, *A Confederate Girl's Diary*, xvi.

26. Dawson, *A Confederate Girl's Diary*, 5.

27. Dawson, *A Confederate Girl's Diary*, 22.

28. Paul A. Cimbala and Randall M. Miller, *The Northern Home Front During the Civil War* (Santa Barbara, CA: Praeger, 2017), 58.

29. Dawson, *A Confederate Girl's Diary*, 77.

30. Dawson, *A Confederate Girl's Diary*, 180.

31. Dawson, *A Confederate Girl's Diary*, 603.

32. Dawson, *A Confederate Girl's Diary*, 152.

33. Dawson, *A Confederate Girl's Diary*, 514.

34. Kate Stone and John Q. Anderson, *Brokenburn: The Journal of Kate Stone, 1861–1868* (Baton Rouge: Louisiana State University Press, 1955), xiv.

35. Stone and Anderson, *Brokenburn*, xiv.

36. Life at Brokenburn in the beginning of the war consisted of visiting with friends and company while waiting for news of family members. On page 24 of Stone's diary, she exclaimed on 10 June 1861, "Oh! to see and be in it all. I hate the weary days of inaction. Yet what can women do but wait and suffer?" By September of 1862, Stone dreaded the lack of activity: "The long rains, the impassable roads, no books, no papers, few letters. Our friends nearly all away, and most of our loved ones in the army. Awful prospect." At first what Stone thought would have been a short war with little disruption to her social life turned into a nightmare of boredom, anxiety, and anticipation.

37. Stone and Anderson, *Brokenburn*, xv.

38. Stone and Anderson, *Brokenburn*, 15.

39. Stone and Anderson, *Brokenburn*, 17.

40. Stone and Anderson, *Brokenburn*, 114.

41. Morehouse and Trodd, *Civil War America*, 43.

42. Stone and Anderson, *Brokenburn*, 258.

43. Stone and Anderson, *Brokenburn*, 293.

44. McCracken, "The Women of America," 697.

45. Taylor Peirce, Donna B. Vaughn, Richard L. Kiper, and Catherine L. Peirce, *Dear Catharine, Dear Taylor: The Civil War Letters of a Union Soldier and His Wife* (Lawrence, KS: University Press of Kansas, 2002), xiv.

46. Peirce, Vaughn, Kiper, and Peirce, *Dear Catharine, Dear Taylor*, 5.

47. Peirce, Vaughn, Kiper, and Peirce, *Dear Catharine, Dear Taylor*, 75.

48. Peirce, Vaughn, Kiper, and Peirce, *Dear Catharine, Dear Taylor*, 85.

49. Peirce, Vaughn, Kiper, and Peirce, *Dear Catharine, Dear Taylor*, 111.

50. Peirce, Vaughn, Kiper, and Peirce, *Dear Catharine, Dear Taylor*, 225.

51. Silber, *Daughters of the Union*, 91.

52. Peirce, Vaughn, Kiper, and Peirce, *Dear Catharine, Dear Taylor*, 350.

53. Peirce, Vaughn, Kiper, and Peirce, *Dear Catharine, Dear Taylor*, 350.

54. Winslow and Mohr, *The Cormany Diaries*, 253.

55. Winslow and Mohr, *The Cormany Diaries*, 253.

56. Winslow and Mohr, *The Cormany Diaries*, 256.

57. Winslow and Mohr, *The Cormany Diaries*, 256.

58. Winslow and Mohr, *The Cormany Diaries*, 258.

59. Winslow and Mohr, *The Cormany Diaries*, 287.

60. Youhn, "You have no idea what I have gone through," 96.

61. Winslow and Mohr, *The Cormany Diaries*, xii.

62. Winslow and Mohr, *The Cormany Diaries*, 406–407.

63. Winslow and Mohr, *The Cormany Diaries*, 408.

64. Winslow and Mohr, *The Cormany Diaries*, 290–291.

65. Winslow and Mohr, *The Cormany Diaries*, 371.

66. Winslow and Mohr, *The Cormany Diaries*, 383.

67. Winslow and Mohr, *The Cormany Diaries*, 546.

68. Winslow and Mohr, *The Cormany Diaries*, 546.

3. The American Plan: How Women Came to Be Viewed as Dangerous

CAROLINE MCLEAN

On Thursday, October 31, 1918, Nina McCall, barely 18 years old, exited a post office near her home in St. Louis, Missouri, when a police officer approached her and told her that she must report for a medical examination. The following day, a distraught Nina reported for a mandatory pelvic exam.[1] Though McCall had never before entered into sexual relations with a man, the medical examiner claimed that she was "slightly diseased" with gonorrhea and ordered her to receive treatment in a detention hospital. McCall spent the following months imprisoned against her will and in excruciating pain from invasive and ineffective mercury treatments. After her release from the detention hospital, medical officials harassed and publicly humiliated Nina for her diagnosis.[2]

While McCall's story is devastating, it was not unique at the time. Thousands of women faced similar experiences as part of a wartime initiative to control the spread of venereal disease (presently referred to as sexually transmitted infections or STIs). In 1918 Congress implemented the Chamberlain-Kahn Act, also called the American Plan. The act, which remained widely in effect until 1950, was utilized as part of a larger initiative to control the spread of venereal disease throughout the United States military.[3] While the American Plan mainly targeted prostitutes, any woman deemed "suspicious" of having venereal disease could be arrested.[4] Women arrested under the American Plan endured invasive medical exams, forced labor, and painful, yet ineffective medical treatments.[5] The American Plan humiliated and traumatized thousands of women during the first half of the twentieth century.

While scholarship on the American Plan remains limited, historians discuss early twentieth-century concepts of "promiscuous" women as delinquent, dangerous, or deviant. However, historians widely disagree on the social status of these so-called "dangerous" and "promiscuous" women.[6] It is important to define the socioeconomic status of women labeled as promiscuous or dangerous in the early twentieth century in order to analyze the impacts of the American Plan on women. It is also important to discuss shifts in public perceptions of women. Scholars such as Mary Odem and Courtney Shah discuss a shift from Victorian age thinking to Progressive era thinking. This shift in thinking supports the central question asked in this chapter: How did social conceptions of delinquent women and sexuality in the early twentieth century lead to the implementation of the American Plan?[7]

In this chapter, I will answer this question by discussing the public perception of promiscuous women in relation to venereal disease, the military's relationship with venereal disease, as well as the reasons the American public thought venereal disease was so widespread. I will rely heavily on reports by medical professionals and the American Social Hygiene Society, sexology and sexual education books, as well as social hygiene propaganda to argue that a general public acceptance of the promiscuous woman as a menace to American society caused by inadequate sexual education led to the implementation of the American Plan.

Local law enforcement first implemented the American Plan in 1918 towards the end of World War I, as a part of an effort to contain and control the spread of venereal disease in the US military. At first, the American Plan only allowed for the arrest of women suspected of prostitution on or near military bases.[8] However, when it quickly became clear that the majority of soldiers contracted venereal disease from women in their hometowns rather than on military bases, authorities extended the American Plan all across the United States.[9] Initially, the American Plan only targeted prostitutes, but it expanded to include any woman reasonably suspected of having a venereal disease. [10] Yet, under the revised version of the American Plan, local law enforcement began to arrest any women that appeared to be sexually impure.[11]

The loose credentials for the type of woman subject to arrest under the American Plan led to the wrongful arrest of thousands of innocent women judged solely on their assumed promiscuity. All women found infected with venereal disease faced quarantine or imprisonment. Law enforcement frequently quarantined women in detention hospitals, prisons, juvenile reformatories, treatment centers, or custodial care homes for the feeble-minded.[12] Officials held infected women in quarantine until deemed "reasonably" cured of infection. However, authorities quarantined many infection-free women. Though free of venereal disease, officials found these women to be sufficiently "promiscuous" or "immoral" to the point that they posed a threat to the well-being of soldiers.[13] Officials continuously contained disease-free promiscuous women because the public viewed promiscuity as a threat to American society.

The Public's Perspective on Promiscuous Women

During the early twentieth century in the United States, the public widely criticized both prostitutes and promiscuous women for their tendency to engage in premarital sex. Many Americans linked a woman's promiscuity with diseases or even hatred. A general public acceptance of these women as the inevitable carriers and cause of venereal disease led to the enactment of the American Plan.

In the early twentieth century, sex education teachers defined prostitution as a "commercialized vice," or the sale of sexual relations to men.[14] Moreover, they associated vice, wicked or immoral behavior, with any prostitute or promiscuous woman. A promiscuous woman, on the other hand, could be any woman with sexually "loose morals" who engaged in any type of sexual activity outside of marriage. Sex education teachers even defined women who kissed or spooned with a man as promiscuous.[15] Terms such as "lady of the night," "delinquent woman," "charity girl," "loose woman," and "promiscuous woman" were all used to define these women of "loose morals" and each of these labels identified a woman as "bad" to the public.[16]

The American public viewed prostitutes and promiscuous women as both medically and morally dangerous. The Official Periodical of the American Social Hygiene Association warned men not to "expose himself to the danger" of venereal disease by engaging in sexual intercourse with an "all-too-likely-infected prostitute."[17] Similarly, a sexology book titled *The Sex Side of Life* warned men not to engage in sexual relations with "ladies of the night" because most of them had "become diseased, and there is, as yet, no way for either them or the men who visit them to be positively safe from infection."[18] Additionally, a propaganda poster titled "Do Not Believe

Him" explicitly warned viewers that "most prostitutes (private or public) have either syphilis or gonorrhea or both."[19] Efforts to contain the spread of venereal disease thus warned men to stay away from these women, because the public believed that they would inevitably contract a venereal disease, and in turn, spread it to unknowing men. The prostitute quickly became the symbol of moral and physical danger.

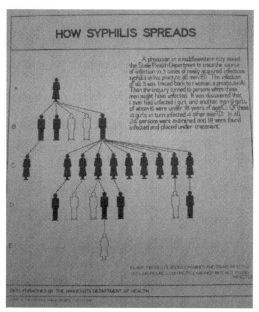

Figure 3.1: This chart shows the results of an epidemiological investigation of cases of syphilis (Poster by ASHA, "How Syphilis Spreads," 1930, Venereal Disease Visual History Archive, https://vdarchive.newmedialab.cuny.edu/items/show/359).

Sexual education materials reinvigorated negative social conceptions of prostitutes and loose women. During the era of the American Plan, public health officials encouraged mothers to teach their sons about sex and venereal disease. After absorbing a mother's lessons surrounding venereal disease, her son "should know enough about prostitution to be on guard."[20] Sex education aimed at teaching young boys and men to live a "pure" life: a life free of venereal disease. A 1918 sexual education book titled *What to Tell Your Boy* explicitly instructed boys to "avoid contact with loose women," in order to maintain pure lives and to avoid diseases. The book also encourages teaching young men "that so widespread is venereal disease ... that not one prostitute in a hundred can escape it."[21] Sex education taught boys to abstain from illicit sexual relations in order to remain healthy.

Propaganda similarly encouraged the public to view prostitutes as dangerously contagious. In *Figure* 3.1, a poster titled "How Syphilis Spreads" depicts a map of 18 people who contracted syphilis. Patient zero of the illustrated outbreak was one single prostitute.[22] Public officials used this poster, and similar ones, as scare tactics to deter men from engaging in potentially dangerous sexual relations. The brochure depicted in *Figure* 3.2 titles "The Venereal Menace: An Exhibit for Adults" also pointed to sex workers as the cause of the disease's spread. The poster directly stated that the causes of venereal disease are "lies about sex," such as minimizing the symptoms of syphilis and the inherent dangers of having sex with a prostitute. This pamphlet also depicts distorted faces of children with syphilis to act as a scare tactic to further discourage the public from engaging in shameful sexual relations.[23] Propaganda used scare tactics that worked to reinforce the idea that all "ladies of the night" carried venereal disease and discouraged sexual engagement with them.

The public blamed the prostitute or promiscuous woman for the spread of venereal disease, rather than the man engaging with her in promiscuous behavior. Though many men in the early twentieth century made clear and conscious decisions to engage in sexual relations with prostitutes or women considered promiscuous, women faced the brunt of the blame for the spread of venereal disease. John Rainsford discussed this issue, deemed "the double standard," in his 1918 sexology book *What to Tell Your Boy*. Rainsford argued that the "double standard" always punished a woman for illicit sexual behavior but rarely punished a man for the same behavior. Under "the double standard" a woman's social position and reputation could be ruined by engaging in improper intercourse. If a woman engaged in premarital intercourse, the public immediately deemed her a promiscuous woman who probably carried a dangerous disease.[24] However, a man rarely faced social consequences for engaging in similar sexual behavior.

Figure 3.2: This brochure shows the PHS version of the "Keeping Fit" poster exhibit for young men (Brochure by the YMCA and USPHS, "The Venereal Menace: An Exhibit for Adults," 1920-1922, Venereal Disease Visual History Archive, https://vdarchive.newmedialab.cuny.edu/items/show/340).

In the years surrounding the implementation of the American plan, the American public linked a woman's promiscuity to venereal disease. They blamed women, rather than men, for the spread of venereal disease and public health officials enforced these ideas through sex education and propaganda. The link that tied promiscuous women and disease together in the minds of so many Americans led to a general acceptance of promiscuous women and prostitutes as dangerous.

Loose Women and Prostitutes in Relation to the Military

Officials also viewed promiscuous women as a danger to the US military. In the early twentieth century, venereal disease constituted a threat to the well-being of the American military. Officials attempted to combat the spread of venereal disease in the military through the education of soldiers and the quarantine of loose women.[25] Widespread fear of promiscuous women's infiltration into and degradation of the military led to social conceptions of women as dangerous to American society.

From the perspective of military authorities, the danger posed by these women was real. According to the sexology book, *The Control of Sexual Infections* by J. Bayard Clark, officials reported 259,612 cases of venereal disease in military men during 1917 and 1918, which resulted in a severe loss of time in military productivity.[26] The presence of sexual infections in the military was certainly a problem. Medical experts reported that "venereal disease uncontrolled results in great military disability and loss in efficiency."[27] Moreover, since the public viewed promiscuous women and prostitutes as the carriers and spreaders of infection, they saw the American Plan's quarantine of infected women as the ultimate way to "protect the health and morals of our men in training."[28] Therefore, officials claimed that the solution to the spread of venereal disease in the military was to solve the "problem of delinquency among women and girls, which we face today as menacing our military strength."[29] Officials attributed the degradation of the US military not only to venereal disease but, by association, to women as well.

Sex education within the military attempted to discourage soldiers from engaging in sexual relations with promiscuous women in order to combat the spread of venereal disease. Propaganda was used to do this. The poster depicted in *Figure* 3.3 titled "Steady buddy–There's a come-back!" was used to warn military men of the dangers of engaging in sexual relations with a "loose" woman. This poster depicts a soldier gazing at an attractive woman. Public health officials used it to promote social hygiene by reminding soldiers about the dangers associated with engaging in premarital sexual relations with any woman, even a deceivingly attractive woman.[30]

Figure 3.3: This poster was meant to warn servicemen about prostitutes and encourage continence (Poster by Social Hygiene Division, Army Educational Commission, "Steady Buddy—There's A Come-Back!" 1918, Venereal Disease Visual History Archive, https://vdarchive.newmedialab.cuny.edu/items/show/331).

Another propaganda poster depicted in *Figure* 3.4 titled "Not in the Line of Duty" depicts an ill, bedridden soldier, sidelined because he contracted a venereal disease. The poster's title refers to the fact that infected soldiers would not be considered injured in the line of duty. Their hospitalization, a sign of dishonor rather than honor, translated to embarrassment for infected servicemen. The poster urged men to refrain from engaging in sexual relations with promiscuous women to avoid humiliation.[31] While propaganda admitted that men could slow the spread of venereal disease by refraining from sex with loose women, women were still seen as the ultimate spreader of venereal disease. In order to control the spread of venereal disease in the military, servicemen were encouraged to avoid these "diseased" women.

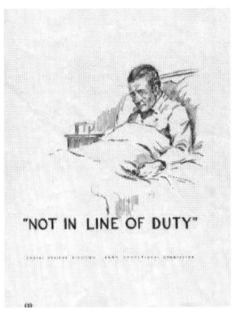

"NOT IN LINE OF DUTY"

Figure 3.4: This social hygiene poster shows a
serviceman in a hospital bed who has been
sidelined because of venereal disease (Poster by
Social Hygiene Division, Army Educational
Commission, "Not in the Line of Duty," 1918,
Venereal Disease Visual History Archive,
https://vdarchive.newmedialab.cuny.edu/
items/show/330).

The quarantine of promiscuous women quickly came to be seen as the
best solution to contain the spread of venereal disease. Throughout the
American Plan, officials dedicated over a million dollars to isolate women
deemed a potential threat to the military.[32] Medical officials reasoned that
"in the case of venereal disease the carriers are human beings. And the
human beings who individually expose the most of the rest of humankind
to this disease are women ... [women] must be cared for where they will
not constitute a military and social menace."[33] Officials thought that the
best way to contain the spread of venereal disease was to physically remove
women from the public. Additionally, due to the tendencies of promiscuous
women to "flock to camp towns," the public thought that women, especially
ones near military camps, needed to be physically restrained from spreading
venereal disease.[34] Furthermore, Martha Falconer, a sexology writer, insisted

that rehabilitation camps were needed in addition to quarantine centers. Falconer argued that the only way to truly prevent the spread of venereal disease was to change the inherent character of promiscuous women and mold them into respectable women by committing them to house and farm work.[35] An overarching theme of promiscuous women as a menace to society persisted during the early twentieth century and resulted in a plan to separate these women from public life and reform their behavior.

The American Plan thus linked patriotism to abstention from sexual relations with prostitutes and or promiscuous women. According to the American Social Hygiene Association, women called "camp-followers" or "hanger-on" types frequently entered the vicinity of military camps with the intention of engaging in sexual relations with soldiers. These women "had the mistaken idea that patriotism demanded that they give the soldier anything that he asked for."[36] However, members of the social hygiene board claimed that these women put military men in direct danger. In fact, officials claimed that women could be patriotic by abstaining from premarital sex with military men. Moreover, they thought that the best way for the average citizen to be patriotic was to "not associate with such women" due to the danger that they presented to the American military.[37] Officials from the American Social Hygiene association encouraged the public to urge against promiscuity in women because it was viewed as a danger to the military, and therefore the well-being of the United States.

Sex Education in the American Plan

Although quarantine was an important component of the American Plan, health officials viewed sex education as the ultimate solution to the problem of venereal disease. Sex education, defined as "all scientific, ethical, social, and religious instruction and influence which directly and indirectly may help young people prepare to solve for themselves the problems of sex," was an important factor of the American Plan.[38] During the American Plan, government and health officials realized the pressing "need for rational sex enlightenment, in combating prostitution and venereal disease, and carrying on a general campaign of sane social hygiene."[39] Health officials also "accepted that the social evil of prostitution is increased by the common ignorance of young people."[40] While the immediate solution to the rapid spread of venereal disease involved isolating prostitutes and infected promiscuous women, public health officials viewed sex education as a necessary long-term solution. If the public could be educated about the dangers of venereal disease and promiscuous women that carried them, then the public would deter from engaging in sexual relations with these women.

During the American Plan, officials saw a need for the movement of sex education into the public sphere. Prior to the American Plan, Americans tended to "[pretend] that sex did not exist."[41] Many public health and government officials criticized the way that Americans used to ignore sex in public life. During the American Plan, public health and government officials realized the need to bring sex education into the public light in order to stop the spread of venereal disease. A World War I era sex education pamphlet titled "Relations with Other Organizations" informed Americans that "the time for silence and drifting is over. The war has forced the issue of sex education."[42] Officials encouraged open discussion about sex in order to inform the public of sexual diseases and deter premarital sexual encounters.

Officials largely used concepts of morality to deter the public from engaging in illicit sexual relations. During the American Plan, health officials saw a need for education because "health and morals have suffered incalculable injury."[43] Due to the abundance of persistent immoral sexual activity in the early twentieth century, officials believed that religion and ethics no longer deterred premarital sexual activity. Officials thought that a re-invigoration of sexual morality through sex education would reinforce practices of sexual abstinence.[44] According to Maurice Bigelow, a 1920s sexology writer, the "reduction of venereal disease must depend on hygienic and moral education which will lead people to avoid the sources of infection."[45] Bigelow and other public health officials used concepts of ethics as a tool to counter the spread of venereal disease by discouraging casual sexual relations.

Sex education programs used fear tactics to deter illicit sexual behavior. Education programs that targeted soldiers specifically pointed to the negative impacts of venereal disease in order to deter them from engaging in sex with promiscuous women or prostitutes. Sex education in the military included "an expansion of the menace of prostitution and of the grave dangers of venereal disease to the men themselves."[46] Social hygiene officials believed that "a man kept from sexual promiscuity by fear of disease ... is a better member of society."[47] Officials leveraged the danger that sexual diseases posed to one's health to deter military men from engaging in reprehensible sexual relations.

The campaign for sex education, however, also targeted the public at large. The Social Hygiene Division of the US Military believed that "ignorance has always been the great ally of venereal disease, and therefore the necessity of putting everyone in the possession of true facts seems obvious."[48] Though sex education programs within the military only directly taught servicemen, the program encouraged them to transfer the information to people in their home community, thereby educating more and more people in the United States.[49] Additionally, officials employed large efforts to educate parents and children in order to expand the scope of sexual education in the United States.[50] Furthermore, many employers spent the time to educate their workforces. US government officials especially encouraged employers with large populations of female employees to teach sex education to their workers.[51] Most employers eagerly employed sex education programs because they realized the potential threat of lost efficiency that venereal disease posed to working-class women and men.[52] Government and hygiene officials found an entirely educated population to be extremely important in the battle against venereal disease in the early twentieth century United States.

Public health officials found the education of children to be important to the sex education initiatives under the American Plan in order to combat illicit sexual behavior of adults later in life. A mother who could properly educate her daughter could deter promiscuity in the girl when she grew up.[53] Officials similarly found it important to educate a boy so that he would "know [his] sure way of escape ... when a bad and beautiful woman lays her wiles to trap a boy."[54] Though the American public furiously debated the idea of employing sex education within schools, officials agreed that parents must be educated about how to teach their own children about sex.[55] The education of children was an important initiative under the American Plan that highlights the longevity of the plan to permanently combat the spread of venereal disease throughout the United States.

Sex education was a principal component of the American Plan. Officials viewed the elimination of venereal disease in the US military as the ultimate goal of the American Plan. The sex education program initiated under the American Plan exceeded the goals of the plan by implementing a long-term sex education campaign to subdue the presence of promiscuity and the spread of venereal disease throughout the entirety of the United States.

A gap exists in the present historical scholarship regarding the social class of women deemed promiscuous and, therefore dangerous, in the early twentieth century in the United States. In her article "Against Their Own Weaknesses," Courtney Shah argues that nonwhite lower-class women were the demographic groups considered dangerous.[56] Mary Odem, in contrast, claims that promiscuous women were young middle-class girls in her book *Delinquent Daughters: Protecting and Policing Adolescent Female Sexuality in the United States*.[57] Furthermore, in her article titled "In Defense of the Nation: Syphilis, North Carolina's 'Girl Problem,' and World War I," Karin Zipf asserts that many well off white women were labeled as delinquent and targeted under the American Plan.[58] Conversely, Ruth Alexander took a different approach in her book *The 'Girl Problem': Female Sexual Delinquency in New York*. Alexander argues that lower-class women and women of different races redefined the place of women in society in a positive light.[59] It is important to close this gap and define the social class of women who were deemed promiscuous in order to reveal the type of women targeted under the American Plan.

I argue that the majority of women that the public deemed promiscuous were working-class or poor women because these classes of women spent time in the streets or the public arena. Prostitutes also called "women of the streets" consisted of lower-class women, who mainly found business while walking the streets.[60] Similarly, the rise of a working-class of unmarried girls during the Progressive era meant that many unmarried young girls roamed the streets unaccompanied. While no longer confined to the home, these working-class women experienced sexual freedom that had never before been attained. However, the American public subjected women who entered the streets to a new wave of sexual criticism that associated their presence on the streets with promiscuity.[61] The 1918 Official Periodical of the American Social Hygiene Association confirms the idea that "venereal Disease is prevalent among public women ... to go with them invites infection."[62] Similarly, the sexology book, titled *The Control of Sex Infections*, found that "the working girl from the shop or factory or the servant class girl" made up "almost three-quarters of the [sexual] tabulations made."[63]

The public thoroughly criticized women who entered the streets to work attributing their position in the public sphere to promiscuity.

Significant scholarship exists that discusses a shift in the way the public viewed women in regard to sexuality. Odem and Shah both discuss a shift from a Victorian age way of thinking about women that regards women as the victims of sexual impurity to a Progressive era way of thinking that blames the individual woman for her promiscuity. Odem and Shah both argue that women transformed from the victim to the delinquent. However, while Odem simply discusses women as delinquents, Shah discusses a shift in perceptions of women from simple delinquents to a danger to society.[64] This shift to the Progressive era thinking is relevant to this chapter, as the American Plan directly blamed women for their promiscuity.

The American Plan embodied the Progressive era way of thinking about promiscuity. The public viewed women as instigators of immoral sexual relations rather than the victims of it. This chapter agrees with Odem's observation that during the Progressive era, the public saw sexually promiscuous women as dangerous rather than simply delinquent. This idea is embodied by the American Plan when officials quarantined women due to the danger that they presented to the United States military.

In the early twentieth century, the American public associated promiscuity in women with disease. Any woman in public life could be arrested and contained simply under suspicion that she might have venereal disease. Authorities arrested Nina McCall simply because someone had complained about her promiscuity.[65]

McCall's experience embodies the disservice of the American Plan. McCall, a lower-class girl who entered the streets on a daily basis, was subject to a wave of criticism regarding her sexuality. Once labeled as promiscuous, authorities also labeled her as a threat to society that needed to be immediately removed. Though Nina had not harmed anyone and had never before engaged in premarital sex, authorities still imprisoned her. Though McCall did not live in the immediate vicinity of military bases, officials still considered her promiscuity a potential threat to the US military. In their eyes, McCall could easily corrupt and infect a soldier on leave.[66]

The sex education plan initiated under the American Plan was an important long term component of the program to combat the spread of syphilis and gonorrhea. Officials used the plan to teach both boys and girls at a young age to avoid promiscuity. Public health officers thought that if girls like McCall had been taught to live a pure life from a young age, then premarital sex, and therefore venereal disease, could be eliminated.

The American Plan is an important part of American history that is rarely discussed today. Under the American Plan, thousands of women were violated through invasive medical examinations and wrongly imprisoned by the United States government. It is important to initiate a discussion of the American Plan in order to educate Americans about the violation of innocent women and to ensure that a similar violation is not repeated.

Discussion of the American Plan is also presently relevant amidst mass testing and quarantines due to the COVID-19 pandemic. Many important questions arise that pertain to ethical considerations under the American Plan. Does the United States have the authority to require its citizenry to submit to mandatory medical tests? Does it have the authority to enforce strict quarantines? Can civil liberties and due process be denied under the threat of an epidemic or pandemic? Historians, lawmakers, and political scientists can study initiatives taken under the American Plan in order to pave a clear and just path to the eradication of infection. They must learn from the mistakes made during the American Plan to ensure that no grave violation of individual freedom or privacy is repeated.

Notes

1. Scott Stern, *The Trials of Nina McCall: Sex, Surveillance, and the Decades-Long Government Plan to Imprison "Promiscuous" Women* (Boston: Beacon Press, 2018), 2–9.
2. Stern, *The Trials of Nina McCall*, 9.
3. Scott Stern, "America's Forgotten Mass Imprisonment of Women Believed to Be Sexually Immoral," History.com, July 21, 2019, https://www.history.com/news/chamberlain-kahn-act-std-venereal-disease-imprisonment-women.
4. Stern, "America's Forgotten Mass Imprisonment of Women Believed to Be Sexually Immoral."
5. Stern, *The Trials of Nina McCall*, 5.
6. Karin Zipf, "In Defense of the Nation: North Carolina's 'Girl Problem,' and World War I," *The North Carolina Historical Review* 89, no. 3 (2012): 1–5, www.jstor.org/

stable/23523735.

7. Mary Odem, *Delinquent Daughters: Protecting and Policing Adolescent Female Sexuality in the United States* (University of North Carolina Press, 2000), 14–18; Courtney Shah, "'Against Their Own Weakness,': Policing Sexuality and Women in San Antonio, Texas, During World War I," *Journal of the History of Sexuality* 19, no. 13 (2010): 9, www.jstor.org/stable/40986335.

8. Melissa Ditmore, *Encyclopedia of Prostitution and Sex Work* (Greenwood Press, 2006), 53.

9. Stern, *The Trials of Nina McCall*, 6.

10. Ditmore, *Encyclopedia of Prostitution and Sex Work*, 55.

11. Stern, *The Trials of Nina McCall*, 7.

12. Ditmore, *Encyclopedia of Prostitution and Sex Work*, 57.

13. Stern, *The Trials of Nina McCall*, 5.

14. John Rainsford, *What to Tell Your Boy: By John Rainsford; A Straightforward Answer to the Difficult Question of a Boy's Sex Education* (Philadelphia: The Penn Publishing Company, 1918), 12.

15. Rainsford, *What to Tell Your Boy*, 11.

16. Mary Ware Dennett, *The Sex Side of Life* (New York: Fifth Printing, 1919), 19.

17. American Social Hygiene Association, *Social Hygiene* (Baltimore: American Social Hygiene Association, 1921), 92.

18. Dennett, *The Sex Side of Life*, 19.

19. YMCA and USPHS, "Do Not Believe Him," 1919, Poster, Venereal Disease Visual History Archive, https://vdarchive.newmedialab.cuny.edu/items/show/382.

20. American Social Hygiene Association, *Child Questions and Their Answers*, 11.

21. Rainsford, *What to Tell Your Boy*, 119.

22. ASHA, *How Syphilis Spreads*, 1930, Still Image, Minnesota Department of Health, https://vdarchive.newmedialab.cuny.edu/items/show/359.

23. YMCA and USPHS, "The Venereal Menace: An Exhibit for Adults," Brochure, Venereal Disease Visual History Archive, https://vdarchive.newmedialab.cuny.edu/items/show/340.

24. Rainsford, *What to Tell Your Boy*, 172.

25. J. Bayard Clark, *The Control of Sex Infections* (New York: Macmillan, 1921), 34–35.

26. Clark, *The Control of Sex Infections*, 34–35.

27. American Social Hygiene Association, *Social Hygiene*, 62.

28. Martha P. Falconer, "The Segregation of Delinquent Women and Girls as a War Problem," *The Annals of the American Academy of Political and Social Science* 79, (1918): 3, www.jstor.org/stable/1013975.

29. Falconer, "The Segregation of Delinquent Women and Girls as a War Problem," 1.

30. Social Hygiene Division, Army Educational Commission, "Steady buddy—There's a come-back!" 1918, Poster, Venereal Disease Visual History Archive, https://vdarchive.newmedialab.cuny.edu/items/show/331.

31. Social Hygiene Division, Army Educational Commission, "Not in the Line of Duty," 1918, Poster, Venereal Disease Visual History Archive, https://vdarchive.newmedialab.cuny.edu/items/show/330.

32. War Department Commission of Training Camp Activities and United States

Public Health Service, *Social Hygiene Monthly* (ASHA Publications: 1918–1919), 178.

33. American Social Hygiene Association, *Social Hygiene*, 21–22.

34. Henrietta S. Additon, "Work Among Delinquent Women and Girl," *The Annals of the American Academy of Political and Social Science* 79, (1918): 1, www.jstor.org/stable/1013974.

35. Falconer, "The Segregation of Delinquent Women and Girls as a War Problem," 5.

36. War Department Commission of Training Camp Activities and United States Public Health Service, *Social Hygiene Monthly*, 178.

37. American Social Hygiene Association, *Social Hygiene*, 127.

38. Maurice A. Bigelow, *Sex Education: A Series of Lectures Concerning Knowledge of Sex in its Relation to Human Life* (New York: Macmillan, 1918), 15.

39. William John Fielding, *Sanity in Sex* (New York: Dodd, Mead and Company, 1920), 12.

40. Bigelow, *Sex Education*, 62.

41. University of Minnesota Libraries, "*Relations with Other Organizations. United States Military. Women's Program. World War I Pamphlets. Box 132, Folder 07,*" Social Welfare Archives, https://umedia.lib.umn.edu/item/p16022coll223:92863/p16022coll223:92705?child_index=0&facets[collection_name_s][], 10.

42. University of Minnesota Libraries, *Relations with Other Organizations*, 10.

43. Bigelow, *Sex Education*, 29.

44. Bigelow, *Sex Education*, 29–30.

45. Bigelow, *Sex Education*, 52.

46. Fielding, *Sanity in Sex*, 66.

47. Bigelow, *Sex Education*, 228.

48. University of Minnesota Libraries, *Relations with Other Organizations*, 1.

49. Fielding, *Sanity in Sex*, 78.

50. Albert Myers Coleman, *Stop, Look, and Think: Our Social System and its Many Dangers* (Boston: National Bureau for Sex Education, 1916), 8.

51. University of Minnesota Libraries, *Relations with other organizations*, 1.

52. Oregon Social Hygiene Society and South Dakota State Department of Health, *A State-Wide Program for Sex Education* (1920), 5.

53. Coleman, *Stop, Look, and Think*, 14.

54. Robert Newton Wilson, *The Education of the Young in Sex Hygiene: A Textbook for Parents and Teachers* (Cincinnati: Stewart & Kidd Co, 1917), 172.

55. Coleman, *Stop, Look, and Think*, 21.

56. Shah, "Against Their Own Weakness," 9.

57. Odem, *Delinquent Daughters*, 15.

58. Zipf, "In Defense of the Nation," 7.

59. Ruth Alexander, *The "Girl Problem": Female Sexual Delinquency in New York* (Ithaca: Cornel University Press, 1995), 3–6.

60. American Social Hygiene Association, *Social Hygiene*, 235.

61. Laura Abrams, "Guardians of Virtue: Social Reformers and the 'Girl Problem,' 1890–1920," *Social Service Review* 74, no. 3 (2000): 5–12, https://www.jstor.org/stable/10.1086/516412?seq=4#metadata_info_tab_contents.

62. American Social Hygiene Association, *Social Hygiene*, 127.

63. Clark, *The Control of Sex Infections*, 27.

64. Shah, "Against Their Own Weakness," 2; Odem, *Delinquent Daughters*, 18.

65. Stern, *The Trials of Nina McCall*, 6.

66. Stern, *The Trials of Nina McCall*, 8–11.

4. Alice Roosevelt and the Rise of the Infamous American Woman

LIV WISNEWSKI

Alice Roosevelt Longworth was the original infamous woman. In a time before celebrities were a part of mainstream culture, she embodied the term. Alice was known for her willful disregard of societal rules. One of the most remembered stories from her White House tenure was the time she climbed the balconies of the White House to smoke, even after being given direct orders not to.[1] She defined her own role as a rule-breaker, wave-maker, and overall publicly interactive woman. Ultimately, Alice's infamy rose from her consistent refusal to conform to society's standards of femininity.

Coming of age in the early 1900s, Alice stood on the edge of a new era for women. She lived through great strides for women's rights, such as the women's suffrage, the appointment of the first woman in Congress, and the establishment of *Griswold v. Connecticut* and *Roe v. Wade*. Her life spanned two centuries and lasted for nearly a century. Throughout it all, Alice was hailed as a cultural icon, a touchpoint for women, and the arbiter of D.C. society. Alice was a lightning bolt through popular culture in American history—explosively bright, shocking in nature, and ephemeral. However, in the decades following her death, Alice sunk further into historical obscurity than her contemporaries. Remembered as the free-wheeling, loose spirited, eccentric daughter of one of the most powerful presidents in United States history, Alice has been relegated to the position of a quirky women's role model at best, and shallow "girl boss" at worst.

Why have we done this? Why is Alice not remembered the way her cousin Eleanor is? Why is she known only by the words said about her, rather than those by her? For a woman so spoken of in her own time, why does she hardly exist in ours? This chapter attempts to expand our understanding of Alice as a public woman and celebrity of the early twentieth century. There are numerous books on the domestic sphere of women as well as the national culture of the United States of the era. There is also a significant amount of literature that covers the respectability of the early twentieth-century American woman, her strides into the public sphere, and the expectations and restrictions placed upon her. The existing writings on these topics do well in granting us a broad understanding of the standards of respectability for a woman of the time. This chapter hopes to contextualize some of that material by using Alice as a touchpoint for the emergence of celebrity culture, and the difference between the public and private worlds of women.

I posit that Alice's infamous nature lead her to be brushed aside; known well in her time, but ultimately disregarded in the records of feminist history. To understand Alice, we have to look at why she was so spoken about. Why was she so interesting to the public? Why did she stay in people's minds and in the newspapers even after the Roosevelt family left the White House? Infamy. Infamy that was inextricably linked to her femininity, or apparent lack thereof. Merriam-Webster defines infamy as an "evil reputation brought about by something grossly criminal, shocking, or brutal."[2] But Alice did not do anything bad, did she? She did not murder anyone, lead a bank heist, or start a political coup. So why was Alice Roosevelt Longworth such an infamous public figure? Alice's infamy is one of a more subtle nature. It is a sort of cultural infamy, which I define as "being well known for diverging from the dominant culture." Cultural infamy still exists today, though it usually takes on more casual forms, such as your favorite reality TV host or a particularly controversial Twitter personality. Alice's insistence on flouting standards of the time, behaving in ways that were distinctly unladylike, and not showing remorse for her actions made her the topic of many "gentle" newspaper takedowns. Even articles that praised her style and life found subtle ways to jab at her for not conforming.

To really understand the cultural infamy that surrounded Alice's life, I will use newspaper articles, private journals, and correspondence, as well as magazines, pop culture pieces, and personal accounts from across her life to examine the ways she flouted traditional femininity and other cultural standards.

Alice Roosevelt Longworth was seventeen when her father Theodore "Teddy" Roosevelt was inaugurated as President of the United States, following the assassination of President William McKinley in 1901.[3] Teddy Roosevelt was never meant to be president. He was placed into the restrictive role of the vice presidency by a party concerned his policies were too much, especially regarding foreign relations. When Leon Czolgosz shot President McKinley at the Pan American Exposition in Buffalo, New York, he did more than give Teddy Roosevelt the presidency; he gave America Alice.

Perhaps in some ways, Alice was the bigger gift. She was loud, spunky, and demanded attention in an era where women were still confined to the home and domesticity. Alice had a storied upbringing. Two days following her birth, her paternal grandmother passed away due to tuberculosis.[4] Eleven hours later her own mother, Alice Hathaway Lee Roosevelt, followed suit. Stricken with grief and unable to care for his newborn baby daughter, Alice's father left her in the care of an unmarried aunt and headed west.[5] Her father only returned years later, following his marriage to his second wife.[6] These early experiences gave Alice the independence that would characterized her the rest of her life.

For America, a first daughter who was practically an adult was a novelty. Both of President McKinley's children had died young, before his presidency, and President Cleveland's children were too young to have a societal impact during his time in office. Alice was seventeen when her father became president. She was an adult with passions and opinions that she could share freely. Many wondered: What was she like? What would she do? Alice immediately marked her independence, without concern for who she might anger or how she might be going against societal expectations of the time.

In 1902, just a few months after her father assumed office, Alice made her social debut with a splash.[7] America's first look at "Princess Alice" was indicative of what would follow. She wore a custom-designed dress in an uncommon blue shade, now known as Alice Blue.[8] She took the country by storm with her good looks and wit, as well as her refusal to meet the standards of femininity of the time. For young women in the early twentieth century, a social debut was a chance to find a suitable young man—Alice spent her social debut party enjoying herself, entertaining who she deemed entertaining, and did not come out of the event any closer to having a husband. Alice was not the soft-spoken, obedient public women the country was accustomed to—and she was not about to change herself.

It was incredibly hard to be an independently minded young woman in 1902, especially one on which the public eye was trained. Before the ratification of the 1920 woman's suffrage amendment, the public sphere belonged to men. For several decades, women had pushed against these boundaries by involving themselves in civic reform movements such as temperance, higher education, and even employment to a point. Still, young women in public were considered disreputable, unrefined, or even trashy because they went against the prevailing restrictions that placed "good girls" or "ladies" at home. The push for progress was fractured and broken into several strands—while progress may be made in one area, the gap between the implementation of progress and the acceptance of that progress was wide. Racial and class divides also played a part in the respectability of a woman, as a higher-class woman would be able to afford to stay home and rely on her husband or father, while women in the working class had to be in public to make a living. A respectable woman was domestic, quiet, private, and above all, avoided vice. These class prescriptions were important to high society of the time, and there was no higher society than the presidential circle. Essentially American royalty, there were strict standards for how women, young and old, in the White House social sphere were supposed to behave.[9]

As a first daughter, these standards applied to Alice. However, an expectation to meet these standards does not always guarantee adherence. Alice grew up outside of the social expectations of this high society, raised by her aunt, a single woman who valued independence, intelligence, and political understanding.[10] Alice was controlled by no one, butting heads with her father and arguing fervently with her stepmother.[11] Before her White House years, Alice threatened to bring shame to the family if her parents attempted to send her off to boarding school.[12] Anyone who may have known Alice prior to the Roosevelt Presidency would have expected her transgressive behavior. Unfortunately, most of America was not afforded that relationship with the glamorous and outrageous new first daughter.

For one, Alice was fond of gambling, especially at the race track.[13] She liked to drink, both privately and in public.[14] She could often be seen getting in and out of cars with men, laughing and being rowdy, headed to parties and other social engagements she chose for herself.[15] She had a penchant for smoking on the White House balconies.[16] Alice was not a demure, high-society lady, ready and willing to uphold the expectations placed upon her by a restrictive society. Alice refused to play by the rules of respectability. Being a high-class woman in the public eye, she was expected to be a purifying influence on the men in her life. The men around her worked in politics—not a place for a woman to begin with—and it was a woman's responsibility to be their haven from the gritty real world. Instead, Alice joined them in that world, seeking yet another form of equality women at the time were barred from. By involving herself in the corrupting influences of drinking and gambling, Alice forced herself into the world of men and distanced herself from the image of the beautiful and pure first daughter that she was expected to take on. Alice rejected any restrictions; and if her father could not tell her what to do, the rest of the country certainly could not.

Moreover, Alice was not a quiet person. Following in her aunt's footsteps, Alice enjoyed participating in her father's cabinet meetings, where she could often be found sitting in the back of the room, running sideline commentary, critiquing ideas, even posing her own.[17] She was vocal and unafraid to hold back her opinions, which was not always welcomed in an era where women could not vote, let alone hold political office. Ideals of traditional femininity still ruled, even in the court of "Princess Alice" and her indulgent father. She may have been able to get away with unruly behavior and disobedience, but a line was drawn at political intervention. Insisting that she was of equal political intelligence went against all of the established rules of gender of the time. The mere idea that she understood political issues, let alone had a better understanding than the men in the room whose jobs were politics was egregious. As one particularly famous story goes: A cabinet member, frustrated with Alice's constant comments and interjections, jokingly threatened to throw her out a window and implored her father to "reign her in or kick her out."[18] Roosevelt responded, "I can do one of two things, I can be president of the United States or I can control Alice. I cannot possibly do both."[19]

Alice's interference in the political realm extended past the White House. In 1905, at age twenty-one, Alice joined William Taft and other politicians on a foreign relations tour through Asia.[20] This trip was the first time Alice had been west of the Mississippi and she intended to pull as much from her journey as she could.[21] Alice recorded her delight at traveling by train and noted the expectations she was supposed to uphold while traveling with a political delegation. Early on she remarked that Taft, in charge of the whole trip, encouraged her to spend time having lunch or tea with the other ladies of the group because "it would be well for [her] to at least seem to have a modicum of interest in the others."[22] Alice profoundly engaged in the journey and was fascinated by following along the route in an atlas she carried and remarked, "I would look at it and think I am actually here at this place on the map."[23] However, the train was only one part of her excitement. As she recorded a stop in Reno wherein some of the men in the party stopped to observe a prizefight, Alice noted her displeasure in not being included on the excursion: "There was no question in those days of a woman going to a prizefight, and our car was switched off and sent on an hour ahead to give the Secretary time to stop for lunch."[24] Alice made acute observations on appropriate local activities for men and women as they traveled across the country, and her remarks paint a picture of a young woman displeased with the expectations placed on her. Alice felt that she had similar interests and talents as the men; therefore, she believed she should be able to participate in the same activities they did.

It was on this trip that Alice met her husband, Nicholas Longworth, a Congressional representative from Ohio and the man many believed would finally tame her spirit.[25] Alice had not met her husband at her social debut and had spent the intervening years inserting herself into places she did not belong, both socially and politically. Longworth was fourteen years older, well established in the American Political system, and a well-known "D.C. playboy." If anyone could match Alice's intense energy, and perhaps rein her into being the demure, high-class woman she was supposed to be, it was Nick. In one of the most famous stories of their time on the trip, Alice jumped fully clothed into a pool rigged upon the deck of their steamer on the voyage to Japan.[26] Alice then implored Nick Longworth to jump in with her, claiming her behavior only would have been outrageous had she first removed her clothes.[27] The press ran with the story, declaring it romantic and dashing. This story softened Alice's appearance to the public, making her seem relatable to the young women back at home. Alice recalled the story herself in her autobiography, claiming that she took precautions to protect her more delicate belongings by leaving her "shoes, watch, and such things that the water would hurt, in the care of onlookers."[28] However, Alice also remarked that "there was not much difference between swimming in a bathing suit and swimming in a linen skirt and shirtwaist," meaning it would have made very little difference what she was wearing at the time, so long as it was appropriately modest.[29] Alice corrected one aspect of the story: the identity of the man who leaped into the pool with her. Despite the press' romantic notions of the man being Nick Longworth, it was instead a childhood friend, Bourke Cockran. Alice noted that Bourke commented on how comfortable the pool appeared and that he was "tempted to go in just as he was." This lead to "a little argument" resulting in Bourke joining her in the water.[30] Rather than a "dashing, romantic" story of lovers and eventual spouses, it was a lighthearted tale of old friends enjoying one another's company while traveling.[31] Those who hoped for Alice to settle down in her match-made-in-heaven romance were unfortunately set up for disappointment.

Despite the popularity surrounding Alice's eccentric behavior, there was no escaping the standards of traditional femininity expected of women in the early twentieth century. Women were expected to adhere to certain social scripts, and women who refused to follow those scripts suffered the consequences. In Alice's time, women were encouraged to be gentle, romantic, quiet, domestic, and never politically or internationally active. Alice flouted each of these conditions from her very first moment in the White House, gaining her a reputation of cultural infamy. She was Princess Alice, well known for her indomitable spirit, her decidedly unfeminine behavior, and her insistence on the truth of her ways.[32] Alice's years in the White House were marked by a relatively fond, yet gently admonishing tone from the press: from referring to her semi-satirically as "Princess," to joyfully recording her misbehavior and commenting on just how outrageous it was that she was allowed to behave that way.[33] America adored hearing about her antics, but at the same time they enjoyed critiquing her for misbehaving. The public loved Alice, even as they sought to editorialize her and make her more into the image they held for a woman of her class.

The White House years were not the last the country heard of Alice, however. President Roosevelt remained in office until 1909, and Alice continued to pull the spotlight. She married Nick Longworth in 1906, in the twelfth wedding ceremony to be held in the White House.[34] Articles across the country remarked on her ceremony, which included the words "to obey" due to the traditional Episcopalian leanings of the pastor.[35] This was uncommon at the time as "many ministers of the gospel do change the word to some other less objectionable term to the modern bride."[36] The irony of Alice agreeing to obey anyone was not lost on reporters. Both across the country and the globe, regular citizens and those in political power celebrated Alice's wedding. In Boston, the bells rang at noon on the 17th of February, and in

Vienna, Austria, and Rome, people telegrammed the White House with their congratulations.[37] It was a new era for the wave-making first daughter, and no one was sure what the addition of a husband would mean for Alice's behavior.

Twenty-two, newlywed, and facing another four years of her father's presidency, what would Alice become? Who would she be? How would she change? The answer: not much. Despite her wedding vows, Alice was not going to obey anyone but herself and she was not going to leave the public eye anytime soon.[38] Alice maintained political connections to people within her father's circles, remained an active participant in political institutions, and continued to charm society with her wit and eccentric personality.[39]

There is a great deal of evidence to suggest that while Alice may have no longer been the young woman who carried a snake around the White House in her purse, she certainly had not settled down. Just because she was a married woman did not mean that she intended to stop her mischief in the nation's capital. A key anecdote on Alice's behavior as an adult includes a prank she played upon a visitor to Congress: Alice placed a tack on the visitor's seat and waited for him to sit on it.[40] The Washington Post stated that the man "jump[ed] into the air with all the force of a bullet discharged from a modern rifle." The first line of the article also referred to the first daughter as "the naughty boy in with the tack."[41] When the Roosevelts left the White House in 1909, Alice supposedly buried a voodoo doll of Nellie Taft in the front yard.[42] She would later be banned from the premises by the Tafts, who became the first, but not the last, family to do so.[43] Alice maintained her younger, wave-making ways throughout her adulthood, still drawing the attention and the adoration of the press and the public.

Despite her marriage, Alice remained fiercely independent. She continued to play by her own rules and flout the standards society tried to set for her. Nick Longworth could no more control Alice than her father had been able to. Before marriage, Nick had somewhat of a reputation for being a "D.C. playboy," and his relationship with Alice was somewhat rocky.[44] Nick and Alice had distinctly opposed political opinions, and Alice, as always, was not one to keep her opinions to herself. In 1912 Alice's father began to campaign for a third term as president; this time under his own party, known as the Bull Moose party.[45] Alice was vocally and publicly supportive of her father's campaign, while her husband backed the sitting president.[46] Alice's convictions were so strong that she endorsed her father in her husband's own district, leading to a deeper rift in their marriage. Although attitudes about women's political involvement were continually evolving and becoming more accepted, it was still considered taboo for a woman to publicly oppose her husband. This action clearly signified Alice's continued free will and disinclination to bend for anyone.

Despite chilly relations, Alice and Nick kept up a good front. In the years after her father's death in 1919, Alice continued to be outspoken, though she did tone down her public disagreements with her husband. Alice remained in the public eye through the befriending of the D.C. political elite and through her prior reputation. Princess Alice did not have to do much to attract the attention of the news sources—when she did, the press continued to use the same teasing tone that had begun in her adolescence.

Even after her teen years, Alice continued to flout the societal standards imposed upon women. The public kept close tabs on Alice, waiting to see when she would settle into the role of domesticity still expected of women. Part of what maintained Alice's infamy as both a young newlywed and adult was her refusal to settle into the obscurity expected of a political wife. No longer the glamorous teenage daughter of the most powerful man in the nation, Alice was expected to take on the responsibilities of a wife and respect the boundaries set by her husband, who was not as lenient as her indulgent father. Instead, Alice maintained her sense of self and her personally curated opinions and continued to make them public knowledge. Although many political and societal restrictions had been relaxed when women gained the right to vote in 1920, there were still certain expectations to be met; expectations that Alice would gladly not meet.

Around the same time that women gained their elective franchise, society started to face a shift towards modernity. Included in this shift was the concept of a celebrity. Ushered in by silent film stars and the increased availability of movies, radio, and television in what became a mass national popular culture, celebrities became cultural touchpoints for the public to relate to. Alice, being a first daughter, achieved this celebrity status early on in her life—being the president's child made her a national touchpoint even before modernity's arrival. And once a mass national culture, and its concomitant culture of celebrity, emerged in the 1920s, Alice remained at its center.

Still, her claim to fame was infamy. Alice and Nick were married for fourteen years before Alice had her one and only child.[47] Born in 1925, Alice's daughter, Paulina, would be the new American Princess.[48] Newspaper articles wrote of how Alice would finally have to obey the whims of someone other than herself. In true Alice fashion, however, there was quite the scandal surrounding her baby daughter. Paulina was the daughter of William Borah, another senator that Alice had an ongoing affair with.[49] Some sources even say that Alice intended to name the baby girl Deborah, which translates biblically to "of Borah."[50]

Although Alice had other engagements to attend to the older she got, she never dropped or curbed her political opinions for anyone. When her cousin, Franklin Delano Roosevelt (FDR), ran for office in the 1930s, Alice stridently campaigned against him saying "the same surname is about all we have in common" and even if she were not a Republican she would not vote for FDR.[51] Alice's political activism and public behavior were no longer a surprise, both to those who knew Alice and to the rest of society. Alice's life lead her through various eras of femininity and eventually, the times caught up with her. Alice was still the arbiter of D.C. society; popular in the press for her famous father and youthful antics, but her public persona now fit more in line with what was acceptable for women. The press turned to retrospectives and the fame from her youth lingered. Alice's complicated relationship with femininity and celebrity culture lasted her whole life, in part because she was ahead of the curve for so many years.

The relationship between Alice, Franklin, and Eleanor Roosevelt was not always tense. Franklin was only a few years older than Alice, and they had been relatively close in their youth, along with Eleanor, Franklin's wife, and another one of Alice's cousins.[52] Throughout their childhood, they spent much time together. Despite the adults in their lives constantly comparing Alice and Eleanor against one another, they managed a sort of friendship. Comparisons between Alice and Eleanor extended throughout Eleanor's time as a First Lady and through history. Eleanor, as the country remembers her, was quiet, demure, and only a political powerhouse in service of her sickly, yet strident husband. Simply, Eleanore was everything that Alice was not.

Perhaps it was Eleanor's status that kept the two of them apart in the annals of history. There is most certainly a gulf between the position of first daughter and First Lady. Perhaps if the two of them had been closer Alice would have been remembered more fondly alongside her cousin, although, it is near impossible to say. Perhaps it is because Eleanor fit herself more neatly into the roles required of a woman of her status, and Alice consistently found herself on the outside of traditional feminine society. It may have been by her own choice, but it has had certain consequences that are impossible to miss in our examination of national culture.

Alice's adult life was touched by several instances of tragedy and at least one bright spot. Her daughter Paulina's life was not particularly happy or long. Despite the public's insistence that Alice take to motherhood, she did not. Paulina grew up with distant parents, married young, lost her husband to hepatitis, and suffered from mental illness including a deep depression.[53] In January of 1957, Paulina died of an accidental overdose of sleeping pills, leaving her daughter Joanna an orphan.[54] This tragedy may have been a turning point for Alice. Despite Alice's poor mothering skills to her own child, she took in her granddaughter and became a devoted caretaker.[55] Alice's granddaughter grew up to be quite the socialite herself, attending presidential social events with Alice and enjoying the type of treatment the public had expected Paulina to receive. Joanna kept her grandmother company throughout the rest of her life and was credited by *American Heritage* for being the source of her grandmother's youthfulness.[56]

Alice's husband died in 1931;[57] she outlived him by just under fifty years, passing away in her Dupont Circle home in 1980.[58] Even in her older years, Alice remained politically active and socially engaged. She attended Congressional hearings regularly, sitting in the general seating and hanging off of every word said.[59] No longer the belle of D.C., Alice finally reigned in her opinions, at least during actual sessions of Congress. She continued to be known for her quick wit, social gatherings, and strong political connections. Alice befriended a long list of Presidents, including Richard Nixon, and kept up with the elite political social scene into her old age.[60]

Some remarked that Alice was the gatekeeper of D.C. society. She had been associated with the community for so long that it had become her de facto role. Alice could be harsh, hard to please, and easy to anger; it was often questioned whether or not it was worse to draw her attention or to be completely ignored by her. One of the most commonly quoted facts about Alice is her love of gossip. She was known to have a needlepoint pillow that said, "if you have nothing nice to say, come over and sit next to me."[61]

The roles of women changed rapidly in Alice's later years. She lived through the civil rights movement, the counterculture of the 1960s and 1970s, the beginning of the AIDS crisis, and the modern beginning of the queer rights movement. Alice saw women transition from being unable to vote, to eventually working outside of the home and even holding political office. It is hard to know exactly what Alice thought of it all—her autobiography had been written decades earlier, and though she was always liberal with her opinions, her younger years drew much more focus than her later ones do. It is hard to imagine, however, that Alice would have had a problem with the evolving and modernized world that young women were now growing up in.

Alice Longworth Roosevelt's life spanned various eras of femininity. In each one Alice flouted convention, broke the rules, and charmed the nation with her raucous personality and vivacious nature. From a young woman insistent on behaving the same way as her male peers, to a wife and mother determined to preserve her sense of self and identity, to the older socialite she became when the times finally caught up to her, Alice forged a path that prioritized her sense of self over societal prescriptions. Alice was the original infamous woman. Her insistence on living life on her own terms won her many admirers and many detractors. It afforded her opportunities within the political world that were not available to most women of her time. Alice's life was one of glamour, as well as infamy.

Alice actively chose to go against the norm. Her circumstances were those of a young woman who could be and do anything she wanted, by virtue of a powerful father and a high-class social network. Alice wanted to be, and was, different. Femininity is often weaponized as a way to keep women in their place. Even today, some cultures and societies still expect women to be quiet, domestic, and virtuous, allowing men to do the hard work of being a part of society. Social norms have shifted for most, allowing women to do important things like vote, own property, and run for office. Many women are no loner required to keep their opinions to themselves on the basis of gender alone.

Alice was not automatically granted this freedom. It was something she had to carve out for herself. Alice cultivated her independence from a young age, and it served her well throughout her life. From a fashionable young woman taking the country by storm, to an older D.C. socialite controlling the scene with her remarks, the nation was clued into her every move. Why has Alice receded in the nation's collective memory? In some ways, she was one of the first liberated American women. Today her behavior would draw no more public ire than your average college student. Perhaps the country was not quite ready to experience Alice when she arrived on the scene.

Either way, Alice and her infamy have given American women a lot. She may not have been the nicest woman in the White House, but she is certainly worth remembering.

Notes

1. Stacy A. Cordery, *Alice: Alice Roosevelt Longworth from White House Princess to Washington Power Broker* (New York: Penguin Group, 2007), 77.

2. *Merriam-Webster*, "Infamy," accessed April 15, 2020, https://www.merriam-webster.com/dictionary/infamy.

3. "The Swearing in of Theodore Roosevelt," The Joint Congressional Committee on Inaugural Ceremonies, https://www.inaugural.senate.gov/about/past-inaugural-ceremonies/swearing-in-of-vice-president-theodore-roosevelt-after-the-assassination-of-president-william-mckinley/index.html.

4. Edmund Morris, *The Rise of Theodore Roosevelt* (New York: Random House, 2010), 229–230.

5. D. Wead, *All the Presidents' Children: Triumph and Tragedy in the Lives of America's First Families* (Atria Books, 2003), 48.

6. Morris, *The Rise of Theodore Roosevelt*, 373–374.

7. Carol Felsenthal, *Princess Alice: The Life and Times of Alice Roosevelt Longworth* (New York: St. Putnam Adult, 1988), 59.

8. John Dinan, "Alice Blue Gown," in *Favorite Songs of the Good Old Days*, ed. Ken Tate & Janice Tate (Berne, Indiana: House of White Birches, 2004), 13.

9. Susan Ware, *American Women's History: A Very Short Introduction* (Oxford University Press, 2015).

10. Wead, *All the Presidents' Children*, 48.

11. Steven Lee Carson, "Alice Roosevelt Longworth," *American History* 40, no. 3 (2005): 38.

12. Edward J. Renehan Jr., *The Lion's Pride: Theodore Roosevelt and His Family in Peace and War* (Oxford University Press, 1999), 47.

13. Wead, *All the Presidents' Children*, 48.

14. Wead, *All the Presidents' Children*, 48.

15. Carson, "Alice Roosevelt Longworth," 38.

16. Cordery, *Alice*, 77.

17. Carson, "Alice Roosevelt Longworth," 38.

18. Carson, "Alice Roosevelt Longworth," 38.

19. Alden Whitman, "Alice Roosevelt Longworth Dies; She Reigned In Capital 80 Years," *New York Times*, February 21, 1980.

20. "Alice in Asia: The 1905 Taft Mission to Asia," Freer Gallery of Art & Arthur M. Sackler Gallery, National Museum of Asian Art, https://asia.si.edu/essays/alice-in-asia/.

21. "Alice in Asia."

22. "Alice in Asia."

23. "Alice in Asia."

24. "Alice in Asia."

25. "Alice in Asia."

26. "Daughter, Fully Dressed, Jumps Into a Swimming Tank On Board a Steamship," *Pittsburgh Post*, Sept. 12, 1905, 1.

27. "Alice in Asia."

28. "Alice in Asia."

29. "Alice in Asia."

30. "Alice in Asia."

31. "Alice in Asia."

32. Margaret M. Lukes, "Princess Alice Bows at Last to Her First Boss," *Salt Lake Telegram*, March 22, 1925.

33. Lukes, "Princess Alice Bows at Last to Her First Boss."

34. "Alice Roosevelt Weds Nicholas Longworth." *Hamilton Evening Democrat*, February 17, 1906.

35. "Alice Roosevelt Weds Nicholas Longworth."

36. "Alice Roosevelt Weds Nicholas Longworth."

37. "Alice Roosevelt Weds Nicholas Longworth."

38. "Alice Roosevelt Weds Nicholas Longworth,"

39. Carson, "Alice Roosevelt Longworth," 38.

40. "Mrs. Longworth's Joke," *New York Times*, May 12, 1908.

41. "Mrs. Longworth's Joke," *New York Times*.

42. Lawrence L. Knutson, "Alice Roosevelt Longworth, Wild Thing," Salon.com, June 7, 1999.

43. Knutson, "Alice Roosevelt Longworth, Wild Thing."

44. Carson, "Alice Roosevelt Longworth," 38.

45. Carson, "Alice Roosevelt Longworth," 38.

46. Carson, "Alice Roosevelt Longworth," 38.

47. Lukes, "Princess Alice Bows at Last to Her First Boss."

48. Lukes, "Princess Alice Bows at Last to Her First Boss."

49. Carson, "Alice Roosevelt Longworth," 38.

50. Carson, "Alice Roosevelt Longworth," 38.

51. "Disclaimer," *Time magazine*, October 1932, time.com.

52. Mark Peyser and Dwyer Timothy, *Hissing Cousins: The Untold Story of Eleanor Roosevelt and Alice Roosevelt Longworth* (Knopf Doubleday, 2015).

53. Carson "Alice Roosevelt Longworth," 38.

54. Carol Felsenthat, *Princess Alice: The Life and Times of Alice Roosevelt Longworth* (New York: St. Putnam Adult, 1988), 59.

55. Felsenthal, *Princess Alice*, 59.

56. June Bingham, "'Princess Alice' Roosevelt Longworth," *American Heritage* 20, no. 2 (1969), https://www.americanheritage.com/princess-alice-roosevelt-longworth.

57. Carson, "Alice Roosevelt Longworth," 38.

58. Carson, "Alice Roosevelt Longworth," 38.

59. Carson, "Alice Roosevelt Longworth," 38.

60. Stephen Hansen, "What Was Once Princess Alice's Palace," *The InTowner*, Sep 10, 2012.

61. Sally Quinn, "At 90, Alice Roosevelt Longworth Didn't Care Who She Offended in This Mean, Funny 1974 Interview," *Washington Post*, March 29, 2016, https://www.washingtonpost.com/news/arts-and-entertainment/wp/2016/03/29/at-90-alice-roosevelt-longworth-didnt-care-who-she-offended-in-this-mean-funny-1974-interview/.

5. Paving Her Own Best Way: Lillian Gilbreth's Journey From Housewife to Career Woman

HELEN HICKMAN

On June 14, 1924, Dr. Lillian Moller Gilbreth was left a widow and tasked with raising her eleven children after her husband's sudden death from a heart attack. Three days later she packed her suitcase, left her children, and sailed across the Atlantic Ocean to give a speech at the London Power Conference. Later, she presided over a session of the World Congress of Scientific Management in Prague on behalf of her husband.[1] Although Lillian adored her husband and grieved his death, she could not let widowhood slow her down. Instead, she worked to provide for her family and prove herself capable of managing the business that she and her husband had built together—on her own. While she and her husband had developed "The One Best Way" to accomplish any and all tasks through their motion studies, Lillian Gilbreth created her own "One Best Way" in order to thrive in the male-dominated fields of business and engineering.[2] This moment began an incredibly successful career in which Lillian managed her husband's engineering consulting business, advised women on domestic efficiency, and became the first female engineering professor at Purdue University, all while single-handedly raising eleven children.

Lillian Gilbreth raised both her children and held a professional career at a time when most women were expected to stay at home. Despite being cast in the role of a simple mother and housewife in the popular memoir and later film *Cheaper by the Dozen* (1948), written by two of her children, Lillian managed much more than her household.[3] Although she never publicly described herself as a feminist, she paved the way for women of the twentieth century with her innovative career and support for other working women. Lillian Gilbreth's story illustrates the ongoing struggle and success of women to balance both a family and a career, despite the societal expectations of her time.[4]

Lillian Gilbreth's story inspired many scholars to write about her life and career. The most notable contribution to the scholarship about her begins with Laurel Graham's monograph *Managing on Her Own: Dr. Lillian Gilbreth and Women's Work in the Interwar Era*. Graham focused on Lillian's career as both a wife and a widow prior to the 1940s.[5] Jane Lancaster explored Lillian's public portrayal, management of her own public image, and the intersectionality of Lillian as both a professional woman and mother in her book *Making Time: Lillian Moller Gilbreth—A Life Beyond "Cheaper by the Dozen."*[6] Most recently, Julie Des Jardins' book *Lillian Gilbreth: Redefining Domesticity* studied Lillian's life and career from her early life through the Great Depression of the 1930s, unveiling how her life illustrated changing perspectives of work and gender roles in American domesticity.[7] This chapter builds on previous scholarship and seeks to answer the following question: How did Lillian Gilbreth help change the workplace for women in the twentieth century as a working mother?

This chapter will explore how Lillian Gilbreth influenced the workplace for women in the twentieth century through her roles as working mother, businesswoman, industrial engineer, and women's advocate that challenged gender roles of her time. Through Lillian's own work, newspaper articles, letters, and memoirs written about her, this chapter will articulate what her roles as both mother and career woman revealed about working women in the twentieth century.

Striving For More

Born in 1878 in Oakland, California, Lillian Moller Gilbreth grew up as a shy and timid young girl with a love of learning.[8] Her parents provided her with a comfortable life, including an education and hired help to manage the household.[9] In her autobiography, Lillian described a Victorian-era upbringing in which "[m]en were thought to be stronger than women—more capable in industry and business—incapable of doing any work in the home."[10] She came of age in an era defined by strict notions about gender roles and acceptable social conduct, especially for women.[11] Her childhood and early life contextualize many of her later reactions to obstacles she faced in her career.

Lillian Moller was a part of an early wave of women at the turn of the century who began to attend college. When she attended the University of California, only 2.7 percent of American women attended college.[12] Even fewer women earned graduate degrees. Only small numbers of women attended college at the time due to cultural attitudes against women in higher education and the expensive cost of attendance that only those with means could afford.[13] Lillian reflected on her college experience during which she thought she would pursue a career in teaching and did not think she would marry.[14] Although an exceptional student, she faced rejection when her school's Phi Beta Kappa chapter did not invite her to join. Lillian noted that no other women had made the list and that a friend had told her "that she had tied with one of the boys, but that someone had said, 'He needs it more' or 'It will be more useful to him.'"[15] Much later she would be invited to join Phi Beta Kappa, but she was disappointed by her rejection as she worked hard for her degree in English. This was just one of many experiences in which Lillian faced obstacles in her career due to her sex.

While her parents hoped she would pursue marriage and motherhood, Lillian initially had other plans. She graduated from the University of California at Berkeley in 1900 and immediately went on to earn her master's degree in literature from Berkeley in 1902.[16] Lillian initially sought to pursue a Ph.D. in literature. However, she changed her plans after meeting Frank Gilbreth at a train station in Boston, traveling with friends for her "Grand Tour" of Europe.[17] In 1904, Frank and Lillian married, building both a family and a business during their twenty years together. In doing so, Lillian sought to pursue an unconventional path for women of her time. Although her plans changed, her education would prove to be integral to her career.

Lillian's children largely shaped her career as she stayed at home to care for them, then eventually left the home to provide for them following her husband's death. Soon after marrying Frank, Lillian became pregnant with their first child and gave birth in 1905. From 1905 to 1922, Lillian carried thirteen pregnancies, giving birth about every fifteen months.[18] One of Lillian's children, Frank B. Gilbreth Jr. described how his parents, while traveling during their honeymoon, "made a pact that they'd have an even dozen children."[19] Frank and Lillian had their dozen children; however, one daughter, Mary, passed away in 1911 from diphtheria.[20] Mary's death left the family deeply saddened, as Lillian described how "it was an experience which an understanding psychiatrist might possibly have adjusted, but it was not adjusted, and it left a permanent scar."[21] Lancaster provides an alternative explanation for the Gilbreths' abundance of children, suggesting that they were "positive eugenicists" who sought to produce a large family to prove they could raise superior children through their efficient methods.[22] Either way, the Gilbreths both adored their children and intrigued others with their tales of raising them. The needs of this large family pushed Lillian to pursue a career following her husband's death, helping to cement her identity as a working mother.

Although Lillian's husband often traveled for work while she remained at home, she played an important role in the Gilbreth business prior to Frank's passing. She and her husband conducted motion studies on tasks such as bricklaying, where "Frank would have been watching the mason's motions, while Lillie was watching the man's dedication to his job." This was unique compared to other early work in industrial efficiency as "it was that emphasis on the *human* side of management that was to make the Gilbreth System unique."[23] As Lancaster notes in her biography of Gilbreth, "Lillian's education was helpful to Frank in at least two ways: she wrote clearly and elegantly, and her training in psychology was to provide an original and important new angle to Frank's work."[24] Lillian's background in psychology and exceptional writing ability provided her husband with the tools he needed to differentiate his work through the incorporation of the human element from others in the field of scientific management.

When Lillian first proposed attending the University of California at Berkeley for college, her father gawked at the idea.[25] In her memoir, she recounted proposing attending college to her parents. Her father told her that "college is only necessary for teachers and other women who have to make their living ... No daughter of mine will have to do that. I can support them—I want to."[26] Lillian's father eventually allowed her to attend college and she not only earned her bachelor's and master's degrees but also later earned her doctorate degree in applied psychology from Brown University in 1915. As the third woman to receive a doctorate degree from Brown University, Lillian and other women of the time paved the way for women in higher education.[27] Lillian's story thus illustrates the struggle women faced in the early twentieth century to earn degrees in higher education and gain opportunities in their careers. After Frank passed away from a heart attack in 1924, Lillian's education and expertise proved vital to providing for her children, continuing her husband's legacy, and forging a new career for herself.

Finding Her Path in A Man's World

As a new widow and single mother, Lillian's role quickly shifted from caregiver to sole financial provider for her children. Lillian was left to manage her children and home in Montclair, New Jersey, on her own. She had worked alongside her husband and had to adapt to running their business and household by herself. Two of her children, Frank B. Gilbreth Jr. and Ernestine Gilbreth Carey, wrote *Belles on Their Toes* (1950), which recounted the adventures of the Gilbreth family following their father's death.[28] In the memoir, Gilbreth Jr. and Carey described how their mother adapted the business to operate without Frank in order to provide for her children and pay for their college educations.

While she was more than capable of the work, others failed to recognize her ability. Gilbreth Jr. and Carey noted that businesses declined to renew their motion study contracts due to their belief that while Lillian "might know the theory of motion study, no woman could handle the technical details of the job or command the respect and cooperation of shop foremen and workers."[29] Lillian largely wrote up her husband's research and published the work under the name L. M. Gilbreth rather than her full name in order to draw attention away from the fact that she was a woman.[30] She faced the conundrum of creating a unique, marketable niche that could interest businesses in hiring her as a consultant.

No matter the obstacles, Lillian had to keep her business running. If she failed, she would face the decision of separating her children to live apart with friends and relatives in order to ease the financial burden.[31] As a result, she adapted the motion study business in new ways. First, Lillian created "The Motion Study Course" in which she invited industrial businesses to send their own engineers and employees to her home in order to learn about efficiency techniques.[32] This provided her with a way to prove her capabilities to businesses.

While Lillian's motion study course did not prove incredibly successful, some notable businesses such as Johnson & Johnson, Sears Roebuck, and R. H.

Macy and Company sent employees to her to train.[33] The connection to the department store R. H. Macy and Company would prove to be particularly helpful. Eugenia Lies, who was a student in Lillian's course and head of the Planning Department at Macy's, allowed Lillian's students to use Macy's Manhattan store as a case study.[34] Not only did Lillian improve worker efficiency and reduce fatigue, but she also improved the experience for shoppers. She created happy customers, and increased sales for the store. Lillian utilized her motion study course in order to demonstrate her efficiency expertise.

Lillian used her experience as a woman to her advantage in order to draw the attention of businesses to her skill set. Other businesses such as Sears Roebuck and Johnson & Johnson took note of her work as they viewed her as an expert on the woman consumer. Johnson & Johnson hired her to improve and conduct market research on Modess sanitary napkins, a new product that female consumers were not convinced were worth purchasing. Lillian's research helped change the sanitary napkin to fit the needs of women, and thus turned them into a viable consumer product.[35] Des Jardins describes how Lillian sought the opinions of women on sanitary napkins and found that female consumers "wanted greater comfort, protection, and inconspicuousness in a product that they could discreetly obtain and throw away."[36] Lillian managed to use her sex and understanding of the female consumer to convince businesses of her expertise. Drawing on conventional notions of femininity, she created a path into the male-dominated field of business. Her sex, once a hindrance, became her consulting business' greatest asset.

Lillian continued to utilize her expertise on the female consumer to her advantage. She knew that businesses would trust her in the realm of domestic affairs, even if they would not trust her in the field of industrial efficiency. Frank and Lillian had applied their time and energy techniques to the household for years. Frank Gilbreth Jr. and Ernestine Gilbreth Carey described how their parents' scientific management company extended into the household: "Dad took moving pictures of us children washing dishes, so that he could figure out how we could reduce our motions and thus hurry through the task."[37] Lillian had long experienced how time and energy techniques could be applied to household tasks. She thus became an expert on household efficiency, even though she could rarely be found in the kitchen.[38] Her son, Frank Gilbreth Jr., recounted in his memoir *Time Out for Happiness* that his mother "couldn't cook, never had done any laundry, didn't know much about sewing or knitting, and never had run a house of her own."[39] In her words, household efficiency "offers a philosophy that will make her work satisfying, a technique that will make it easy, and a method of approach that will make it interesting."[40] With eleven children, running an efficient household was a necessity. Lillian utilized this knowledge in order to attract the attention of women seeking to streamline their own households.

By 1926, Lillian Gilbreth had begun to share her household advice with the general public. She wrote an article for *Good Housekeeping* magazine in which she discussed how homemakers could reduce fatigue.[41] In her article, Gilbreth suggested that women could reduce fatigue by making "a survey of her working conditions with a view to eliminating unnecessary expenditures of time and energy."[42] She provided a series of questions that homemakers could use to evaluate ways in which they could change the household to reduce fatigue: "are soap, towels, and other bathroom supplies stored at hand or in some distant cupboard downstairs? Are drawers too deep, or just deep enough for their purpose so that articles stored in them are easily accessible?"[43] Additionally, Lillian wrote and published *The Homemaker and Her Job* in which she applied her methods of psychology and efficiency to the household in the form of advice to women.[44] In *The Homemaker and Her Job*, she described housekeeping as "the science, the universal likeness, the necessary activities which must be carried out in order that one may have more time and energy for the rest."[45] The following year in 1928, she also published *Living With Our Children* where she advised American women on how to best manage the household and raise children.[46] For example, Lillian asserted that "'living with should mean living together. If our plan enables us to live together happily and look forward to having children live with each other and with us together, then it has passed the tests and is worth trying."[47] Thus, these advice books further established Lillian as an expert on female consumers in the eyes of businesses and a superwoman figure in the eyes of American women.

Lillian's pivot to household efficiency advantageously utilized the sexist nature of businesses to create a niche for herself in the marketplace. While she faced the immense pressure of supporting her children in order to keep them together and continue her husband's legacy, Lillian became an expert in household efficiency that would remain with her throughout her career. Even into the 1950s, Lillian cast herself as a household efficiency expert in articles she wrote such as "You can be a timesaving expert, too!" for magazines such as *Better Homes and Gardens*.[48] In these articles, she suggested families utilize a "regular family council that has meetings and makes decisions, or informally where every member is consulted and helps as best he can to solve the problems."[49] While Lillian Gilbreth would always be a mother, it would be difficult for her to break away from this understanding of her identity as she sought to utilize her expertise in industrial efficiency.

A Pioneer in Engineering

In October of 1926, Lillian Gilbreth spoke at a psychological dinner in New York. Professionals from various industries and associations were in attendance at the dinner. Through this experience, she learned of the uphill battle it would be to work as a woman in a man's professional world. She recounted this experience in her autobiography where she wrote that "the chairman gave both men their title of 'Doctor' but carefully called Dr. Marston 'Miss' and Dr. Gilbreth 'Mrs.'[50] While Lillian largely downplayed the interaction in her autobiography, the experience clearly stayed with her as she chose to include the story. She already dealt with businesses refusing to renew their contracts, however, the chairman's diminishment of her expertise in a public setting made a lasting impression.

Lillian successfully remarketed her consulting business and gained recognition from professionals in her field. In 1929 she attended the World Engineering Conference in Tokyo as the only female delegate from any country.[51] The same year, she concluded the Motion Study Course as she found other sources of income.[52] By 1930 Lillian had gained a steady stream of consulting work to keep the family afloat.[53] With her finances stabilized, she was able to focus her work on advancing her engineering research and would join Purdue University as a faculty member.

In 1935 Lillian accepted a position as the first female full professor of management at Purdue University, in West Lafayette, Indiana.[54] Her children chose to stay at their home in Montclair, New Jersey, so Lillian left to work without them.[55] While teaching at Purdue, her work opened opportunities for women to break into male-dominated fields.

People both within and outside the Purdue community largely respected Lillian and viewed her appointment as a sign of progress for both women and the university itself. For example, a June 1935 letter written from C.R. Dooley, an oil industry expert, to Dr. Edward C. Elliot, Purdue University president, compares Gilbreth to newly appointed Purdue faculty member Amelia Earhart. In the letter, Dooley wrote in regard to Earhart's appointment saying, "this reminds me of the appointment of Mrs. Gilbreth to the faculty, some months ago. I just want you to know that these two appointments give me a thrill in feeling that the University is stepping right ahead in the line of progress."[56] Dooley's letter illustrated that just as Earhart was a pioneer in the field of aviation, Lillian Gilbreth was a pioneer for women in engineering. This comparison of the two highlights how both women broke into fields previously inaccessible to women.

Lillian Gilbreth and Earhart both lived and worked at Purdue in the mid-1930s where their mutual admiration of one another led to a close friendship. Before Lillian began working at Purdue, a reporter noted that the two women actually resembled one another, to which Lillian replied, "I'm so glad, because I'm one of her ardent admirers."[57] Earhart later included a photo of Frank and Lillian in her 1924 scrapbook and told a friend that "the most rewarding part of my time at the University is my association with Lillian Gilbreth."[58] The friendship between both of these women demonstrates how Lillian networked with other professional women seeking equality.

Earhart and Lillian lived and worked closely together while in residence at Purdue. Earhart was hired as a special career counselor and aviation advisor for women at Purdue University from 1935 to 1936. While not a normal faculty position, Earhart spent several weeks living in residence at Purdue per year giving lectures and advising students.[59] A student living in Duhme Hall, the only women's residence hall at the time on Purdue's campus, described how Lillian and Earhart both lived and worked at Purdue in Duhme Hall at the same time.[60] Lillian also wrote a letter to Earhart in which she warmly welcomed her to Purdue.[61] While Lillian and Earhart did not work in the same departments, both women had to prove themselves within their own fields. More publicly defiant of gender norms, Earhart sought to improve the climate for women at Purdue during her time in residence.[62] When Earhart disappeared in July 1937, Lillian took over Earhart's role as a career counselor to women.[63] Lillian was much older than Earhart at fifty-seven years old in 1935, while Earhart was thirty-eight years old. Both Lillian and Earhart provided young female students at Purdue with a real example that they could break into fields previously limited to men.

Although Lillian largely enjoyed her experience at Purdue, it was not always easy being the only woman professor in the School of Engineering.[64] For example, Marvin Mundle, a colleague of Lillian's who she often worked with, repeatedly embarrassed Lillian in front of others. Mundle would ask Lillian to complete complicated mathematical equations, and Lillian would have to admit that Frank had always handled the calculations.[65] Despite Mundle's attempts to diminish Lillian's capabilities, Lillian found a place at Purdue where she remained teaching, when not consulting, until her retirement at the age of seventy.

Lillian initially established her career through the use of female stereotypes that confined her to work in certain areas of business deemed acceptable to women. After proving her capability, she largely abandoned these stereotypes and sought to demonstrate that women were just as capable as men in the field of engineering. Through her determination, she became an engineering pioneer as one of the first women to break into the male-dominated field of engineering, opening doors for other women to do the same.

Lillian Gilbreth and 1930s Feminism

Contributing in her own way, Lillian Gilbreth sought to support women with more subtlety than others of her time. Her son, Frank Jr., described how "although she believed in women's rights with all her heart, she believed just as strongly that no lady should make a spectacle of herself."[66] His description of his mother suggests that Lillian worked to advance women's rights through her own brand of feminism.

Lillian did not publicly declare herself a feminist. Choosing to forge a new path in her own way, Lillian supported women in their endeavors without a label, adhering to a brand of feminism that developed in the 1930s with the emergence of the modern working woman. Her work during this time presents the consistent themes of mentorship and working towards the advancement of other women in their professional careers.

Her contemporaries often described Lillian as a feminist. In 1929, Edna Yost wrote of how Lillian's work interjected a sense of feminism into the masculine field of engineering. Yost noted that Lillian provided a sense of femininity as she incorporated the "human element" of the worker through her blend of psychology and management principles to engineering.[67] Describing Lillian's contributions to industrial management, Yost noted that "the whole profession undoubtedly owes part of its remarkable growth in prestige of recent years to its attempts to inculcate this once-thought-to-be feminist point of view into industrial life. Far from effeminizing the profession, it has helped to give it increased importance in life."[68] Yost's interpretation of Lillian's work described how Lillian applied a feminist perspective to the masculine field of engineering that became an industry-wide standard.

Lillian also worked to advance equality for women through various women's groups. As chairman of the American Women's Association, Lillian presented the Women's Medal Award to Amelia Earhart in November 1932. Earhart kept a newspaper clipping of an article describing Lillian's address before presenting the award: "Dr. Gilbreth, an engineer, social worker and the mother of eleven children, analyzed women's place in the new social order. She emphasized the need for emotional serenity, adaptability, and sufficient rest to balance all her activities."[69] Lillian's mention of women in "the new social order" suggests that she was aware of the changes taking place for women during the 1930s.[70] Notably, Earhart collected this newspaper clipping before she crossed paths with Lillian at Purdue. When she received the medal, Earhart remarked that she was "proud to receive it," and that "she was interested in the fact that it was designed by women for a woman."[71] Lillian's involvement with women's groups demonstrated her support for the advancement of women during the 1930s.

Lillian's work as chairman for the American Women's Association and her public recognition of Earhart's achievements that challenged gender norms illustrate how Lillian advanced women's accomplishments in a public setting. With her own accomplishments in a sphere dominated by men, Lillian could have chosen to quietly and solely advance her career. Instead, she chose to celebrate and uplift other women. In a speech given after Lillian's death, Helen Schleman stated that "she knew that it took caring, understanding, and support on the part of women who had arrived in the professional and work world of men to make opportunities for other women—if very many were ever to be successful at breaking the age-old barriers. She understood 'sisterhood' long before it was popular."[72] Schleman's words demonstrated how Lillian utilized her own success to help other women she encountered during her career. Lillian Gilbreth understood that women needed to build networks and that those who managed to succeed needed to help open the doors for others.

Lillian became more publicly known as newspapers wrote about her interesting life as a mother of eleven children. A journalist described Lillian as the "most famous career-mother in the country."[73] Americans were aware of Lillian and her superwoman capabilities as she was able to balance a career and an exceptionally large family all on her own as a widow. Journalists frequently interviewed Lillian; she provided an intriguing human-interest piece for readers.[74] The popularity of Lillian's story suggests that the public had difficulty reconciling how a woman could manage a career and family by herself. This very notion proved to be intriguing as most women could only imagine this for themselves, rather than act on it in their lives. These portrayals of Lillian as the perfect homemaker who meshed scientific principles with household responsibilities perhaps allowed female readers to view Lillian only as an ideal—something to strive for but not attain for themselves. Yet, while journalists framed Lillian's accomplishments in ways that seemed unattainable to most women, Lillian herself worked in her own way to support women in their career and professional endeavors.

Through her commitment to helping other women, Lillian became a mentor and role model for women at Purdue University. For example, part of her work as a professor at Purdue involved teaching part-time in the School of Home Economics.[75] By this time, she was an older woman and had much wisdom to share with her students. Scholars noted that "Lillian became Dean of Women, Dorothy Stratton's greatest influence" due to her time working at Purdue.[76] Stratton later described her experience with Gilbreth: "most of us have, I think, a limited capacity as to the number of people we can care for. Dr. G seemed to be able to take a personal interest in and care for many. She could reach across educational barriers, social barriers, race barriers, sex barriers, age barriers, and find common ground."[77] Lillian used her time at Purdue to not only further her own career but also to help other women along the way.

Helen Schleman, the Director of the Women's Residence Hall where Lillian lived while at Purdue, also fondly reflected on Lillian's presence on Purdue's campus. Schleman praised Lillian, stating that those who knew her at Purdue "loved her not so much because she was great, but because she was appealingly human."[78] Thus, Lillian not only advanced the field of engineering through her professorship at Purdue but also influenced the lives of women through her compassion and mentorship.

Lillian often spoke publicly about how she wished other women could find success in their careers. A newspaper article described Lillian as an advocate for women who had "a want to push her profession of engineering as far as she can and a genuine wish to see women of first-class work in engineering, or in any other field they enter."[79] She was a feminist in her own way, seeking to make home life easier for the housewife and opening doors for women in the workforce. However, Lillian herself also managed to blend her identities as career woman and housewife in a way that challenged the gender norms of the 1930s.

Conclusion

Ultimately, Lillian Gilbreth represented the conundrum many women continue to face today as they struggle to find a balance between raising a family and excelling in a career. However, Lillian managed to do both with quite a few more children than most mothers. Her initial years of becoming an expert on household efficiency and female consumers following her husband's death were pivotal to her success in the male-dominated fields of business and engineering. Lillian transformed the greatest hindrance of her consulting business, her gender, into the greatest asset of her consulting business as she became an expert on the woman consumer.

As a professor at Purdue University, Lillian became a mentor to women and inspired younger generations of women that they could pursue both a career and a family. Her close acquaintance with feminist Amelia Earhart suggests that Lillian was exposed to and part of a network of women striving for equality. While not publicly defining herself as a feminist, Lillian was a part of 1930s feminism in which the modern working woman emerged.

Working as an advocate for women in her own way, Lillian continually supported women in their endeavors, both within their homes as homemakers and within the workplace throughout the 1930s and beyond. While not publicly declaring herself a feminist, she supported both homemakers and working women through her household advice books, by advocating for female consumers, and assisting women's advocacy groups. Lillian proved herself to be an advocate for women as she recognized her privilege in breaking through barriers that prevented other women from advancing in their careers.

Thus, Lillian Gilbreth created her own "One Best Way" throughout her career both in response to her own family's necessity and in support of other women.[80] Though she may have appeared conventional in her roles as a diligent housewife and doting mother, Lillian combined her expertise in the separate spheres of engineering and domesticity in unconventional ways in order to ease the burden of women in the household. Through this combination, Lillian entered engineering, a field that very few women had ever managed to enter. Her career and life present interesting contradictions in which she had to navigate as she asserted herself in the realms of engineering, business, and academia.

Notes

1. Frank B. Gilbreth, Jr. and Ernestine Gilbreth Carey, *Belles on Their Toes* (New York: Thomas Y. Crowell Company, 1950), 2–7.
2. Lillian Moller Gilbreth, *The Quest of the One Best Way: A Sketch of the Life of Frank Bunker Gilbreth* (Easton: Hive Publishing Company, 1973), 5.
3. Frank B. Gilbreth, Jr. and Ernestine Gilbreth Carey, *Cheaper by the Dozen* (New York: Thomas Y. Crowell Company, 1948).
4. Jane Lancaster, *Making Time: Lillian Moller Gilbreth—A Life Beyond "Cheaper by the Dozen"* (Boston: Northwestern University Press, 2004), 18.
5. Laurel Graham, *Managing on Her Own: Dr. Lillian Gilbreth and Women's Work in the Interwar Era* (Norcross, GA: Engineering & Management Press, 1998).
6. Lancaster, *Making Time.*
7. Julie Des Jardins, *Lillian Gilbreth: Redefining Domesticity* (Boulder, CO: Westview Press, 2013).

8. Lillian M. Gilbreth, *As I Remember: An Autobiography* (Norcross, GA: Engineering & Management Press, 1998), 16.

9. Lancaster, *Making Time*, 22.

10. Gilbreth, As I Remember, 52.

11. Des Jardins, *Redefining Domesticity*, 14.

12. Des Jardins, *Redefining Domesticity*, 22.

13. Des Jardins, *Redefining Domesticity*, 22.

14. Gilbreth, As I Remember, 21.

15. Gilbreth, As I Remember, 72.

16. Jill Lepore, "Not So Fast: Scientific Management Started as a Way to Work. How Did It Become a Way of Life," *New Yorker*, October 5, 2009.

17. Frank B. Gilbreth Jr., *Time Out for Happiness* (New York: Crowell, 1971), 7.

18. Lancaster, *Making Time*, 97.

19. Gilbreth, *Time Out for Happiness*, 96.

20. Gilbreth, As I Remember, 119.

21. Gilbreth, As I Remember, 119.

22. Lancaster, *Making Time*, 98.

23. Gilbreth, *Time Out for Happiness*, 92.

24. Lancaster, *Making Time*, 85.

25. Gilbreth, As I Remember, 66.

26. Gilbreth, As I Remember, 66.

27. Lancaster, *Making Time*, 160.

28. Gilbreth and Carey, *Belles on Their Toes*.

29. Gilbreth and Carey, *Belles on Their Toes*, 94.

30. Frank B. Gilbreth and L. M. Gilbreth, *Applied Motion Study: A Collection of Papers on the Efficient Method to Industrial Preparedness* (Easton: Hive Publishing Company, 1973).

31. Gilbreth and Carey, *Belles on Their Toes*, 95.

32. Gilbreth and Carey, *Belles on Their Toes*, 94.

33. Edna Yost, *Frank and Lillian Gilbreth: Partners for Life* (New Brunswick: Rutgers University Press, 1949), 319.

34. Julie Des Jardins, *The Madame Curie Complex: The Hidden History of Women in Science* (New York: Feminist Press at the City University of New York, 2010), 78.

35. Des Jardins, *The Madame Curie Complex*, 79.

36. Des Jardins, *Redefining Domesticity*, 126.

37. Gilbreth and Carey, *Cheaper by the Dozen*, 2.

38. Gilbreth and Carey, *Belles on Their Toes*, 110.

39. Gilbreth, Jr., *Time Out for Happiness*, 1.

40. Lillian M. Gilbreth, *The Homemaker and Her Job* (New York: D. Appleton and Company, 1927), vii.

41. Lillian M. Gilbreth, "Have You A Restful Home?: A Message to Homemakers," *Good Housekeeping*, August 1926.

42. Gilbreth, "Have You A Restful Home," 1.

43. Gilbreth, "Have You A Restful Home," 1.

44. Gilbreth, *The Homemaker and Her Job*.

45. Gilbreth, *The Homemaker and Her Job*, 20.

46. Lillian M. Gilbreth, *Living With Our Children* (New York: W. W. Norton & Company, Inc., 1928).

47. Gilbreth, *Living With Our Children*, 48.

48. Lillian M. Gilbreth, "You Can Be a Timesaving Expert, Too," *Better Homes & Gardens*, June 1954.

49. Gilbreth, "You Can Be a Timesaving Expert, Too," 78.

50. Gilbreth, *As I Remember*, 212.

51. Gilbreth, *As I Remember*, 219.

52. Yost, *Frank and Lillian Gilbreth*, 328.

53. Gilbreth, *As I Remember*, 222.

54. Angie Klink, *The Dean's Bible: Five Purdue Women and Their Quest for Equality* (West Lafayette, IN: Purdue University Press, 2014), 74.

55. Klink, *The Dean's Bible*, 75.

56. C. R. Dooley to Dr. Edward C. Elliot, June 3, 1935, Archives and Special Collections, Purdue University Libraries.

57. Lancaster, *Making Time*, 301.

58. Lancaster, *Making Time*, 301.

59. Susan Ware, *Still Missing: Amelia Earhart and the Search for Modern Feminism* (New York: W. W. Norton & Company, 1993), 209.

60. Wilma Jean Kay, "Oral History Interview with Wilma Jean Kay," interview by Katherine Markee, Purdue University Oral History Program Collection, Purdue University Libraries, Archives and Special Collections, November 15, 2007, http://collections.lib.purdue.edu/oralhistory/POH0708026(Kay).mp3.

61. Lillian M. Gilbreth to Amelia Earhart, n.d., George Palmer Putnam Collection of Amelia Earhart Papers, Purdue University Libraries, Archives and Special Collections.

62. Ware, *Still Missing*, 209.

63. Lancaster, *Making Time*, 302.

64. Yost, *Frank and Lillian Gilbreth*, 340.

65. Lancaster, *Making Time*, 302.

66. Gilbreth, *Time Out for Happiness*, 35.

67. Edna Yost, "The Intelligent Sex," *The North American Review* 228, no. 3 (1929): 343.

68. Yost, "The Intelligent Sex," 7.

69. "Mrs. Putnam's Feat Praised as She gets Medal Award of Women's Association," November 17, 1932, George Palmer Putnam Collection of Amelia Earhart Papers, Purdue University Libraries, Archives and Special Collections.

70. "Mrs. Putnam's Feat Praised."

71. "Mrs. Putnam's Feat Praised."

72. Klink, *The Dean's Bible*, 78.

73. Mary Margaret McBride, "Woman Would Want Same Life: Lillian Gilbreth Would Have Career and 11 Children Again," *Roanoke Times*, April 14, 1935.

74. Graham, *Managing on Her Own*, 174.

75. Gilbreth, *As I Remember*, 232.

76. Klink, *The Dean's Bible*, 69.

77. Klink, *The Dean's Bible*, 76.

78. Klink, *The Dean's Bible*, 76.

79. Jane Dixon, "She Changed Her Career: Dr. Lillian Gilbreth Gave Up Literature to Join Husband as an Engineer," *Richmond Times-Dispatch*, January 25, 1931.

80. Gilbreth, *The Quest of the One Best Way*.

PART II

WARTIME OPPORTUNITIES

6. Fighting Nazis: A Collective of Trailblazing American Women in the 1930s and 1940s

SAVANNAH LAWHORNE

The old black and white photo pictured below (*Figure 6.1*) might make one wonder, what do these girls all have in common? The answer is, they were all refugees from Europe during World War II, cared for by an American woman named Lois Gunden.[1] During the 1930s and 1940s, World War II divided society and chaos enveloped the world. During the war, various heroes and villains emerged and epic tales of the front lines spread around the world. However plentiful the stories of heroes are, there is one group whose tales go collectively untold: American women like Gunden who fought Nazism.

Figure 6.1: *A group of girls living at the Ville St. Christophe children's home, where they were cared for by Lois Gunden, ca. 1941 (Photo courtesy of the US Holocaust Memorial Museum).*

Many scholars have discussed men who physically fought on the front lines in Germany. Scholars have also published literature about American women who stepped up to the plate on the home front and worked in factories when their husbands enlisted. Some scholars have even written about European women and their families who hid Jews in their homes in the Netherlands and Poland.[2] Missing in the discussion, however, are the American women who used their power and agency to take a stance against Nazism and anti-Semitism. The women against Nazism fought against cultural odds and raised awareness in the American public of the horrors happening in Europe.

In this chapter I will tell stories of both individual women and women's organizations: Lois Gunden, The Women's Division of the American Jewish Congress, and Dorothy Thompson. I will reveal how they went against the status quo to break societal norms for women and how they used their positions to fight Nazism. Finally, I will explain the effect these women had on the war as a larger picture of history. In order to accomplish this, I will use primary sources such as letters, interviews, newspaper and magazine columns, and books. I will also examine secondary sources such as articles from websites like the United States Holocaust Memorial Museum as well as journals and books by other scholars. In this chapter I argue that American women held a vital, yet often overlooked role in spreading awareness and advocating against Nazism throughout the 1930s and 1940s.

***

Women who took on industrial work during the World Wars challenged the public's understanding of appropriate jobs for women. As men enlisted to fight and left the factories for military service, the need for women to enter the workforce increased. Nevertheless, many men were displeased to find women playing such a large role as wage laborers. Described as biologically soft and only fit for domestic work, many considered it unnatural for women to work in the railway industry or in a factory. But it was not only industrial work where women's place was in dispute. The realm of public office was considered masculine as well: in the decades preceding World War II over ten thousand men held positions in public office, compared to only about two hundred women. And in jobs increasingly deemed "feminine," such as clerical and secretarial work, women found themselves facing occupational dead ends. Men clearly held the upper hand in the public sphere during the decades that preceded World War II.[3]

Born on February 25, 1915, in a small town in Illinois, Lois Gunden was a typical Mennonite woman.[4] She graduated from Goshen College in Indiana and then taught French from 1939 to 1941 and from 1944 to 1958.[5] But as World War II approached, Gunden saw an opportunity to use her suppressed talents. When the Mennonite Central Council asked Gunden to go to France to work with refugee children in October of 1941, she readily packed her bags and traveled to Europe.[6] Well trained in language and culture and gifted with natural maternal instincts, Gunden was a perfect fit for a lifesaving operation abroad. She used her skills to show the world the importance of women caregivers, paving the way for other Mennonite women to follow in her footsteps.[7]

Contextually, 1941 marked the middle of World War II, one year since France became occupied by Hitler's Nazi regime. France, as it was known by the Allies, had completely changed. As the French government fled and re-stationed abroad, Nazis gained control of the northern part of the country. The Nazis instituted Vichy France, an easily influenced government in the southern region of France. According to scholar Aliza Luft, "everything was different. There were Nazis everywhere. There were swastikas dangling from classic French buildings. They emptied out the museums. They took control of other museums, and filled it with Nazi propaganda, and used them as headquarters of Nazi offices."[8] Soon after establishment, the Vichy regime pushed anti-Semitic legislation.[9] The France that Gunden found was not the easygoing country known today.

While the Nazi reign in France terrified most, Lois Gunden did not shy away. In her first encounter with war-ravaged Europe, Gunden recalled "a German bomber [who] came toward us this morning as we were on Deck drinking bouillon. It circled over us a couple of times and then flew on. That was our first sign of war in Europe."[10] This greeting foreshadowed future events because it would not be Gunden's last encounter with the Nazis. Gunden soon arrived at the Villa St. Christophe children's convalescent home in Canet-Plage, France.[11] Sick children from a nearby refugee camp called Rivesaltes filled the convalescent home, which had a capacity of only sixty beds. Most of these children were refugees of the Spanish Civil War who reunited with their parents in cycles. The refugee camps began to transform as the harshness of Nazi rule increased in Canet-Plage. Nearby camps soon filled with Jewish children waiting for deportation to concentration camps.

When Gunden realized the devastation, she decided to risk her own life to save the children. Though frightened, Gunden challenged the French government and Nazi laws.[12]

On August 9, 1942, Gunden wrote into her diary, "Mary informed me about the return of Polish and German Jews to Poland where death by starvation awaits them."[13] Gunden, aware of the fate that awaited Jews in the East, chose to act with this information. In Vichy France, where Gunden now lived, the French police rounded up Jewish children and their families to send to Drancy in the northern Nazi-occupied territory. From Drancy, Nazis shipped Jews to Auschwitz. It became obvious to Gunden that the Jewish children in Rivesaltes would die, so Gunden decided to fight Nazi brutality. Children in homes like St. Christophe were usually under the age of sixteen. Oftentimes, French Police would not even check to see if the children were Jewish or not in order to meet a transport quota from the refugee camps. Gunden knew that she would be the perfect person to hide these children, as she could speak French and use that skill to converse with police. In order to combat further Nazi atrocity, Gunden agreed to hide Jewish children in St. Christophe with the help of her Quaker friend, Mary Elms.[14]

Next, Gunden faced the challenge of how to quickly execute her plan to save the children. When the children first arrived at St. Christophe, they did not reveal their Jewish origins to anyone per their parents' instructions. Gunden did not tell anyone about the children's Jewish backgrounds to ensure their protection during police searches. One day, Gunden was out for a walk when an officer approached her wanting to take several children who were rumored to be Jewish. Gunden convinced the officer that those children were away from home for a bit, and that he should come back later. When the police officer returned Gunden told him the children were not ready to be deported because their clothes were wet and that he should, again, come back later. Gunden hoped that the officer would eventually meet his quota elsewhere if she kept delaying him. This theory proved true, as the officer did not return a third time. It is without a doubt that Gunden would have continued this charade until the officer decided not to return. Gunden cared for these children for over a year, and her everyday courage and quick thinking protected many Jewish children throughout the Holocaust.[15]

Gunden's fight against the Nazis put her life, and a safe return to America, at risk. Gunden quickly realized that hiding the same Jewish children for too long posed two problems: First, continuously caring for the same sixty children would not allow her to save additional children. Second, keeping healthy and able children in the home's services would look suspicious.[16] To combat these risks, Gunden began to send some children through an "underground railroad" for Jewish children escaping from refugee camps.[17] Organizations like the OSE (Œuvre de Sécourse aux Enfants or, in English, Mennonite Aide for Children) took hidden children and re-homed them in rural private homes, catholic worship centers, and OSE camps.[18] Although it was the best solution for the children, membership in this underground system posed a great threat to Gunden; at any time, officers could arrest both Gunden and the workers at St. Christophe.

As the war dragged on, formal relations between Vichy France and the United States fell apart, complicating all escape plans from France to America. Travel services like the one that Gunden took to get to France ceased as the war went on. Faithful as always, Gunden stated, "if God wants me to return, he will provide a way."[19] Even when offered an escape route back to America by friends in the Mennonite Central Committee, Gunden refused to leave the Jewish children.[20] Although each day spent in France made her escape less likely, Gunden refused to leave without completing her mission.

Gunden saved many children, but not without facing consequences. On January 27, 1943, after the Nazis overtook southern France, authorities arrested Gunden and deported her to Germany as a prisoner of war.[21] Before her arrest, Gunden hired a new overseer for St. Christophe to ensure that the children would be taken care of. She left him the entirety of her savings in order to supply the children with their daily needs.[22] Gunden spent an entire year at Baden-Baden camp.[23] Gunden's memoir, At *Brenner Park Hotel*, shows that she did not lose her unshakable spirit while interned. While most people would complain about being held against their will, Gunden's only complaint was that she could not help more children. Gunden stated that "most of us felt that, at best, what we were doing [for the children] was only a substitute for the much more important duties that would otherwise have been ours."[24] Allied forces liberated Gunden on March 14, 1944 and returned her to Goshen, where she returned to her university teaching job.[25] While her internment could have been fatal, Gunden felt it was worth it to be able to save the children.

Over the course of two years, Gunden willingly embarked to war-torn Europe, broke the law to hide Jews, fought for defenseless children, and kept her mind focused on helping people even at the risk of imprisonment. Gunden's memoir closes with a line that perfectly sums up her life, character, and work: "Mankind can live together as brothers when nations will have learned to build their policies upon goodwill and understanding rather than hatreds and selfishness."[26] This awe-inspiring advice came from a woman who knew the true meaning of bravery and understanding. Although she was from a time when society expected women to be silent helpers, Gunden proved that she could give great meaning to her work and become a woman that was not to be silenced by Nazis.

Gunden was only a single person in the larger fight against an epidemic of hatred, but there were also groups of American women who came together as a collective to fight Nazism and Anti-Semitism. One of the most prominent groups that did this was the Women's Division of the American Jewish Congress (AJC). The Women's Division of the AJC rejected statements that their voices were less than those of men and proved to the world that domesticity and protest were not to be separated.

According to their website, "the American Jewish Congress has been a legacy organization of the Jewish community for over 100 years, working to defend Jewish interests at home and abroad through public policy, advocacy, legislation, and the courts."[27] The AJC held their first meeting in Philadelphia just after World War I ended in pursuit of protecting Jews and Americans worldwide. When the horrors of the Holocaust and the true Nazi agenda became known, the AJC wrote a memorandum to President Franklin D. Roosevelt that showed their activism against Nazism. The opening to this memorandum, written on December 8, 1942, stated that Americans have been made aware and sit in horror at Hitler's call for the extermination of all Jews, in addition to the two million already killed. The letter went on to demand that Democracies must come together to defeat Hitler, as they are the only political systems that hold the power to do so. The AJC urged the president to intervene with the following statement:

> We ask you now once to raise your voice—on behalf of the Jews of Europe. We ask you again to warn the Nazis that they will be held to strict accountability for their crimes. We ask you to employ every available means to bring solemn protest and warning to the peoples

of the Axis countries so that they may be deterred from acting as the instruments of the monstrous designs of their mad leaders.[28]

Along with this urge, the AJC also asked the president to make the world aware of the situation in Europe and urge them to stand accountable with America to end Nazism. Letters like this one are just one strong example of what the AJC did to keep Americans charged against Nazism.[29] Men often received credit for diplomatic letters like this one, but it was the women's division who did the ground work on America's front lines. The Women's Division did not consist of the average housewives that most people think about during the interwar period. Although these women were nuanced to society, they did not lose sight of their femininity, and this is what made them such a powerful force.

The AJC as a whole stood for women's rights. Leaders of the organization supported increasing the involvement of women in the AJC.[30] Although the AJC took a stance for women in the political arena, women still faced discrimination and hardships throughout the 1930s and 1940s. During this time, women were expected to take on a domestic role while men were expected to oversee politics and protests. Despite this, the women of the AJC made their voices heard in order to protect other Jewish people suffering in Europe. [31]

The AJC held partial responsibility for a boycott when Hitler rose to power in Europe in 1933. The boycott, which affected all German goods imported into the United States, occurred in response to the National Socialist German Workers Party's anti-Semitic platforms.[32] The Women's Division of the AJC led the protests of this boycott. These Jewish women handled most of the day-to-day work that was required of such a large national protest. They organized activists within communities and held the picket signs themselves, actively breaking cultural norms for women at the time.[33]

The Women of the AJC did more than protest; they also developed refugee centers and lobbied politicians. The president of the AJC Women's Division in the 1930s and 1940s, Louise Waterman Wise, along with other women of the AJC, developed refugee shelters for Jews that fled Germany for America, ensuring they had access to shelter, food, and other essentials. This refugee program touched the lives of thousands of European Jews after their arrival in the United States.[34] The Women's division also lobbied for the creation of visas for those trying to escape Nazism and come to America, helping them flee war and potential death.[35] The women of the AJC always rose to the occasion to provide much needed services for Jews during the Holocaust.

The women of the AJC embraced their femininity in order to further help Jews. Society considered women to be caretakers, and these women embraced the label in a positive light by building shelters, providing home-cooked meals for people in need, and knitting blankets for soldiers and civilians on the front lines of battle. During the war, these women sold war bonds, created Jewish orphan sponsorships programs, and helped the American defense department. In doing so, they demonstrated they were capable of embracing important domestic work while also leading successful social and political campaigns.[36]

Unrelenting in their role to serve the Jewish people, the Women of the AJC played a major role in the lives of many European Jews while bringing the atrocities of the war to the attention of the American people. Without their work, thousands of Jewish men, women, and children would have suffered and died. These women used their femininity to change the world while also revolting against the societal limitations of what was appropriate for a woman to do outside of her home.[37] These women were indeed heroes.

Dorothy Thompson was a female journalist who detailed every moment of the frontlines for those listening back home. In the 1930s, female journalists were often tasked with writing domestic columns.[38] Thompson, however, wrote about subjects that were largely unfamiliar to the female pen. She showed the world that a woman could write about more than trivial household matters.

Throughout her entire life, Thompson resisted societal and sexist constraints. In her adolescence, Thompson advocated for women's suffrage and repetitively fought for the underdog. After her stint in the suffrage movement, Thompson decided to take her speaking and writing skills to the journalism field. In the 1930s and 1940s, Thompson was a journalist for numerous media outlets, including *The New York Evening's Post*, where she was eventually promoted as European chief. Always involved in political matters, Thompson quickly found an interest in covering European current events, especially as the war began and Hitler rose to power.[39]

Thompson repetitively put herself in dangerous situations if it meant that she could warn the world of a growing threat. For example, in 1931, Thompson accepted the opportunity to interview Hitler right before he rose to power as the Fuhrer of Germany. The interview, published as "I Saw Hitler," criticized Hitler, as Thompson urged her readers to "imagine a would-be dictator setting out to persuade a sovereign people to vote away their rights."[40] Germany kicked Thompson out of the country for her article, and she became the first exiled journalist in the interwar period.[41]

Thompson said that at first glance, Hitler seemed like a person that world powers would not take seriously, but that this should not be the case. Thompson observed the situation in Germany as something dire. She warned the nation and the world, stating that "by 1930 it is impossible any longer to laugh off Hitler."[42] Thompson told of the desperate German economic situation. She told of how citizens looked for a savior and found one in Hitler. Thompson warned that Hitler essentially owned the German state. She reported on deaths in the country under his rule and showcased his violent propaganda. Hitler told Thompson about his feelings on groups such as Communists and Catholics, and he told her of his plan for Germany and the abolition of the Weimar Government.[43] While most of the world was still trying to figure out who Hitler was, Thompson already knew. Hitler took control of Germany soon after she interviewed him, and Thompson felt that it was her duty to warn the world.

Thompson wrote a column called "On the Record," which was published in over 170 different newspapers.[44] According to an article written about her, "back in the United States, Thompson mounted a one-woman crusade against the Nazis. She denounced the German government frequently and vigorously in her syndicated column."[45] Thompson placed herself on the front end of some of the greatest events of World War II and kept the nation up to date. Thompson's column was published three times a week[46] and she covered everything from Hitler's interactions with the Czech people[47] to anti-Semitism[48] to Vichy France.[49]

Thompson quickly rose to fame and she used her influence to relay messages to the American people. Instead of basking in her notoriety, she used her platform to educate readers.[50] The American people were largely complacent at the start of World War II, with isolationist policies keeping Americans largely disconnected from foreign affairs at the time.[51] In her book, *Let the Record Speak*: Thompson stated that "Americans must choose,"[52] calling on Americans to force their public officials to take action and take a second look at policies that may harm the United States, and the world, in the long term. Thompson urged citizens to reconsider the United State's Neutrality Act before Pearl Harbor even happened.[53] In another of her "On the Record" articles, Thompson spoke about how America's identity and privilege differed from European nations. Thompson used this angle to compel readers to notice their status in the world and to try to make them more aware of its effect.[54] Thompson used the acknowledgement of privilege and information as a tool against complacency toward the Nazis.

Thompson received vast recognition for her achievements, as she was even featured on the cover of Time Magazine. The article named her the second most influential woman in American history, behind Eleanor Roosevelt. There was even a Broadway Musical called *Woman of the Year* created about her life.[55] Despite all odds, Thompson became a powerful female in journalism. Thompson compelled Americans to face the threat of the Nazis and take action against them.

Lois Gunden, The Women's Division of the AJC, and Dorothy Thompson each represent American women who showed courage and strength in the fight against Nazism. Lois Gunden paved the way for female aid workers. The Women's Division of the AJC made America aware that women are capable of both domestic work and political campaign, and Dorothy Thompson showed the world that a female could take on the front lines of journalism. Their actions tested cultural norms for women, yet they did not crumble under pressure. These women collectively saved thousands of lives and held the world accountable for the horrors of the Holocaust.

Notes

1. "A Children's Home in France Lois Gunden," United States Holocaust Memorial Museum, United States Holocaust Memorial Museum, accessed February 22, 2020, https://exhibitions.ushmm.org/americans-and-the-holocaust/personal-story/lois-gunden.

2. "'Women of Valor,' Stories of Women Who Rescued Jews During the Holocaust" Yad Vashem, accessed May 3, 2020, https://www.yadvashem.org/yv/en/exhibitions/righteous-women/index.asp.

3. Nancy F. Colt, *No Small Courage: a History of Women in the United States* (Oxford

University Press, 2004).

4. "Lois Gunden Clemens," Clemens, Lois Gunden (1915-2005), Obituary, Mennonite Weekly Review, accessed April 2, 2020, https://mla.bethelks.edu/mediawiki/index.php/Clemens,_Lois_Gunden_(1915-2005).

5. Mary Jean Gunden, "Letters from Lois: Goshen College," Goshen College News & Events, Goshen College, November 8, 2013, https://www.goshen.edu/news/2013/11/08/letters-from-lois/.

6. Miller, "Rescuing Jewish Children."

7. Joe Miller, "Rescuing Jewish Children: The Story of Lois Gunden," Mennonite Central Committee U.S., October 14, 2019, https://mcc.org/centennial/100-stories/rescuing-jewish-children-story-lois-gunden.

8. "Questions of Complicity: France and the Nazi Occupation," Facing History and Ourselves, accessed April 2, 2020, https://www.facinghistory.org/resource-library/video/questions-complicity-france-and-nazi-occupation.

9. Facing History and Ourselves, "Questions of Complicity: France and the Nazi Occupation."

10. Miller, "Rescuing Jewish Children: The Story of Lois Gunden." (This letter transcription provided on the website was provided to the website by Mary Jean Gunden. "Lois Gunden Clemens" letters and diary are held by Mennonite Church USA Archives, 3145 Benham Ave, Suite 1, Elkhart, IN 46517.)

11. A Convalescent home is essentially a home that provides welfare and daily care for someone who is unable to help themselves. In this case these were displaced children who were too young to be on their own and needed protecting. Definition by Charlotte Gerber, "Should You Place Your Disabled Child in a Youth Nursing Home?" Verywell Health, March 19, 2020, https://www.verywellhealth.com/youth-nursing-homes-1094453.

12. Miller, "Rescuing Jewish Children."

13. Miller, "Rescuing Jewish Children."

14. "Lois Gunden: A Righteous Gentile," The Mennonite: A Publication of Mennonite Church USA Providing Anabaptist Content, September 1, 2013, https://themennonite.org/feature/righteous-gentile-lois-gunden-righteous-gentile/.

15. Miller, "Rescuing Jewish Children: The Story of Lois Gunden."

16. American and French relief organizations were allowed to operate under Vichy rule as long as they were providing services that were accepted by the government and under their laws. The women at St. Christophe would not be allowed to house healthy children in an orphanage setting if they were operating under the government as a convalescent home.

17. The Mennonite, "Lois Gunden."

18. Miller, "Rescuing Jewish Children."

19. The Mennonite, "Lois Gunden."

20. Miller, "Rescuing Jewish Children."

21. Gunden, "Letters from Lois."

22. Miller, "Rescuing Jewish Children."

23. Gunden, "Letters from Lois."

24. Lois Gunden, At Brenner Park Hotel (Akron, PA: Mennonite Central Committee, 1945).

25. Miller, "Rescuing Jewish Children."

26. Gunden, *At Brenner Park Hotel.*

27. "About," American Jewish Congress, accessed April 5, 2020, https://ajcongress.org/about/.

28. Delegation of Representatives of Jewish Organizations, "Franklin Roosevelt Administration: Jewish Organizations Press the President to Act," Jewish Virtual Library, accessed April 5, 2020, https://www.jewishvirtuallibrary.org/jewish-organizations-press-fdr-to-act-december-1942.

29. Delegation of Representatives of Jewish Organizations, "Franklin Roosevelt Administration."

30. Stuart Svonkin, "American Jewish Congress," Jewish Women's Archive, February 27, 2009, https://jwa.org/encyclopedia/article/american-jewish-congress

31. Moshe Gottlieb, "The Anti-Nazi Boycott Movement in the United States: An Ideological and Sociological Appreciation," *Jewish Social Studies* 35, no. 3/4 (1973): 198-227, www.jstor.org/stable/4466779.

32. Gottlieb, "The Anti-Nazi Boycott Movement in the United States."

33. Rona, Sheramy. "'There Are Times When Silence Is a Sin': The Women's Division of the American Jewish Congress and the Anti-Nazi Boycott Movement," *American Jewish History* 89, no. 1 (2001): 105-21, www.jstor.org/stable/23886208.

34. Svonkin, "American Jewish Congress."

35. Sheramy, "'There Are Times When Silence Is a Sin.'"

36. Svonkin, "American Jewish Congress."

37. Sheramy, "'There Are Times When Silence Is a Sin.'"

38. Joanna Scutts, "The Evolution of the Advice Column," Medium, Medium, August 10, 2018, https://medium.com/s/story/the-evolution-of-the-advice-column-4676167c4317.

39. "Dorothy Thompson," United States Holocaust Memorial Museum, accessed April 10, 2020, https://exhibitions.ushmm.org/americans-and-the-holocaust/personal-story/dorothy-thompson.

40. Dorothy, Thompson, "I Saw Hitler!" *Nash's Pall Mall Magazine* 89, (468) (05): 46-107.

41. "Dorothy Thompson."

42. Thompson, "I Saw Hitler!"

43. Thompson, "I Saw Hitler!"

44. Kristin Hunt, "Dorothy Thompson, the Journalist Who Warned the World About Adolf Hitler," Mental Floss, June 11, 2019, https://www.mentalfloss.com/article/583332/dorothy-thompson-journalist-who-warned-world-hitler.

45. Hunt, "Dorothy Thompson, the Journalist Who Warned the World About Adolf Hitler."

46. "Dorothy Thompson."

47. Dorothy Thompson, "On the Record: 'Brutal' Czechs to be Blamed," *Washington Post* (1923-1954), Sep 22, 1938.

48. Dorothy Thompson, "On the Record: The Race Against Freedom," *Washington Post* (1923-1954), Mar 07, 1941.

49. Dorothy Thompson, "On the Record: Hitler's Lost War," *Washington Post* (1923-1954), Feb 12, 1941.

50.   James F Winder, "On the Record," Radio Days - Dorothy Thompson, Radio Days, March 29, 2014, http://www.otr.com/thompson.html.

51.   Michael J Kirkhom, "Dorothy Thompson: Withstanding the Storm" *The Courier - Syracuse University* 23, no. 2 (Fall 1988): 3–21. https://surface.syr.edu/cgi/viewcontent.cgi?article=1218&context=libassoc.

52.   Dorothy Thomson, *Let the Record Speak*, (Boston: Houghton Mifflin, 1939).

53.   Thomson, *Let the Record Speak*.

54.   Dorothy Thompson, "An American Credo: Conception of Human Rights," *Washington Post* (1923-1954), Jul 05, 1940.

55.   "Dorothy Thompson," RUSC Old Time Radio - over 35,000 OTR shows, R U Sitting Comfortably?, March 29, 2008, https://www.rusc.com/old-time-radio/articles/Dorothy-Thompson.aspx?t=1354.

7. The All-American Girls Professional Baseball League: The New Women of World War II

MADISON SHEEHAN

Since the late nineteenth century, baseball has been America's pastime, but its existence was threatened in the 1940s by the Second World War. With U.S. entry into the war, millions of men joined the military, leaving absences in a variety of jobs, including baseball. During this tumultuous time, women were called to step into a man's role–including that of a baseball player. In 1943, Philip Wrigley, the owner of the Chicago Cubs men's professional baseball team, called upon women to fill the vacant spots that were left by the male baseball players. Wrigley and President Franklin Delano Roosevelt felt that America needed their favorite pastime in such a trying time.[1] It was made clear by Wrigley from the beginning that women would not replace male players, but would become their own entity. It was not considered appropriate for men and women to play sports together, and men's sports were deemed too strenuous for women.[2] However, the women eventually proved they were just as capable of playing baseball as men and were widely regarded as a replacement for the male players.

The All-American Girls were largely forgotten until the mid-1990s when the movie A *League of Their Own* was released. However, even with renewed interest, their cultural impact has not been widely researched. These women exist in the Baseball Hall of Fame, a few specific books on the All-American Girls, and minimal paragraphs in books about women during World War II, but extensive research on their history is lacking. These women exist in the Baseball Hall of Fame, a few specific books on the All-American Girls, and minimal paragraphs in books about women during World War II, but extensive research on their history is lacking. This chapter offers a closer look into the history of the AAGPBL, revealing the profound impact these women left on American society and culture.

The All-American Girls Professional Baseball League both showcased and challenged traditional female roles during World War II. The players successfully joined a male-dominated field while proving that wives and mothers could balance their jobs and domestic responsibilities. Players' interviews and quotes, images, league documents, and newspapers are the best sources to explain the experiences these women had and to give an explanation of how the social climate was when they played. However, the background information found in historical monographs is just as important. In order to understand how these women transcended the roles laid out for women in sports and into their own baseball league, certain questions need to be asked. How did they become an acceptable replacement for the men? How did they meet or break the expectations of women during World War II? How did baseball challenge their ability to meet the standards of a wife and mother? How did they gain popularity? What does their popularity say about war's impact on social and cultural ideals? All of these questions are important ones to ask to determine the impact these women ultimately had.

Joining a Man's World

World War II was a time when women moved into the workforce and took jobs that were previously held by men. The move into male-dominated jobs was not an easy one, even though the jobs needed to be filled. Evelyn Steele wrote in 1943 that "employers were discouraged from employing women at tasks above their strength."[3] This "strength" was not only a reference to a woman's physical strength but also their mental strength and intelligence. Business and political leaders assumed that women could not possibly do the same job as men and that factories needed to be "adapted to the capabilities of women."[4] The factories were forced to change to try and meet the assumed "needs" of women to be as productive as men. Evelyn Steele also wrote that the only jobs appropriate for women during this time were military service, industrial jobs, tools of the trade, nursing, engineering, technical jobs, civil service, transportation, retail, and volunteer services.[5] While some of these occupations were traditionally male jobs, women were needed to fill the vacancies. Baseball was not seen as a job that was appropriate for young women.

Philip Wrigley came up with the idea of the All-American Girls Professional Baseball League (AAGPBL) in 1942 when several professional male baseball players left the league to support the war effort. These baseball players were either drafted, joined the military, or took up other war jobs.[6] Franklin Delano Roosevelt, President of the United States, influenced Wrigley when he wrote a letter to the commissioner of baseball, Judge Landis. Roosevelt wrote, "I honestly feel that it would be best for the country to keep baseball going. There will be fewer people unemployed and everybody will work longer hours and harder than ever before. And that means that they ought to have a chance for recreation and for taking their minds off their work even more than before."[7] Roosevelt expressed the people's desire to be able to relax in their time off and not have to worry about the war going on around them. He thought that baseball was a great way to distract the public and wanted it to continue. Since the president was the one who made the request, Wrigley felt it was his patriotic duty to have the sport continue.[8] Moreover, since the men's league was losing players by the day, he decided that women were the next best choice to fulfill the president's request.

Wrigley's plans were not supported by many people in the baseball community when it was initially presented. As historian June Sochen argues, at the time most physical activities were viewed as unhealthy for women and could damage their reproductive capabilities.[9] There were some physical activities considered appropriate for women, and supporters advocated for them. As long as the activity did not include too much competitiveness or was too strenuous on the body, critics deemed them appropriate for women to compete in.[10] For example, many women wanted to play basketball, but playing the same version of basketball as men did was deemed inappropriate. Female players operated within strict game restrictions: they could not steal the ball from each other, they played in a limited zone on the court, and they were only allowed to hold the ball for three seconds. The idea was that these women would be happy because they could play sports, but it also satisfied critics because they played in a "feminine" way.[11] This was the balance that Wrigley himself had to achieve when he created a women's baseball league.

Wrigley needed his baseball women to fit the expectations of women at the time so they would be accepted as an alternative to men's baseball. Wrigley stated that, "The All-American Girls Softball League is created with the highest ideals of womanhood in mind."[12] The highest ideals of womanhood meant that these women behaved and looked like society thought they should be. To ensure he achieved these ideals, he made sure they looked and acted feminine through the use of the "Charm School" and their uniform design. Wrigley also created conduct rules that further enforced many policies on how society expected women to act and hired chaperones as extra insurance that the young, single women had protection from the world.

Wrigley wanted his women perceived as feminine because they were entering into what many considered a man's job. According to writer Melissa McEuen, women were important people to the war effort, but "a desirable appearance from the neck up remained the purview of young, impressionable women, who were led to believe the nation's health and ultimately its peace would depend on their efforts."[13] This meant that society expected women to look their best in order to help end the war. Wrigley applied this very philosophy to his own league by first only recruiting women that were already pretty. Wrigley did not want to pick any "butch" women because that would have garnered thoughts that those women were lesbians, which was something he wanted to avoid entirely.[14] Wrigley wanted his players drawn away from the traditional thought of what professional women's softball players looked like. Wrigley picked women who were petite and attractive with most players being between 5'2" and 5'6" in height and weighing between 116 and 145 pounds.[15] Of course, there were a few players that fell outside these limits, but the majority fit into these measures.

Once the league chose a player, she was sent to what was called "Charm School." This was where the newly recruited players would go during their spring training to learn how to be a "proper" lady. At Charm School, they received a handy guidebook that taught them everything they needed to learn. The beginning of the guidebook included a foreword that gave players the essentials of what they should include in their beauty kit. The guidebook said to "Remember the skin, the hair, the teeth and the eyes. It is most desirable in your own interests, that of your teammates and fellow players, as well as from the standpoint of the public relations of the league that each girl be at all times presentable and attractive."[16] The Charm School followed the feelings of the time that women needed to keep everything from the neck up in good condition. It also suggested that women had to be attractive in order to gain attention from the public. The guidebook continued by giving "After-Game Care Routine" and also a general "Morning and Night" routine that would keep them healthy and presentable.[17] The women were never given a break from the required routines and were expected to complete them. They were told that they were never allowed to not look their best, which meant even in their leisure time.

Well-groomed hair was a requirement of any proper lady, and the women of the AAGPBL were no exception to this rule. The guidebook emphasized a player's hair and called it "Woman's Crowning Glory."[18] The name itself indicated how important the hair was to the league because they used such highly elevated language. The guidebook even said, "But above all, keep your hair as neat as possible, on or off the field."[19] So, not only were these women required to keep their hair nice off the field, the expectation was that their hair would be perfect on the field, even when they were running and getting sweaty. Long hair was something that set the women apart from the men. In 1945 a rookie named Joyce Hill complained that she and her teammates would have practice in the morning and then have to shower and curl their hair before the night games.[20] The players did not have a lot of downtime between their morning practices and their games in the evening, but they had to uphold the requirement to style their hair in order to look presentable for the game.

The mouth was also a point of emphasis for the Charm School and for the time period in general. Lipstick became a staple during World War II because Americans believed it represented "democracy and freedom" and also symbolized femininity in a "man's job."[21] The women in the AAGPBL attempted to fit into a man's world while also attempting to remain feminine, which made lipstick important. Along with lipstick, there were other expectations of how women in the workforce should look.

Society felt that women needed to dress in feminine attire for their traditionally "male" jobs. An article from *Good Housekeeping* titled "How a Woman Should Wear a Uniform" discussed the ways that women should wear a military uniform. However, many of these tips applied to women in many other professions during this time. The first line made the writer's argument clear by asserting that men did not like it when women wore uniforms.[22] By saying this, the article attempted to shame women into not working by insinuating that men considered women unattractive if they worked in uniforms. The article continued by saying that women should wear their hair shoulder-length and have it curl up at the bottom, make sure they wear a little makeup to look fresh, and wear short heels.[23] The expectation for women was to present themselves as feminine while also remaining professional.

Wrigley had the same policy when he created the uniform for the women of the AAGPBL. Since Wrigley decided that it was his "patriotic" duty to keep baseball going, it is not surprising that he took a similar view to dressing his women as the military dressed theirs. Wrigley requested that his players wear skirts and designed them to look similar to a figure skating uniform.[24] Figure skating, with its emphasis on poise and concealed delicacy, was an appropriate sport for women. To model the AAGPBL uniforms after them was to suggest that these women were just as feminine as figure skaters. Additionally, the uniforms were extremely impractical for baseball. Many women complained that the skirts impeded their throwing motion while they pitched and there was no protection for their legs, which led to lots of cuts on their legs from sliding. The uniforms were not the only thing that was impractical for these women; acquiring the gear necessary to play baseball was a challenge.

Sporting goods were difficult to find for women in general, but to find baseball gear for women was nearly impossible. One player did not own a pair of baseball cleats because stores only sold men's cleats. Her feet were very small, so it was difficult for her to find a pair of men's baseball cleats that fit her. In the end, she was able to find an extremely small pair of men's cleats that she was able to wear for the season.[25] The lack of baseball gear for women speaks largely to the fact that baseball was considered a man's sport.

Even though society viewed baseball as man's sport, Wrigley did not allow his women to act like men. Wrigley created codes of conduct that reminded the women of what he and society expected of them, and the league threatened fines if they broke any of the codes. The first two rules focused on the appearance of the players. The first rule said to "always appear in feminine attire when not actively engaged in practice or playing ball."[26] The second rule said that "Boyish bobs are not permissible ... longer hair [is] preferable to short hair cuts. Lipstick should always be on."[27] The first two codes of conduct reflected the need for Wrigley's players to appear feminine wherever they were. Wrigley also required that the women did not drink or smoke in public, and a strict curfew of 12:30 a.m. was enforced.[28] The curfew was for the safety of his players because it was thought that women should not be out late at night on their own since that was when prostitutes would roam the streets. Wrigley wanted to create the "all-American girl" image which meant that his girls were feminine, fragile, sweet, and wholesome.

The codes of conduct were not the only way that Wrigley would accomplish this image. Wrigley acquired the help of chaperones to not only enforce the codes to the girls but to appear as protection from the world. Chaperones were assigned to one team to control the behavior of the players. The chaperones also presented themselves as a comforting presence for many parents who were worried about their young, single daughters going into the world alone. Sophie Kurys recalled that her family only let her join the league because there was a promise of a chaperone.[29] The men within the league, and society, justified the close watch of the girls because they claimed they were preserving the virginity of the players.[30] The men in society thought that women were weak, vulnerable, and needed protection from the world. However, chaperones were not only a comfort for the parents but also for the players. The chaperones served as their surrogate mothers and even became friends with many of the players.[31] They wanted to create a place where the players were comfortable and they could enforce rules to match the ideals of women at the time.

The women of the league met several ideals for women at the time. However, they went against several other ideals—the most obvious of which was joining a male profession, one that was not necessarily ready to accept women. Men felt that the women would struggle to play baseball because it was a "man's sport." However, these women proved themselves able to compete.

When the league first started in 1943, the rules were more similar to softball than they were to baseball. The only difference was that Wrigley slightly extended the lengths of the base paths, increased the distance of the pitcher's mound, required the teams to play with nine players instead of ten, and used a ball slightly smaller than a softball.[32] However, as the women continuously proved that they were capable of playing like men, the league's rules became almost identical to those of men's baseball. The women proved themselves as early as 1944, when a small-sized ball was used in games and base paths were lengthened.[33] They proved themselves further in 1946, when the league created a new rule that allowed the players to begin throwing overhand, or sidearm, like the men did.[34]

In many ways, the women acted similarly to men in an unladylike demeanor.

The most common time for unladylike behavior was during their games. The women of the league frequently talked back to managers and argued with umpires, who were always men. Subordination to men was the expectation of women, so it was very unladylike to talk back. One player, Marge (Callaghan) Maxwell, recounted a time when she screamed back at her manager in defense of her actions on the field instead of standing idly by and letting her manager humiliate her.[35] Another former player, Elizabeth "Lib" Mohan, described an incident with her manager that caused her to quit. She felt the manager was unfair to one of her teammates, so she got in his face and told him that he was not being fair to her teammate.[36] Another incident in 1944 found Praire Pepper punching an umpire in the face after being called out at second base because she felt the umpire blew the call.[37] There were instances in which the girls would stand up for themselves against men and authority figures, which was uncommon for women at this time.

The women of the league were also famous for their on-field arguments and fights with other players. In 1944, Gabby Ziegler ran over an opponent while running to second base, and in the next inning, an opponent ran over Ziegler. The players cleared the benches on both sides after this incident. During the next play, a catcher was run over and knocked out.[38] These women played with the utmost competitive spirit, which was extremely inappropriate for women participating in sports. However, the inappropriate behavior of players was not only limited to the playing field.

Some players constantly broke the rules by going on unapproved dates and staying out past curfew. One of the most notorious players known for her rebellious nature was Faye Dancer. Dancer continuously bragged to teammates about her boyfriends in different towns.[39] She dated a mobster that proposed to her, but she rejected the offer and kept the ring for herself.[40] Dancer went against most ideals for a woman at the time because she held so much of men's attention. She was also famous for an incident where she climbed onto a fire escape by stacking up beer kegs and then used her nail file to stab a hole in the window screen to get back in her room after curfew.[41] Dancer broke the rules of the club and society because she stayed out late at night with men, which was not appropriate for women. Another woman, Daisy Junor, snuck out with the neighbor boy to go dancing, even though this was highly discouraged.[42] These women constantly broke different rules that separated them from the other women of their time.

Mothers and Wives at Work

The women of the AAGPBL joined the workforce even though it was not in a traditional field of work. They were subject to the same scrutiny that other working wives and mothers dealt with. The "government propaganda and policy encouraged women to alleviate manpower shortages incurred by the war through employment in traditional male vocations. Yet the necessity of women's employment in 'male' jobs did not alter social expectations for their continued traditional feminine roles of wife, mother, and homemaker."[43] Society encouraged women to take the traditional "male" jobs that had been left vacant, but these women were still expected to be good wives and mothers.

Most women's magazines during this period gave women suggestions on how they should behave as working wives and mothers, but some also discouraged women from having jobs at all if they were wives or mothers. According to an article called "Women and War," women caused wars to end because they helped the men to become more sympathetic. The article emphasized, however, that the home should be a woman's top concern.[44] The article suggested that the war continued because women were not in the home to console the men around them. The women needed to stop working and return to the home to change the public opinion about the war. Another article, "Mother's Our Only Hope," focused more specifically on the role of the mother. The author of this article claimed that youth delinquency is the fault of working mothers. They said that the mother should only work if it was absolutely necessary because their main war job was to raise children.[45] Women taking factory jobs received no praise but were instead reprimanded because they raised "delinquent" children. The author explained that a mother should always have meals ready for her children in order to make them come home and stay out of trouble.[46] However, a woman who worked would likely not be home during the days to provide lunch for her kids. Or if she worked the night shift, she would not be home for dinner. There was also the expectation that women would be home to feed their husbands upon their arrival home from work. The article "Starting from Scratch" explained that any good wife needed to plan her meals ahead of time so they would be ready as soon as her husband got home.[47] The article insinuated that any woman who did not have dinner ready as soon as their husband got home should be embarrassed. These women were deemed poor wives.

Society also had other concerns about working wives. The article "You Can't Have a Career and be a Good Wife" directly attacked the idea of women having jobs. The author claimed that two-career couples would never work out for a multitude of reasons: men felt bad because they were no longer the sole provider, women would get ideas while they worked which took away from supporting their husbands, and women looked younger when they did not have to work.[48] Many held this sentiment since magazines printed it as a serious article.

Baseball further challenged the expectations of women's roles. Society generally expected women to be wives and mothers, but some female baseball players made more money than their husbands or even became the sole providers for their households.[49] During the war years, female players often signed contracts from forty-five dollars to as much as eighty-five dollars per week to play in the league for a season. However, men's salaries averaged around forty dollars per week during this time period, so many female baseball players likely made more money than their fathers, brothers, and spouses.[50] Society considered it demeaning for women to make more than their husbands. Despite this, Audrey (Haine) Daniels continued to play baseball in 1951 after having a baby the prior year because her husband could not find a job.[51] Dottie (Wiltse) Collins wanted to retire after having a child, but she continued playing because her family needed the income.[52] These women continued to work during their marriages due to their circumstances rather than because they sought to challenge society's view of the appropriate role of women.

Baseball also forced the members of the league to be on the road frequently, which meant they could not be at home to raise their children or be present for their husbands. The baseball season ran from the end of May up until mid-August. Half of their games were road games, so they were gone for days at a time.[53] While a lot of the girls were not from the city in which they played, there were players who decided to settle down in their team towns because they had children or husbands. Their absence meant that they were not home to put food on the table for their husbands and children every night. Even when they played home games after the war, most of the games were at night, which still meant they missed dinner. The time commitment for baseball also meant that they were not home very often to raise their children (if they did have children). According to society, they would be raising delinquent children who would eventually cause havoc on society from a lack of motherly attention and care. Of course, this was not entirely true for these women.

These women were still able to have meaningful and close relationships with their families. While the women of the league were criticized for not being good wives or mothers, they were still doing things that would have considered them good parents or wives. Many of the women who were married and played in the league asked their husbands for permission to play. Daisy Junor initially rejected her offer to play in the league in 1943, but in 1944, her husband gave her permission to play in the league because he knew that is what she wanted to do.[54] Another woman, named Mary Baker, promised her military husband that she would quit when he returned from service because that is what a good wife would have done. Mary's husband realized how upset she was about having to stay home, so he told her that she should go have fun and do what she loves to do.[55] These women conformed to the societal expectations of wives by asking for permission from their husbands to play in the league.

Women were also able to be good wives or mothers because their children and husbands would follow the team on their road trips. When the husbands came on the road trips, they were often put to work helping out the team.[56] Additionally, the husbands and children would attend home games if they were from the area. Jean Faut was pictured many times while holding her son after games. Faut revealed that she did hire another woman to take care of her son while she played, but she took care of her son in the off-season or whenever she was home. Additionally, when her son was five years old, he rode along on the bus with her and her teammates.[57] Several other players came into the same situation as Faut because they still wanted to play baseball after having children. Dottie (Wiltse) Collins had her first child in 1948, but she played baseball until she was almost four months pregnant. Collins sat out the 1949 season to raise her child but returned in 1950 to continue playing. However, before Collins played again, the league allowed her to remain in her hometown to stay with her child.[58] Audrey (Haine) Daniels got married in 1948, had a baby in 1950, and then continued to play in 1951. In her 1951 season, she only played in the home games because she wanted to be at home with her husband and child.[59] Helen Callaghan had a child, took a year off, and then returned to play. She eventually decided to retire because she wanted to have a big family.[60] Many of these women decided to have children after they got married, but they were also able to continue playing baseball. These women set many new standards for what it meant to be a working mother and wife. They proved they could still have successful marriages and also raise their children.

Popularity of Women

Wrigley knew when he created the AAGPBL that he would have to compete with the women's softball leagues already established across the Midwest. He determined that the best way to do this was to make his players the exact opposite of the softball women. He knew that the public would respond best to players who matched the ideals of society. Softball players wore pants or shorts while they played, which made them appear more masculine.[61] Softball was also faced with a stigma for being inappropriate because, in the early days, teams would go by names like "Slapsie Maxies Curvaceous Cuties" or "Num Num Pretzel Girls."[62] So, Wrigley created his rules of conduct, the uniforms, and chose attractive women to play in his league to present them as appropriate. Staged photographs were very common and often showed the women putting on make-up during a game. Wrigley also monitored the media closely in the early years in an attempt to promote positive views. The media during World War II focused on crafting "scenarios detailing a feminine ideal that was found or nurtured overwhelmingly in domestic environments."[63] Wrigley attempted to follow the same philosophy. The married women and the ones with children were extremely popular in the media.[64] They were often photographed performing domestic tasks such as doing their laundry.

One of the first national media sources to cover the AAGPBL was *Life Magazine* in 1945. The article talked positively about the women in the league agreeing that the girls met the ideals of feminine athletes. It also talked extensively about the achievements of women in the sport.[65] This article supported the way that the league was going and the women in it. The league wanted to show that their players were still feminine, but they were also successful athletes.[66] The league proved its own success when *Life Magazine* published this article about the league and its support for the league.

The local newspapers were equally as supportive of these women and their successes. In 1948 the Chicago newspaper *The Auburn Parker* wrote, "Thus far, they [Colleens] also have shown that they can play a good brand of girls' baseball...the type that appeals to the crowd."[67] The Colleens were a traveling team in the league that did not have a hometown and traveled all over the Midwest to play. The crowds were coming to watch, and this paper deemed that the Colleens were playing good, real baseball.

The AAGPBL did not rely only on gameplay for attendance to their games. They also played several charity games and benefit games, especially during the war years. Wrigley decided it was a good opportunity to promote his new girl's league in 1944, when he offered a benefit game for the Red Cross members, blood donors, and military members. Attendance to the game was free for these members, and they had designated special seats to watch the girls.[68] Patricia Brown recounted the kinds of charity events the Colleens supported in 1950. In Ohio, they played two games in support of the local high school band. In Lynchburg, Virginia, the girls played a doubleheader in support of the Boys Club Building Fund, and they also played in Roanoke, Virginia, to benefit the Roanoke Optimist Club.[69] *The Dixon Evening Telegraph* also reported about how the Rockford Peaches and the Fort Wayne Daisies hosted a benefit for the newly returned veterans in 1946. Out of 3,000 attendees, at least half were veterans.[70] The girls supported local causes and helped to create interest in the league by supporting causes of interest to the community.

The league eventually garnered interest from their fans in their team's hometown, which continued after the war. Vivian Kellog explained that even in 1946 they still drew in a huge crowd for their championship game.[71] In 1948, 910,747 people attended league games, a record for the program.[72] Even though the women were thought of as a placeholder until the men returned, they became a popular source of entertainment for their fans. There were even places where the women's teams attracted more interest than the men's teams. The women in Fort Wayne attracted more fans than the men in their area.[73] The most impressive example came when the women began their spring training in Cuba in 1947. The AAGPBL had spring training with the Brooklyn Dodgers—a men's professional baseball team. However, the Cubans were more interested in watching the women instead of the men; the women's team attracted over twenty-five thousand fans to their training sessions.[74] So, the women attracted a fair amount of attention during their good years, even while having to compete with men's baseball.

The biggest supporters of the women were the communities in which they played. The league required the towns in which they played to raise money to start the team.[75] The communities were in small towns, but the smaller towns were more supportive of their teams.[76] Since the towns were much smaller, it was easier for teams and players to become more personally involved with their communities.[77] This led to dedicated fans who would come to every home game. One woman recollected that when she was a girl, she would collect every news article about the Fort Wayne Daisies and used to go to many of their games.[78] The players also advocated for young girls, like the fan with her scrapbook. They encouraged young girls to play baseball and were even able to organize leagues in the communities for the girls to play in.[79] They helped show the next generation that they too could break barriers.

Conclusion

The All-American Girls Professional Baseball League was the brainchild of Philip Wrigley in 1943 and grew to become a popular recreation for fans until its end in 1954. These women answered the call to serve their country by filling in for the men while they were away. However, baseball was not considered an appropriate wartime job for women. In order to be accepted as a replacement for men, they were molded to fit many ideals and standards of the day, such as appearing feminine in the workplace and maintaining the archetype of a successful wife and parent.

Femininity in the workplace for these women meant that they wore skirts, had perfect makeup and hair, and performed domestic tasks for the camera. They learned all of these tasks through a league-required program known as "Charm School." The league also focused on their wives and mothers to ensure that the image they wanted for the league was broadcasted to the public. Even though the women of the league followed the rules required of them, they enjoyed, on occasion, breaking the rules.

The women of the league enjoyed the times in which they could bend or even break the rules that had been set for them. They did not allow the preconceptions about women in sports to hold them back from playing their hearts out, and they likewise did not allow a curfew to hold them back from meeting men. The women of the league presented the ability for women to maintain a job while also being a good wife and mother at the same time.

Even though the AAGPBL has not been widely researched, the organization still had a large impact on women's history. The women of the AAGPBL broke barriers, paving the way for future women in the workforce, women in sports, women in baseball, and working mothers alike.

Notes

1. Margot Fortunato Galt, *Up to the Plate* (Minneapolis: Learner Publishing Company, 1995), 11.
2. Marilyn Cohen, *No Girls in the Clubhouse: The Exclusion of Women from Baseball* (Jefferson, NC: McFarland and Company, 2009), 46.
3. Evelyn Steele, *Wartime Opportunities for Women* (New York: EP Dutton and Co., 1943), 43.
4. Steele, *Wartime Opportunities*, 43.
5. Steele, *Wartime Opportunities*, 43.
6. Lois Browne, *Girls of Summer: In Their Own League* (Toronto: Harpers Collins, 1992), 12.
7. Franklin Delano Roosevelt to Kenesaw Mountain Landis, January 15, 1942.
8. Browne, *Girls of Summer*, 23.
9. June Sochen, *Enduring Values: Women in Popular Culture* (New York: Greenwood Press, 1987), 118.
10. Sochen, *Enduring Values*, 118–119.
11. Sochen, *Enduring Values*, 118–119.
12. Carol J. Pierman, "Baseball, Conduct, and True Womanhood," *Women Studies Quarterly*, 33, no. 1/2 (2005): 68.
13. Melissa A. McEuen, *Making War, Making Women: Femininity and Duty of the American Home Front, 1941–1945* (Athens: University of Georgia Press, 2001), 8.
14. Browne, *Girls of Summer*, 61.
15. Merrie Fidler, *The Origins and History of the All-American Girls Professional Baseball League* (Jefferson, NC: McFarland and Company Publishing, 2006), 187.
16. Ester Sherman, "A Guide for All-American Girls: How To ... Look Better, Feel Better, Be More Popular," 1.
17. Ester Sherman, "A Guide for All-American Girls," 2.
18. Ester Sherman, "A Guide for All-American Girls," 3.
19. Ester Sherman, "A Guide for All-American Girls," 3.
20. Galt, *Up to the Plate*, 24.

21. McEuen, *Making War, Making Women*, 45.

22. "How a Woman Should Wear a Uniform," *Good Housekeeping*, August 1942, 21.

23. "How a Woman Should Wear a Uniform," 21.

24. Emily Yellin, *Our Mothers' War: American Women at Home and at the Front During World War II*, (New York: Simon & Schuster, 2004), 301.

25. Patricia I. Brown, *A League of My Own: Memoir of a Pitcher for the All-American Girls Professional Baseball League* (North Carolina: McFarland and Company Inc., 2003), 26.

26. "Rules of Conduct," All-American Girls Professional Baseball League, http://www.aagpbl.org/history/rules-of-conduct.

27. "Rules of Conduct."

28. "Rules of Conduct."

29. Sophie Kurys, interview by Gordon Olson, transcript, Veterans History Project, Grand Valley State University, September 26, 2009.

30. Cohen, *No Girls in the Clubhouse*, 57.

31. Fidler, *The Origins and History*, 166.

32. Fidler, *The Origins and the History*, 71.

33. Fidler, *The Origins and the History*, 71.

34. Browne, *Girls of Summer*, 110.

35. Jim Sargent, *We Were the All-American Girls: Interviews with Players of the AAGPBL, 1943–1954* (Jefferson, NC: McFarland & Company Inc., 2013), 78.

36. Sargent, *We Were the All-American Girls*, 72.

37. Browne, *Girls of Summer*, 74.

38. Browne, *Girls of Summer*, 74.

39. Galt, *Up To the Plate*, 69.

40. Browne, *Girls of Summer*, 55.

41. Browne, *Girls of Summer*, 55.

42. Browne, *Girls of Summer*, 65.

43. Fidler, *The Origins and History*, 62.

44. "Women and War," 1940, reprinted in *Women's Magazines 1940–1960: Gender Roles and the Popular Press*, ed. Nancy A. Walker (Boston: Bedford/St. Martin's, 1998), 33.

45. J Edgar. Hoover, "Mother's Our Only Hope," *Woman's Home Companion*, January 1944, reprinted in *Women's Magazines 1940–1960: Gender Roles and the Popular Press*, ed. Nancy A. Walker (Boston: Bedford/St. Martin's, 1998), 46.

46. Hoover, "Mother's Our Only Hope," 46.

47. Grace L. Pennock, "Starting from Scratch," *Ladies' Home Journal*, April 1940, reprinted in Nancy A. Walker, *Women's Magazines 1940–1960: Gender Roles and the Popular Press*, 147.

48. "You Can't Have a Career and Be a Good Wife," *Ladies' Home Journal*, January 1944, reprinted in Walker, *Women's Magazines 1940–960: Gender Roles and the Popular Press*, 71–75.

49. Fidler, *The Origins and History*, 199.

50. Galt, *Up to the Plate*, 16.

51. Sargent, *We Were the All-American Girls*, 42.

52. Sargent, *We Were the All-American Girls*, 36.

53. "Rockford Peaches pocket schedule, 1943," Women in Baseball, Baseball Hall of Fame.

54. Browne, *Girls of Summer*, 108.

55. Browne, *Girls of Summer*, 109.

56. Browne, *Girls of Summer*, 64.

57. Jean Faut, interview by James Smither, Women in Baseball, Grand Valley State University, August 10, 2010.

58. Sargent, *We Were the All-American Girls*, 36.

59. Sargent, *We Were the All-American Girls*, 42.

60. Sargent, *We Were the All-American Girls*, 80.

61. Fidler, *The Origins and History*, 57.

62. Browne, *Girls of Summer*, 16.

63. McEuen, *Making War, Making Women*, 7.

64. Cohen, *No Girls in the Clubhouse*, 50.

65. "Girl's Baseball: A Feminine Midwest League Opens its Third Professional Season," *Life Magazine*, June 4, 1945, 63–65.

66. Cohen, *No Girls in the Clubhouse*, 47.

67. "Colleens Come Home Saturday: Play Racine," *The Auburn Parker*, May 20, 1948.

68. Fidler, *The Origins and History*, 54.

69. Brown, *A League of My Own*, 51.

70. H. A. Hoff, "Mt. Morris," *Dixon Evening Telegraph*, August 27, 1946.

71. Sargent, *We Were the All-American Girls*, 57.

72. Fidler, *The Origins and History*, 137.

73. Fidler, *The Origins and History*, 47.

74. Sophie Kurys, interview by Gordon Olson, Veterans History Project, Grand Valley State University, September 26, 2009.

75. Nelson Yomtov, *The Belles of Baseball: The All-American Girls Professional Baseball League* (Minnesota: Essential Library, 2016), 32.

76. Jim Sargent, *We Were the All-American Girls*, 35.

77. Browne, *Girls of Summer*, 90.

78. Nancy O'Rear, 1945–1954, *All-American Girls Professional Baseball League Collection*, Grand Rapids Public Museum.

79. Browne, *Girls of Summer*, 102.

8. Seeing Eleanor: The First Lady of the World

OLIVIA WOOD

Eleanor Roosevelt said, "do what you feel in your heart to be right—for you'll be criticized anyway. You'll be damned if you do, and damned if you don't." This is a powerful statement from a phenomenal woman of the twentieth century. Eleanor Roosevelt set a precedent during her time as First Lady of the United States by using the press and a media presence to make her publicly accessible.

Eleanor was born in New York City on October 11, 1884. She was raised by her grandmother after the death of her parents when she was young.[1] In 1905, she married Franklin D. Roosevelt, who was her fifth cousin. He would become the thirty-second president of the United States in 1933. Eleanor Roosevelt took the role of the First Lady much more seriously than her predecessors, and because of this, she reshaped the role forever.

Eleanor Roosevelt completely altered the role of the First Lady because she was so open to the public. Prior to her tenure in the White House, the job of the First Lady was not as open and as active as it is today. Even though she was the true visionary, there were some women who set the bar in the White House before her. Roosevelt's predecessors usually portrayed the domestic role of the First Lady; they were the typical housewife, but on a larger scale. The duties of the First Lady were really set in stone by Dolley Madison, wife of James Madison. She helped President Thomas Jefferson, a widower, with household management of the White House during his Presidency.[2] Once Madison's husband was elected president, she set the tone for the first ladies that followed her. "She fortified her role of hostess by the visual effect of both the executive mansion and her own person"[3] Dolley Madison truly created the standard for all the first ladies after her until Roosevelt came along. Roosevelt was not someone who wanted to be a typical First Lady. She simply did not want to be tied down to the domesticity that came with the job. She wanted to be different than any other First Lady before her, and she did this successfully.

Throughout history, scholars have written a lot about Roosevelt. Some of these scholars have written detailed histories of her entire life, and others have written works that were based on one particular influential point in her life. Most scholars focus on the many political roles she had while she was the First Lady and afterwards. Her political activities are incredibly important to study because she was such an influential part of Franklin Roosevelt's administration. She was also a trailblazer for the roles of American women.

I believe my work will add to this continuously growing study of Eleanor Roosevelt. This chapter will discuss multiple points within her political life; I will examine each of her roles individually and discuss why the public's view of her changed throughout her political career. By focusing on her time as the First Lady, as a member of the United Nations Commission for Human Rights, and as the ceremonial Chair of Kennedy's Presidential Commission on the Status of Women, we will learn how her actions influenced public opinion. This chapter will also demonstrate that Roosevelt was a controversial figure during her time as the First Lady. However, as she stepped into her career with the United Nations and later the Kennedy administration, she was viewed as a very highly esteemed political figure.

Active First Lady

Before Roosevelt became the First Lady, she was not always active in political society. In 1913, Roosevelt moved to Washington D.C. when her husband joined Woodrow Wilson's administration as the Assistant Secretary of the Navy. At first, Roosevelt was unsure about Washington D.C., but she soon realized that there she would be able to grow her political awareness.[4] Fran Burke wrote, "She learned to handle new situations and new associates—especially politicians and members of the press."[5] Once World War I started, Roosevelt became involved in many different relief agencies which brought her further into the public eye.[6] She fell in love with the idea of helping others and continued to find ways to do so. Roosevelt would soon find it as a way to escape from her daily life. In 1918, she discovered that her husband was having an affair with another woman. Despite the infidelity, the two remained married, and Roosevelt stood by her husband's side as his political ally, advisor, and eventually caregiver.[7] Still, this did not change her newfound sense of independence. Once the affair occurred, Roosevelt became more independent and became increasingly involved in many social reforms and politics.

In the face of tragedy, Roosevelt would pick up the pieces and continue to push herself and her family to achieve extraordinary goals. In 1921, the Roosevelt family went on vacation to New Brunswick, Canada. During this vacation, Franklin Roosevelt became incredibly ill, complaining of lower back pain. Jean Edward Smith wrote that his physician believed, without a doubt, that Franklin Roosevelt had contracted poliomyelitis, more commonly known as "polio."[8] Roosevelt kept up with her husband's affairs during his recovery, which took months. His arms and back muscles would eventually recover, and he was able to get himself into a wheelchair with some assistance. However, due to the nature of the disease, he would require his wife's assistance and care for the rest of his life. After a break from politics due to this polio diagnosis, Franklin Roosevelt ran for governor of New York and won in 1928. During this time, Roosevelt became active in the women's division of the State Democratic Committee to ensure her husband's politics remained at the forefront of his campaign, despite his health troubles. Franklin Roosevelt would successfully run for the presidency in 1932, making his wife "the most politically active and influential First Lady in history."[9]

When her husband won the presidency in 1932, Roosevelt was initially terrified. She worried that her social and political life would be lost as most of the previous first ladies, who were solely perceived as hostesses.[10] For this reason, Roosevelt decided that she was not going to follow in the footsteps of any other First Lady. In paving her own way, she became the new model for American first ladies. She would take on a number of roles unusual for a First Lady, and because of this, she was a very controversial figure during her time in the White House.

Roosevelt was quite open with the goals she believed her husband's administration should achieve. She disagreed with lowering taxes because of the large amount of "social needs and wanted relief policies extended to provide work and new training for the unemployed."[11] Roosevelt also believed the isolationist policies the country had at the time were economically dangerous. Her view of isolationism had become unpopular among politicians.[12] When Franklin Roosevelt took office amid the Great Depression, his main goal was to get the American people through the economic crisis. He did this by establishing what is known as the "New Deal" within his first one hundred days in office. The New Deal was a series of federal programs that would help restore the American economy and the American spirit. Some of the popular programs Franklin Roosevelt created through the New Deal included the Social Security Board, the Tennessee Valley Authority Act, and the Federal Deposit Insurance Corporation.[13] One of Roosevelt's first acts as the First Lady was touring Washington D.C.'s alley slums with Charlotte Everett Hopkins, a major civic activist.[14] She was completely shocked at what she saw, and her experiences helped develop the legislation that would create the Alley Dwelling Authority.[15] Roosevelt was skeptical, yet hopeful, of everything that went on within her husband's first one-hundred days in office. She was afraid not every part of the government would agree with one another, but she was "impressed by the initial spirit of cooperation."[16] Roosevelt would not be impressed with every way her husband would handle certain issues during his time as the President of the United States.

There was one thing Roosevelt was disappointed about when it came to the New Deal, and it was the fact that "Eleanor believed democracy depended on housing, health care, and education. And virtually all of it discriminated against women."[17] She was such an influential part of her husband's presidential decisions, she begged him to appoint more women to public offices. This would lead to Franklin Roosevelt's appointment of Frances Perkins as the new head of the Department of Labor.[18] Roosevelt was also able to pressure her husband to allow "Rose Schneiderman to join the NRA Labor Advisory Board, Sue Sheldon White and Emily Newell Blair to the NRA Consumer Advisory Board, and Jo Coffin to become an assistant public printer."[19] While Roosevelt influenced the decisions on the policies and appointments her husband made, she also spoke and appeared in public on his behalf plenty of times.

Roosevelt had a special ability to be empathetic towards people who were struggling. This was especially true for the people involved in the struggle for civil rights. Roosevelt was deeply upset about the atrocities occurring within the United States, and she would stand with many key figures of the civil rights movement. One issue that Roosevelt focused on as soon as she took on the role of the First Lady was the terrible lynching that was still taking place throughout the United States. There had been twenty-eight lynching's in 1933, and this was not acceptable to Roosevelt. So, she partnered with the

NAACP to pass a federal anti-lynching law.[20] Vernon Jarrett, an American journalist, was interviewed about Roosevelt and how she worked to help the African American community. When Jarrett was asked if Roosevelt was behind Franklin Roosevelt's popularity with African Americans, he stated, "Mrs. Roosevelt became Franklin Roosevelt's secret weapon."[21] Jarrett would go on to talk about Roosevelt's involvement with the NAACP, saying that because the National Association for the Advancement of Colored People (NAACP) was considered a radical left-wing organization, Roosevelt was continuously investigated by the FBI. It was known that the FBI was anti-Eleanor Roosevelt.[22] Roosevelt endorsed the Southern Conference on Human Welfare and she attended a convention with Mary McLeod Bethune in Birmingham, Alabama. She was told by police officers she could not sit with Bethune because Birmingham had outlawed integrated seating, so she moved a chair into the middle of the aisle.[23] In 1939, Roosevelt would publicly resign as a member of the Daughters of the American Revolution (DAR) after they refused to rent out a theatre to a famous African American opera singer, Marian Anderson. Two months after this incident, Roosevelt invited Marian Anderson to sing at the White House for the King and Queen of England.[24] She would continue to connect and support the African American community throughout the country.

One of the things that made Roosevelt different from any other First Lady was that she communicated with the American public in many different ways. She held press conferences, hosted radio broadcasts, gave lectures, traveled all over the nation, and even expressed her opinions in her daily newspaper column.[25] Two days after officially becoming the First Lady of the United States, Roosevelt held a press conference with female reporters in the Treaty Room. She would continue to do this weekly, discussing actions and programs in an effort to encourage women to become more politically active.[26] Roosevelt's press conferences were unique because she only allowed female reporters into them. In fact, there was an open ban on any male reporters attending the press conferences.[27] Roosevelt also looked to communicate with the American people through a magazine column. She was contracted with a monthly magazine called *Women's Home Companion.* Roosevelt had a column called "I want you to write to me," which allowed the American people to ask her questions. Roosevelt would return to writing monthly newsletters in the *Women's Democratic News*, also known as WDN, in February 1933.[28] Roosevelt was so passionate about being able to talk with the American people during her time as First Lady; she communicated through her writing and becoming a radio sensation.

On December 7, 1941, Japan bombed the American Pacific Fleet in Pearl Harbor, Hawaii. That night it was Roosevelt who took to the radio to address the American people before Franklin Roosevelt addressed Congress. She stated clearly and calmly, "Japan's airships were bombing our citizens in Hawaii and the Philippines and sinking one of our transports on its way to Hawaii."[29] She went on to speak directly to the women of the country, sharing empathy with them because she, too, had a son on a destroyer and her other children lived near coastal cities. She also states in her message that she will put the White House on the same food and gas rationing system as the rest of the nation.[30] Roosevelt also spoke to the young people—she told them that their abilities were about to be tested and that she believed in them. She built rapport with the American people this way. Roosevelt knew this would change the lives of every American citizen. She knew of the changes in daily life that lied ahead. She would become a symbol guiding the American people throughout World War II.

Roosevelt was appalled by the Japanese internment camps that were established throughout the United States. She voiced her protest to the public and even asked the Attorney General to fight the absurd policy with her husband.[31] But the majority of the American people were anti-Japanese, and because of this, she lost the battle to shut them down. Roosevelt did not just try to protect Japanese Americans, but she also tried to protect Jewish children across Europe.

Roosevelt went to work trying to help the people abroad during the trying war times. She was a strong supporter of the Wagner-Rogers Bill, which would allow Jewish children to emigrate to the United States to flee the violence of the Nazi regime and the persecution of Jewish people throughout Europe. The state department did not support this bill, causing Roosevelt to join the many Jewish-American leaders in speaking out about the crisis.[32] She learned of the horrible things happening to Jewish people across Europe and believed it was the duty of the United States to aid these people. While Roosevelt was deeply invested in wartime issues, she focused on women that were left behind during the war. For example, Roosevelt visited African American female workers that were living in Lucy D. Slowe Hall in

Washington, D.C.[33] Her goal was to inspire American women to become more involved during wartime.

Roosevelt's role as First Lady ended after twelve years when her husband passed away in 1945. She was an extremely controversial figure during her time as the First Lady of the United States. Minorities in the nation largely praised her work, while she was disliked by the patriarchal society that surrounded her during this time period. Even though her ideals were frowned upon by some, she still was able to pave the way for future first ladies.

The United Nations

Despite the fact that many people, including Roosevelt herself, believed that her political activity would end with the death of her husband, this was definitely not the case. In 1946, Roosevelt would be asked by President Harry Truman to become the United States' first delegate to the newly founded United Nations (UN).[34] Roosevelt was hesitant at first to take on the position because she did not believe she was qualified enough.[35] However, ultimately she accepted and throughout her time with the United Nations, from 1946 to 1952, Roosevelt remained an important political activist. Roosevelt was no longer tied to the role of First Lady, and this caused her to become more outspoken about politics and social reforms. As time went on and American society began to change, the public's view of Roosevelt changed as well.

Due to the end of World War II, the UN's Commission on Human Rights was created in 1946 to establish a universal doctrine of human rights. The abuse of human rights by the Nazi regime during this time spawned this commission. The world wanted to make sure that nothing like World War II would ever happen again. Roosevelt, having been a firm supporter of human rights during her time as First Lady, seemed a perfect fit for such a commission. The first meeting of the UN's Commission on Human Rights was held on January 27, 1947. The meeting included representatives from eighteen nations who unanimously selected Roosevelt to be the chair of the Commission.[36] It was easy to see that Roosevelt was the most important member of the Commission simply because of who she was. She was not only the former First Lady, but also an important figure in humanitarian works.[37]

The Commission decided that its first order of business was to create an international bill of rights. This is when problems immediately began to arise.

The creation of the Commission was mainly due to the atrocities that occurred just a few years before and during World War II. In her speech to the General Assembly of the UN, Roosevelt states, "The realization of the flagrant violation of human rights by Nazi and fascist countries sowed the seeds of the last World War, have supplied the impetus for the work."[38] The traditions of communist countries began to clash with western democratic traditions. The representatives from the communist countries, such as the Soviet Union and Yugoslavia, did not support the rights of the individual, which is something that was very important to representatives from the democratic countries, such as Roosevelt. A minor official from the Soviet Union questioned Charles Malik's "Four Basic Principles." This Soviet official, Valentin Tepliakov, stated, "The rights of the individual must be seen in relation to the individual's obligation to the community ... which is the main body that provides for his existence."[39] But she did not just struggle with representatives within the Commission, she also struggled with people from within the United States government. It is believed that she clashed with Robert Lovett, who was the Under Secretary of State. Lovett did not believe a declaration would help or serve a purpose for the United States.[40] Roosevelt went back to work when she realized what a problem the differing ideals, both in and out of the Commission, would be.

Finally, after a year of convening, debating, and compromising, the Commission had completed the Universal Declaration of Human Rights. They took the Declaration in front of the United Nations General Assembly on December 9, 1948. The president of the General Assembly at the time was Herbert Evatt, from Australia. Evatt stated that, "Eleanor was the person who, with the assistance of many others, has played a leading role in this work."[41] Once Roosevelt took the floor of the General Assembly, she urged them to adopt the Declaration that she and the other members of the Commission had worked so hard on. She stated to the members of the General Assembly that she hoped the Declaration would be as important as the proclamation of many different declarations of rights, such as the declarations in France and in the United States.[42] The Declaration declared that all humans are born free and with rights regardless of sex, race, religion, or language. The Declaration also outlawed slavery, cruel and unusual punishment, and it established asylum in other countries.[43] On December 10, 1948, it was officially adopted by the United Nations. Roosevelt's continuous hard work finally paid off.

Throughout her time working with the United Nations, Roosevelt was still writing and broadcasting to the nation she loved. She found it much more freeing because she could speak out on issues that she would normally avoid as the First Lady. Now she was free to talk about causes she was passionate about including intolerance, progressive causes, civil rights, and even her work with the Commission on Human Rights.[44] Roosevelt knew the impact she had on the United States and its people. She believed that through discussing intolerance, racism, and human rights on air that she would make the American people better aware of what was going on around them. She continued to broadcast her political opinion across the country because she wanted her critics to know she was not planning on backing down. Roosevelt never backed down from a challenge, and she became increasingly confident in herself as she progressed through her career.

After seven years of working as a delegate for the United Nations, Roosevelt resigned in 1953. She did this so that the new President, Dwight Eisenhower, could choose someone he wanted in her place.[45] However, she continued to volunteer with the United Nations within the United States. She would also continue to be an important supporter of the Democratic Party. She was an important member of the Democratic Party as Democratic nominees often needed her support in order to win the nomination. This is when the unlikely friendship between Eleanor Roosevelt and John F. Kennedy came into play in the 1960s. She would find herself once again in the political spotlight because of this friendship–one that would turn into something much more important in women's history.

Working with President Kennedy

Kennedy would have to try very hard to earn the support of Roosevelt, even after he won the election in 1960. Roosevelt did not care for Kennedy and at first, and would not support him as a Democratic candidate. Roosevelt "opposed Kennedy's nomination in 1956 because she thought he avoided taking a stand on the Senate censure of Joseph McCarthy and on enforcing civil rights legislation and court decrees."[46] But she also adamantly refused to support the Republican nominee, Richard Nixon. She would not campaign for Kennedy until the final days of the campaign when she realized they needed to put their differences aside and begin to work together. She made appearances on multiple occasions, asking for people to vote for Kennedy in the election because she believed in him.[47] She wrote a letter to a woman named Mary Lasker discussing her conversation with Kennedy. Roosevelt was extremely interested in what Kennedy had to say about his plan to expand social security, which was something close to her heart because her husband had started the program during his presidency. Roosevelt had been in politics for almost four decades by this time, and as a result, the American people trusted her opinion. Even though they were unlikely partners, they managed to move past their differences to make what they saw as "the new frontier."[48]

Once Kennedy took office in 1961, their relationship only grew. Roosevelt attended Kennedy's inaugural address and wrote him a letter thanking him for allowing her to be there. She said she felt a sense of gratitude and liberation after his inaugural speech.[49] Kennedy went right to work when he took office, wasting no time. Within two months of taking office, Kennedy had seven important legislations sent to Congress.[50] These pieces of legislation included aid to depressed areas, an extension of unemployment benefits, a 25 percent increase in the minimum wage, medical care for the elderly, and federal aid to education.[51] These were legislations that Roosevelt supported willingly. Within six weeks of being in office, Kennedy invited Roosevelt to the White House when he issued an executive order that would make the Peace Corps a reality. Roosevelt was very pleased to see that Kennedy sympathized with Martin Luther King Jr. This was one issue that the two agreed on, as they were both strong supporters of the civil rights movement and human rights as a whole. Roosevelt had started out working with African Americans in the 1930s and 1940s during her time as the First Lady. While he was being backed by Roosevelt, Kennedy was also highly praised by the younger generation for standing up against the atrocities that were starting in the South. Everyone could see the mutual respect between Kennedy and Roosevelt, and this respect would continue to grow with time.

On December 14, 1961, Kennedy proposed the executive order to create the PCSW, better known as the President's Commission on the Status of Women. He proposed this commission to look into what improvement was needed when it came to the status of American women. The Director of the Women's Bureau in the Department of Labor, Esther Peterson, was concerned that the administration was not helping American women. Kennedy believed he knew the right woman had to take on the job at hand, and that woman was Roosevelt. Kennedy requested that Roosevelt serve as the head chair of this newly created commission.[52] This commission not only would mitigate some of the hardships that women face, but it would also push for an Equal Rights Amendment to be added to the Constitution. The Commission was put together with the secretaries of the departments of commerce, agriculture, labor, health, education and welfare, the Attorney General, the Chairman of the Civil Service Commission, and twenty members appointed by the president, including a total of fifteen women and eleven men.[53] Some of the members were educators, writers, leaders of organizations, members of the House and Congress, and union leaders. Roosevelt truly believed that this commission could do the job it was created to do, and she discussed this in her newspaper column, "My Day," on February 16th, 1962. Roosevelt was focused on how to help benefit women without hurting their children. Since most women were still working within the home, there had to be a way to make sure American children were not negatively affected. The Commission looked at the expansion of employment, legislation, political, civil, and property rights for women. Roosevelt spoke at a congressional hearing on behalf of the Commission to show their support of the equal pay legislation for women.[54] Roosevelt was making her final effort to make sure women would be able to be on the national front in all aspects of life. She wanted to make sure people knew that women were capable of doing anything a man could do, and this was her way to show it. This role would be the last public humanitarian role Roosevelt would undertake before her death.

Even though Roosevelt passed away before the completion of the report, she was still memorialized by the other members of the Commission. The report, titled "American Women," was given to Kennedy on Roosevelt's birthday in 1963. The report openly discussed the inequalities and the injustices that American women faced. The Commission weighed in on a lot of different aspects that they believed needed improvement in order to help American women. They believed that education was the biggest issue, and they did not just need to focus on higher education, but also education for the younger girls of our nation.[55] They went on to say that in order to allow women to get a better education and reenter the workforce, there would need to be some type of child care services and that there would be deductions for the child care expenses for working mothers.[56] The Commission also discussed the disadvantages women faced in the workforce. They found that most employers during this time believed that women were more unpredictable than male workers. They also discovered that women were filling the jobs that were the lowest-paying. The Commission looked into the number of women that held public office, and it reflected a low proportion of women in these positions. They stated that American women should be encouraged to fill these public office positions at local, state, and national levels and that they should not experience discrimination due to their sex. This report helped end the exclusion of women from jury services, from owning property or businesses, and even legal control over their own earnings.[57] The Commission was able to uncover an enormous amount of discriminatory acts towards American women, and they were able to come up with recommendations to fix these issues. They were able to finish what Roosevelt started. At the very beginning of the report given to Kennedy, there is a quote from Roosevelt, and it states how she believed that eventually there would be nothing in the way of stopping women from achieving their goals because of all the hard work that was being done in the United States to fix it.

Conclusion

Eleanor Roosevelt was an inspiring political figure. She accomplished things in her life that she never thought she could. She went from a shy and quiet girl to a politically opinionated woman who spoke her mind. Her voice and ideas were heard around the world. She had a love for her country so strong that you could hear it with every word she spoke. She also loved all people. It did not matter where you came from or what your story was, she would care for them regardless. Roosevelt was admired by many, and she was known as the "First Lady of the World."

However, Roosevelt started out as a highly controversial figure at the beginning of her lifelong political career in the 1930s, when she became the First Lady. She questioned the typical social norms of her time, and many Americans did not agree with that. She marched to the beat of her own drum, and she learned not to care what people thought of her. Once she stepped into the role of the First Lady, she began to learn her place in the world. She helped the American people get through the Great Depression by pushing her husband to create the New Deal. She would continue to help the American people through the second World War. She was able to understand their troubles and empathize with them. She was able to reach out to them regularly and talk to them through her broadcastings and writings, continuing to do this throughout the rest of her life. She would end her time as First Lady and move into her role as a member of the United Nations Commission for Human Rights. She would play a leading role in creating and drafting the Universal Declaration of Human Rights. She would remain at the forefront of the Democratic Party and the political world in general. She would eventually find an unlikely friendship with the new president. He would ask her to run his newly created Presidential Commission on the Status of Women, and she would take on this role proudly because she was always a supporter of women's rights. She would not live to see the completion of the report, however, she was with the commission in spirit the entire time they pressed on. They were able to hand in the report to Kennedy on what would have been Roosevelt's birthday, and they dedicated the report in her honor. By the end of her life, she was one of the most well-respected women in the world and one of the most highly esteemed political figures in history.

Roosevelt was a controversial figure during the 1930s and even in the 1960s. But why was she controversial? It was mainly because of the time period she lived in. Most women during this time were still confined to only working within the home. Women were remaining in their homes, confined to the realm of domesticity. As time progressed and World War II began, women emerged from their homes and entered the workforce while the majority of men were away at war. But one thing remained the same and that was Roosevelt's presence. From the 1930s to the 1960s, Roosevelt was able to reach into the homes of the American people and pull them into the outside world.

Notes

1. "Eleanor Roosevelt Biography," FDR Presidential Library & Museum, https://www.fdrlibrary.org/er-biography

2. "FirstLady Biography: Dolley Madison," National First Ladies' Library, http://www.firstladies.org/biographies/firstladies.aspx?biography=4.

3. "First Lady Biography: Dolley Madison."

4. Debra Michals, "Eleanor Roosevelt," National Women's History Museum, 2017, https://www.womenhistory.org/education-resources/biographies/eleanor-roosevelt.

5. Fran Burke, "Eleanor Roosevelt, October 11, 1884–November 7, 1962 – She Made a Difference," *Public Administration Review* 44, no. 5 (1984): 365–72, 10.2307/975987.

6. Michals, "Eleanor Roosevelt."

7. Michals, "Eleanor Roosevelt."

8. Jean Edward Smith, FDR (New York: Random House, 2007), 189.

9. Michals, "Eleanor Roosevelt."

10. Blanche Wiesen Cook, *Eleanor Roosevelt: The Defining Years*, (New York: Viking, 1999), 9.

11. Cook, *Eleanor Roosevelt: The Defining Years*, 11.

12. Cook, *Eleanor Roosevelt: The Defining Years*, 11.

13. "Great Depression Fact," FDR Presidential Library & Museum, https://www.fdrlibrary.org/great-depression-facts.

14. Mary Jo Binker, "Eleanor Roosevelt's 'My Day': Causes," White House Historical Association, https://ww.whitehousehistory.org/eleanor-roosevelts-causes.

15. Binker, "Eleanor Roosevelt's 'My Day': Causes."

16. Cook, *Eleanor Roosevelt: The Defining Years*, 70.

17. Cook, *Eleanor Roosevelt: The Defining Years*, 70.

18. Michals, "Eleanor Roosevelt."

19. A. M. Black, "Roosevelt, Eleanor," Social Welfare History Project, October 17, 2017, https://socialwelfare.library.vcu.edu/eras/great-depression/eleanor-roosevelt/.

20. Cook, *Eleanor Roosevelt: The Defining Years*, 177.

21. "Eleanor Roosevelt and Race," Public Broadcasting Service, https://ww.pbs.org/wgbh/americanexperience/features/eleanor-jarrett/.

22. "Eleanor Roosevelt and Race."

23. Black, "Roosevelt, Eleanor."

24. "First Lady Biography: Eleanor Roosevelt," Eleanor Roosevelt: National First Ladies' Library, http://ww.firstladies.org/biographies/first-ladies.aspx?biography=33.

25. "Anna Eleanor Roosevelt," The White House, https://www.whitehouse.gov/about-the-white-house/first-ladies/anna-eleanor-roosevelt/.

26. Harris & Ewing, photographer, *Eleanor Roosevelt with group of women*, 1932, photograph, Library of Congress, https://www.loc.gov/item/2016890059/.

27. "First Lady Biography: Eleanor Roosevelt."

28. Binker, "Eleanor Roosevelt's 'My Day': Causes," 10.

29. "Eleanor Roosevelt Pearl Harbor Attack Radio Address," C-SPAN, https://www.c-span.org/video/?419692-1/eleanor-roosevelt-pearl-harbor-attack-radio-address.

30. "First Lady Biography: Eleanor Roosevelt."

31. "First Lady Biography: Eleanor Roosevelt."

32. "First Lady Biography: Eleanor Roosevelt."

33. Roger Smith, photographer, *Washington D.C. Eleanor Roosevelt visiting Lucy D. Slower Hall, women's dormitory for Negro war* workers, 1943, photograph, Library of Congress, https://www.loc.gov/item/2017854156/.

34. Blanche Wiesen Cook, *Eleanor Roosevelt: The War Years and After* (New York: Viking, 2016), 549.

35. John Sears, "Eleanor Roosevelt and the Universal Declaration of Human Rights," FDR Presidential Library & Museum, https://www.fdrlibrary.org/human-rights, 7.

36. Sears, "Eleanor Roosevelt and the Universal Declaration of Human Rights," 5.

37. Mary Ann Glendon, *A World Made New: Eleanor Roosevelt and the Universal Declaration of Human Rights* (New York: Random House, 2003), 33.

38. The WPA Film Library, "Eleanor Roosevelt Reads the Universal Declaration of Human Rights, ca. 1948," Films On Demand, July 8, 2014.

39. Glendon, "A World Made New: Eleanor Roosevelt and the Universal Declaration of Human Rights," 40.

40. Sears, "Eleanor Roosevelt and the Universal Declaration of Human Rights," 10.

41. Sears, "Eleanor Roosevelt and the Universal Declaration of Human Rights," 10.

42. The WPA Film Library, "Eleanor Roosevelt Reads the Universal Declaration of Human Rights."

43. "Universal Declaration of Human Rights," United Nations, https://www.un.org/en/universal-declaration-human-rights/.

44. Stephen Smith, "Eleanor Roosevelt: The First Lady of the Radio," *American RadioWorks*, November 10, 2014, http://www.americanradioworks.org/segments/eleanor-roosevelt-radio/.

45. "Eleanor Roosevelt Biography," FDR Presidential Library & Museum, https://www.fdrlibrary.org/er-biography.

46. Allida Black et al., eds., *Eleanor Roosevelt, John Kennedy, and the Election of 1960: A Project of The Eleanor Roosevelt Papers* (Columbia, SC: Model Editions Partnership, 2003), https://erpapers.columbian.gwu.edu/.

47. Allida Black et al., *Eleanor Roosevelt, John Kennedy, and the Election of 1960*.

48. Cynthia Ellen Harrison, *On Account of Sex: The Politics of Women Issues, 1945–1968*, (Berkeley: University of California Press, 1988), 70.

49. Allida Black et al., *Eleanor Roosevelt, John Kennedy, and the Election of 1960*.

50. Allida Black et al., *Eleanor Roosevelt, John Kennedy, and the Election of 1960*.

51. Allida Black et al., *Eleanor Roosevelt, John Kennedy, and the Election of 1960*.

52. Michals, "Eleanor Roosevelt."

53. Maurine Hoffman Beasley and Holly Cowan Shulman, *The Eleanor Roosevelt*

Encyclopedia (Westport, CT: Greenwood Press, 2001), 409.

54. Beasley and Shulman, *The Eleanor Roosevelt Encyclopedia*, 409.

55. "American Women," Commission on the Status of Women, https://www.dol.gov/wb/American Women Report.pdf

56. "American Women."

57. "American Women."

PART III

POPULAR CULTURE AND MODERN WOMEN

9. "Funny Like A Guy": Women in American Standup Comedy

ELIZABETH SHOLTIS

In September 2015, Ali Wong walked onstage to perform her Netflix special, *Baby Cobra*, while seven and a half months pregnant. She immediately addressed her visible pregnancy and then set up a series of jokes about how female comics rarely return to work after having a baby, whereas male comics return almost immediately. "They'll get onstage a week after [having a baby] and be like 'guys I just had this baby ... it's so annoying and boring!' and all the dads in the audience say, 'that's hilarious! I identify!' And their fame just swells."[1] While Wong's special was notable for her honest and accurate jokes about motherhood and pregnancy, it also marked a significant milestone in the progression of women in standup comedy. When Joan Rivers appeared pregnant on television in 1967, producers told her explicitly not to mention her pregnancy, believing it would be considered impolite.[2] The history of women in standup is a recent one. Women in the profession today still make some of the same arguments for themselves that they did twenty years ago.

In the 1970s, standup comedy was emerging as a mainstream form of entertainment. After evolving from vaudeville acts, standup comedians booked clubs in major cities and performed amongst singers and dancers as mainstream entertainers. Television talk shows and variety shows popularized in the 1950s and 1960s, like *The Ed Sullivan Show* and the *Tonight Show*, also hired comedians to appear and perform, exposing audiences to standup comedy from the comfort of their living rooms. These advancements in technology allowed comedy to become more accessible to people all over the country, integrating itself into the mainstream media.

At the same time, second-wave feminism encouraged women to challenge the 1950s housewife model and enter into the workforce as well as the public eye. While many women had jobs at this point, the jobs available to women were highly gendered: women could be secretaries but not executives, women could be teachers but not professors, women could be comedic sidekicks but not stars in their own right. Second-wave feminists advocated for women to challenge these societal norms and prove that they deserved the same kinds of jobs and opportunities as men.

Despite the cultural importance of female comedians, there have been few historical studies of women's experiences in the world of American standup comedy. Many articles have been written on women in comedy from an anthropological standpoint or as a lens to view feminist theory. *Hysterical! Women in American Comedy* is a collection of essays that cover comedians from 1940 through the present and focus on a myriad of topics relating to them. For instance, the eighth chapter, "Moms Mabley and Wanda Sykes: 'Ima Be Me'" examines in part how the two comedians "used the microphone to both assert their agency and enact their own unique brands of activism."[3] *Comic Venus: Women and Comedy in American Silent Film* by Kristen Wagner examines the ways in which "silent comediennes played an important role in a societal reconceptualization of femininity and gender roles."[4] Similarly, other material on the history of standup comedy as a whole exists but tends to leave women out of the story, reflecting the reality of the profession as it was a predominantly male enterprise. The podcast *The History of Standup* argues that the growth of American standup comedy was driven by changes in technology that allowed comedians to get their work to audiences in different ways.[5] All of these works provide context for the story of women in American standup comedy.

In this chapter, I will explore the ways in which female comedians challenged ideas about what it meant to be a "funny woman" in order to make a space for themselves in comedy from 1970–1990. I will explore this topic through a series of thematically oriented "case studies" of women who performed standup comedy during this period, highlighting the work of Phyllis Diller, Lilly Tomlin, Joan Rivers, and Elayne Boosler. These sections will examine how each of these women took the societal norms and expectations of their time and both challenged them and worked within them to make a name for themselves in comedy. This chapter aims to argue that rather than creating their own space in the comedy world, the first women in standup comedy had to break into the boy's club of comedy. Early female comics did this by parodying what men thought women should be. Eventually, women in the industry argued that they should be considered comics that just happened to be female, instead of a separate class of "women comics."

The Set-Up: Standup's Historical Context

The history of standup comedy is a fairly recent and male-dominated one. Standup emerged from the comedic acts of the vaudeville circuits, traveling variety shows that featured everything from burlesque to slapstick comedy. Standup comedy first appeared as comedians performing monologues in these vaudeville shows. It came to be different from other forms of comedy because the comedians spoke as themselves, not as a character and without props or costumes. The comedian would stand alone on stage and simply tell funny jokes by being themselves. Some of the first standup comedians included Jack Benny, Bob Hope, George Burns, Fred Allen, Milton Berle, and Frank Fay.[6] As the genre grew in the 1950s and 1960s, comics ventured into politics, sex, and religion with their jokes, which gave audiences the impression that standup comedy was taboo and not the kind of thing women and children should listen to. This mentality and the lack of women performing standup perpetuated the idea that comedy was for men. Jokes frequently featured the comedian's wife and were made at the expense of women for being vain, vapid, or shallow. By making their jokes about women, male comics told America that women themselves could not be funny, but instead must be the butt of a joke.

At almost the same time, second-wave feminism in America was gaining momentum. As women entered the workforce, they began to push for greater rights and equality in the workplace. In 1963 Betty Friedan published *The Feminine Mystique*, a book demonstrating that many women were unhappy with simply being housewives and homemakers, despite what mainstream media would have people believe. Friedan's book is credited with sparking the second-wave feminist movement, which sought to build on the progress of first-wave feminism by advocating for more than just suffrage. The second-wave feminist movement took up issues such as sexuality, family, the workplace, and official legal inequalities. This movement brought attention to gender inequality and provided opportunities for women to enter fields they previously believed impenetrable, and comedy was no exception.

Getting in Character: Phyllis Diller and Lily Tomlin

Whether or not character work can be considered standup comedy is a greatly contested question amongst comedians and critics. Most people consider standup comedy to be distinct from other forms of comedy in the sense that the comedian is not performing a character, but rather is standing on stage as themselves telling jokes that are ostensibly about their life. In the case of women standups, however, Phyllis Diller is widely regarded as one of the first female standup comedians and says that she herself uses a character onstage. Lily Tomlin is also known specifically for her character work, yet in an interview with Steve Allen published in the *Los Angeles Times* discussing his book *Funny Men*, Allen admitted that he would include Lily Tomlin among the starts of standup comedy.[7] It would seem from these labels that the debate over what is or what is not considered standup is not as hotly contested among women comedians. Female standup comedians frequently use character work. In fact, Diller and Tomlin's careers demonstrate how character work was essential in allowing women to burst into the field of comedy. This section aims to examine how Diller and Tomlin used typically feminine characters to break into the male-dominated field of standup.

Diller, first appearing in 1955 at The Purple Onion, was part of a vanguard of female comedians who, despite their skill, had to learn the ropes without a female role model. Already a wife and mother of five, Diller had gotten into comedy at the age of thirty-seven, which was later than most comedians. While no clubs specifically catering to comedians existed yet, clubs like The Purple Onion hired many different types of entertainers, and to get a spot at the Purple Onion meant that you were a serious performer.[8] In an NPR interview, Diller explained that as a new comedian, she had no idea what she was doing.[9] There were no women in standup comedy that she could draw from and she had no role models.

As Diller performed more and more shows, however, a comedic persona began to solidify in the shape of a surreal version of the 1950s housewife. This persona was heavily reliant on Diller's costuming. She emerged on stage in shapeless short dresses, dramatic makeup, and hair teased into a disheveled mop. In an NPR interview, Diller held a cigarette holder in her gloved hands and said, "all clowns wear gloves—even Mickey Mouse." The aesthetic of Diller's persona was designed to allow her to be both a woman and funny. Her baggy dresses hid what she described as a near-perfect figure, and her ugly makeup covered a pretty face. The appearance of Diller's character allowed her to establish that she was funny before opening her mouth.

Diller's jokes were rapid-fire and based on a caricature of white suburbia. Her comedic style mirrored that of Bob Hope. The material for her jokes consisted largely of self-deprecation and jokes about "Fang," a character she had created as her persona's husband. Her jokes about Fang had to do with him being lazy, stupid, and drunk. For example, "I asked him to lower the thermostat. He put it six inches above the floor."[10] Most of her jokes had this style: set-up, punchline. Years later in an interview, comedian Paula Poundstone explained that Diller's jokes were not exceptionally funny, but she got laughs because she was able to bombard the audience with them. [11] Her material caricatured the suburban housewife and her husband: "[my neighbor] is always bragging about how you can eat off her kitchen floor—you can eat off my kitchen floor! There's mustard, ketchup, baked beans." Jokes like this confronted the expectations of women to be perfect homemakers. Diller's persona was everything a 1950s housewife was not supposed to be. In this way, her humor provided men with jokes that reinforced stereotypes they were familiar with and provided women with an alternative version of femininity. Her male contemporaries made wife jokes, and Diller's "Fang" allowed her to make the same kind of material, making fun of herself as a wife as well as of her husband.[12] Diller's material had something for everyone, which enabled her to become as popular as she did.

Diller designed every element of her act to avoid scrutiny. Her jokes were rapid-fire so that there was no time to be heckled or to analyze her mistakes. "I don't have hecklers," she once said in an interview for the New York Times early in her career: "My timing is so precise, a heckler would have to make an appointment."[13] Her costuming was purposefully ugly so that no one could comment on what she was wearing or what she should have been wearing. She could not be sexualized in her shapeless dress and disheveled hair. She was, according to a 1989 New York Times article, the "ultimate exponent of smiling comic self-deprecation."[14] By already representing everything wrong with a suburban housewife, no one could criticize her for not being pretty, not proper enough, or not wearing the right thing.

Almost twenty years after Diller's debut, comedian Lily Tomlin would take Diller's lead, becoming one of the most famous character comedians of all time. Lily Tomlin has been described as "one of the most dangerous and revolutionary comedic performers to emerge in the 1970s."[15] She is known widely for her character work and for being able to disappear into the many characters she has created over the years. Tomlin made her debut in 1969 on *Laugh-In*, a sketch comedy show that "made fun of the social and political issues of the late 1960s and early 1970s."[16] Tomlin was not a mainstream performer, and her work was heavily influenced by her involvement in the feminist movement and the gay liberation movement. Her characters were inspired by the idiosyncrasies that Tomlin saw in everyone around her. On *Laugh-In* and in her shows, she appeared as the characters she had created: Ernestine, a brash telephone operator; Edith Anne, a five-and-a-half-year-old girl; Susie the Sorority Girl; and many more. These characters are all examples of how Tomlin could make jokes with women at the center and also be considered funny to men.

Through Ernestine the telephone operator, one of Tomlin's most popular characters, Tomlin was able to use stereotypes of femininity to criticize large corporations and politics, as well as how mainstream America viewed women. In one bit on *Laugh-In*, Ernestine calls General Motors. Tomlin begins the bit with Ernestine thinking that General Motors was a person, rather than a company. She continues with a series of short jokes at the expense of General Motors. For example, after realizing she had made a mistake in assuming General Motors was a person, she delivers the line "oh, of course, now I recall. That's a switch, isn't it? Someone recalling General Motors."[17] The joke references the 1971 recall of 6.7 million vehicles made by General Motors after the discovery that a fault in their engines caused vehicles to accelerate unprompted.[18] In her delivery, Ernestine moves so quickly through lines that the audience hardly notices the biting and critical nature of her comments. In this way, Tomlin plays into feminine stereotypes of women being dumb or shrill in order to deliver serious commentary on society. Tomlin's jokes as Ernestine are similar to Diller's in the sense that they are mostly short one-liners without much setup, but Tomlin's interaction with the person on the other end of the phone makes it different. The jokes build on each other and while the first few gags are at Ernestine's expense–her snort, her hair, the way she says "one ringy dingy" while she waits for the person to answer–by the end of the bit the audience is laughing about the jokes that Ernestine is making. By easing audiences into Ernestine's humor, Tomlin was able to show America that women could deliver funny jokes too.

Each of Tomlin's characters had their own set of aesthetic flaws that mocked cultural understandings of womanhood, but in ways that still held on to their dignity. Tomlin's characters were not purposefully ugly in the way that Diller's comic persona was, but they certainly were not meant to be sexualized. Even Susie the Sorority Girl was never scantily dressed or made to be an object of sexual desire. In one bit where Fred Fraternity asked Susie to get in the back of his car, she replied that they could after they were married.[19] She is inherently unsexual with her large round glasses and modest clothing. Ernestine had a scrunched face, a snort when she laughed, and a signature 1940s hairdo despite the fact that her character was contemporary.[20] Each of Tomlin's characters was visually as funny as the jokes they told. Their visual appearance was essential to their delivery.

For two women using characters to break into comedy, Diller and Tomlin's comedic styles varied vastly. Part of this had to do with the different political atmospheres present when each woman came into comedy. Diller, entering the comedy world in the late 1950s, generally told conservative jokes that catered to everyone. They did not have much depth or irony, but were instead delivered one right after the other. Tomlin, conversely, came onto the scene in the late 1960s amidst a culture of protests and political activism. An activist herself, Tomlin's work carried a much more overt political tint. Ultimately, however, both women were able to use their comedy to make a comment on the role of women in society.

"Keep Your Femininity and Give it to Them"

Joan Rivers was the first woman to gain national recognition for standup comedy without using a character. While also dabbling in acting and writing, Rivers began her comedy career in the early 1960s in the clubs of Greenwich Village, including such well-known venues as The Gaslight, The Bitter End, and The Duplex.[21] After performing at these clubs and as a comedic actress in movies and plays, Rivers booked herself a spot on the Tonight Show on February 17, 1965, which brought her into the national spotlight and skyrocketed her career. Rivers appeared on the Tonight Show seven more times between February and September that year.[22] She quickly became a regular guest on the show, eventually even guest hosting. This exposure granted her opportunities for appearances on many other talk and variety shows, such as The Ed Sullivan Show. Rivers recognized that she was unique in being a woman doing traditional, non-character-oriented standup. "Women are finally making it," she said once in a guest lecture at Lee Strasberg's Theater Institute: "I have a motto: keep your femininity and give it to them."[23] This section aims to explore how Rivers navigated ideas about women, gender, and sexuality to carve out a place for herself in the comedy world.

Because Rivers chose not to use a character, her physical appearance differed significantly from that of Diller and Tomlin. When Rivers appeared on stage, she was pretty—her makeup was done, her hair and outfits were stylish and feminine, and her figure was well-defined. Her carriage was different too. She appeared meeker, shyer than Diller and Tomlin who rather burst onto the stage and fired joke after joke. Rivers would wring her hands and nervously fiddle with her fingers onstage as she delivered her jokes. Her jokes also differed from those of comedians who performed as characters. Rather than delivering short gags with a setup, punchline structure, River's jokes were embedded in stories about her life. For example, in one show in 1966, she tells a story of her "old maid cousin" who gets married at seventy-two to a man twenty years older. While describing the wedding, Rivers delivers the line "we threw rice, and orthopedic shoes," and the audience erupts in laughter.[24] Like Diller, Rivers' comedy could take a turn toward self-deprecation as she frequently told stories of her being a fat child or hopelessly single: "because I was so fat I didn't have any friends. 'Cause nobody could get close enough to me to realize I was fun."[25] Despite Rivers' decision to be pretty and feminine in her acts, early in her career she used self-deprecation and displayed a less confident carriage than her male contemporaries. This allowed Rivers to follow the model of "female humor" set before her while also challenging the idea that funny women had to be ugly or flawed.

After her first appearance on the *Tonight Show*, Rivers' confidence grew, her nervous mannerisms vanished, and she began to use self-deprecation more pointedly to challenge traditional expectations of women. On one appearance on the *Tonight Show* from 1980, she is interviewed by Johnny Carson. He asks her about the boa she is wearing and she makes several gags off of the question. When Carson asks if it is made of fox fur, she says, "well actually it's squirrel, [my husband] thinks it's fox but I never saw a fox with a nut in its hand." This retort allows her to stray away from a stereotypically feminine conversation about clothing and provides her with an opportunity to get laughs instead. In an interview with Bob Monkhouse in 1983, he asks her if being the top comedy star in America has robbed her of "the joys of being a homemaker." Rivers replies, "oh sure! I really missed *that*," and rolls her eyes and pretends to gag. She then makes a series of jokes about how she hates housework and is ill-equipped for it: "the recipe said separate two eggs I put one on the chair, one on the floor." Through these jokes, Rivers is able to embrace her femininity while also refusing the specific role society laid out for her. In this bit, she does not put down women who are homemakers. Rather, she calls attention to the fact that not every woman enjoys housework.

It might be easy to see Rivers as a vehement feminist, being the first woman to do this kind of standup. However, her public persona did not focus on empowering women to follow in her footsteps. Much of Rivers' career involved pleasing the men who controlled it. After bombing her first appearance on the *Tonight Show* with Jack Paar, she needed to make a comeback. When she came onto the Tonight Show again with Johnny Carson, she was everything Johnny Carson thought a woman should be. Men found her funny because she was willing to make fun of other women, just like a male comedian. In the *Tonight* appearance from 1980, when asked again about her boa, she says, "actually it's Elizabeth Taylor's belt," and when the audience reacts, she screams, "What?! What?! It's not my fault she's fat! I didn't shove the potatoes in her mouth."[26] This comment demonstrates Rivers' desire to set herself apart from other women in show business. By separating herself from other women and by adhering to men's expectations of her, Rivers was able to make a space for herself as a woman in comedy.

This duality of Joan Rivers would exemplify the debate between women doing comedy over their title as a "female comic" rather than a comic who happens to be a woman. On one hand, Joan Rivers was the first woman to do standup in this way, as herself rather than a character. On the other hand, Rivers did not pursue comedy to make a political argument, and later in her career, she took to bashing other women in entertainment as her jokes became more and more famous for being rude. In the years that would follow the height of Rivers' career, a debate amongst women in comedy would rise over whether or not women should be proud of being a "woman comic" or whether the term was derogatory in nature, separating women in comedy from men who were simply referred to as "comics." Joan Rivers remains an icon of women in American comedy despite the fact that she was willing to put other women down to advance her own success.

Elayne Boosler and The Question of "Female Comics"

During the 1980s, standup comedy in America experienced a period of rapid growth that became known as "the boom years." It was in this period that specific venues for comedy emerged based on the rise in popularity of comedy shows in other clubs. The increase in venues provided an increase in opportunities for aspiring comics–women included.[27] As the popularity of comedy clubs rose, some clubs decided to dedicate rooms solely to women standup comedians. One such room was The Belly Room, a room inside the notorious Comedy Store in West Hollywood.[28] Mitzi Shore owned and operated the club. She came into ownership of the club as a result of her divorce from Sammy Shore. Despite being a woman herself, Mitzi Shore had a tumultuous relationship with many women comics. When she opened the Belly Room, female standup comedians were divided in their opinions of the creation of a venue specifically for women.[29] Debate is still present in discussion over women in standup, as many performers prefer to be labeled simply as "comedians" rather than "female comedians."

On the debate over "women's rooms" in comedy clubs, Elayne Boosler firmly believed that having special clubs designated for women would ghettoize female performers. She refused to play at Mitzi Shore's Belly Room, saying, "I'm a woman who's a comic, not a woman comic."[30] She wanted to be considered equal to her male colleagues and felt that being labeled a "woman comic" put her at a disadvantage. Boosler was the first female comic to "make waves" since Joan Rivers. She started her career as a waitress at The Improvisation comedy club where she met comedian Andy Kaufman, who convinced her to pursue standup.[31] By 1985, Boosler was the first woman to have her own hour-long standup special on cable. She financed the show herself, as the cable networks did not believe people would watch a woman's special.[32] That special and its success, according to the biography on Boosler's website, "is widely credited for blowing open the gates of TV for female standup comedians."[33] This section aims to explore how Boosler challenged the model of female standup embodied by her predecessors in the field.

Boosler's comedic style was much different from that of her predecessors, though their influence was clear. She delivered her jokes as herself and based on her own experiences, much like Joan Rivers and many contemporary male standup comedians. Like Lily Tomlin, Boosler was not afraid to joke about politics: "I'm surprised we have to be here [at Comic Relief]," she quipped in 1989, "I thought the Republicans were supposed to fix *everything!*" [34] But more than that, she drew on inspiration from the men she saw telling jokes. Boosler was not doing "single girl" jokes and her humor was not self-deprecating. Instead, Boosler's jokes were observational: "I live in New York and I have six locks on my door, but I only lock three of them. I figure no matter how long someone sits there and picks the locks, they're always locking three." [35] This is not to say that Elayne did not make jokes about the difference between men and women. In her first appearance on *The David Letterman Show* in 1982, Boosler did a bit about her time as a waitress, saying, "I never liked when women would order through the man. I used to put both of the plates down in front of the man." [36] Nevertheless, her jokes were not about her being a woman; she just happened to be a woman in them.

The combination of embracing her femininity and also taking up challenging social topics in her jokes was what made Boosler stand out from the female comics before her. Robin Williams, notable actor and comedian, commented on Boosler's "veiled" delivery, saying, "it seemed kind of 'oh gosh, oh golly!'–but at the same time, her jokes were tough. As Letterman would say, she's funny like a guy." [37] This was a comment on the way that Boosler, unlike the women before her, could throw out a joke about IUDs or casual sex, something that would not have been possible for comedians just ten years before, and the audience would not think twice. A contemporary once described her as "the comic emblem of women's liberation." [38] Boosler's refusal to be a woman first and then a comic second embodied the spirit of the women's liberation movement, which advocated for women to not be defined or confined by their gender. While the work of women standup comedians before Boosler is notable, many of the women who would come into comedy during the Boom Years would cite her as an inspiration: "in order to have a lot of women after Elayne, you had to have Elayne." [39]

Boosler's appearance onstage was different than the women who came before her. Because she was not playing a character, she had no consistent costume like Diller and Tomlin, but she also, unlike Joan Rivers, never wore dresses onstage. According to an interview with comedian and writer Margaret Smith, "none of the women were wearing dresses on stage."[40] Boosler was no exception; she never performed in a dress but rather would choose a pantsuit or a jumper, sometimes jeans and a blouse. Her makeup was always done but never unnatural or particularly glamourous. She looked like a normal woman, not a sexualized Hollywood star. This helped Boosler's delivery: She was talking about being a normal woman, therefore, she should look like one.

Ultimately, Boosler challenged the model of female standup by telling jokes that were not about her being a woman but rather took up more topical social issues without using a character. Boosler's jokes were tough and pointed but hidden behind feminine charm and dazzling wit. She represented herself as she was: a regular New York woman. She told jokes about her life and the things she experienced, and she embraced her femininity in a way that created jokes that both men and women could appreciate. Boosler refused to be labeled as a "woman comic" because she was not a comedian for women. Elayne Boosler was a comedian for everyone.

Conclusion

The phenomenal success of these women's careers would pave the way for the female comics of the twenty-first century. When Joan Rivers performed while she was pregnant, she was given specific instructions not to mention her condition.[41] The word "pregnant" was not allowed on cable. Today, Ali Wong has two comedy specials where she is not only visibly pregnant, but almost half of her jokes are about her experiences being pregnant. Phyllis Diller and her surreal housewife persona made room for Lily Tomlin and her characters who served as inspiration for the women who would become famous doing characters on sketch comedy shows like *Saturday Night Live*. Joan Rivers' career showed women that they were allowed to be funny, and Elayne Boosler showed them that they did not have to only make jokes about being a woman or at the expense of other women. After Elayne Boosler and the comedy boom of the 1980s, many more women would find their way into comedy. The comedy boom was not just opportune for straight white women, but for minority women as well. Throughout the 1980s and 1990s, many gay female comedians would rise in popularity: Ellen DeGeneres,

Wanda Sykes, and Tig Notaro, to name a few. A number of women representing racial minorities such as Margaret Cho, Whoopi Goldberg, and Mo'Nique, also began to make names for themselves during the comedy boom. The success of twenty-first-century female comics and their impact on modern media is largely reliant on the careers of early female comedians.

While Elayne Boosler and Lily Tomlin used comedy to engage in direct political commentary, none of the women outlined in this chapter pursued comedy solely to push boundaries or to advance women's rights. They did it because it was their passion and they wanted to make a name for themselves, which they all accomplished in different ways. While other stories of women breaking into male-dominated spaces do so to lead the way for their gender, some of the great female comedians did so without regard for other women and the advancement of their sex. Phyllis Diller, Lily Tomlin, Joan Rivers, and Elayne Boosler were not "nasty women" in the sense that they were out for the advancement of women, rather, they were not interested in the criticism of others, which disrupted the social dynamic of their time and set an example for other women to follow suit.

Notes

1. *Ali Wong: Baby Cobra—The Pregnant Female Comedian | Netflix Is A Joke*, Youtube Video, accessed April 13, 2020, https://www.youtube.com/watch?v=XY9h-0x1Oao.

2. Wayne Warga, "Joan Rivers—Not Silent, but Deep," *Los Angeles Times: 1923–1995*, February 4, 1973.

3. Bambi Haggins, "Moms Mabley and Wanda Sykes: 'Ima Be Me,'" in *Hysterical! Women in American Comedy*, (Austin: University of Texas Press, 2017), 207–232.

4. Kristen Anderson Wagner, *Comic Venus: Women and Comedy in American Silent Film* (Wayne State University Press, 2018), 8, https://muse.jhu.edu/book/58634.

5. Wayne Federman and Andrew Steven, "The History of Standup," The History of Standup, accessed February 21, 2020, https://www.thehistoryofstandup.com.

6. Federman and Steven, "The History of Standup."

7. Cecil Smith, "Funny Men—and Lily Tomlin," *Los Angeles Times: 1923–1995*, January 27, 1975.

8. Yael Kohen, *We Killed: The Rise of Women in American Comedy* (Picador, 2013), 11.

9. "Fresh Air Remembers Comedian Phyllis Diller," NPR, accessed April 6, 2020, https://www.npr.org/2012/08/21/159557879/fresh-air-remembers-comedian-phyllis-diller.

10. NPR, "Fresh Air Remembers Comedian Phyllis Diller."

11. Kohen, *We Killed*, 159.

12. NPR, "Fresh Air Remembers Comedian Phyllis Diller."

13. Arthur Gelb, "Phyllis Diller: A Female Bob Hope," *New York Times*, 1961.

14. Stephen Holden, "Phyllis Diller's New Targets," *New York Times*, 1989.

15. Kohen, *We Killed*, 35.

16. "Rowan & Martin's Laugh-In–YouTube," 1968–1973, accessed April 8, 2020, https://www.youtube.com/channel/UCEK8vZlzR1tPg2WOlZ59r8w.

17. "Ernestine the Telephone Operator Calls General Motors," 1972, YouTube video, accessed April 8, 2020, https://www.youtube.com/watch?v=RT4__Nz5HWY.

18. Jerry M. Flint, "6.7 Million Cars Face G.m. Recall," *The New York Times*, December 5, 1971, https://www.nytimes.com/1971/12/05/archives/67-million-cars-face-gm-recall-but-company-denies-safety-defect-in.html.

19. "Suzie Sorority Dates Fred Fraternity" 1968–1973, YouTube video, *Rowan & Martin's Laugh-In*, accessed April 8, 2020, https://www.youtube.com/watch?v=Pr5FdNiDJX8.

20. "Ernestine the Telephone Operator Calls General Motors."

21. Kohen, *We Killed*, 11.

22. "Comedienne Joan Rivers Signed By NBC Television," *The Chicago Defender*: 1921–1967 (Chicago, Illinois), September 18, 1965.

23. Warga, "Joan Rivers–Not Silent, but Deep."

24. "Joan Rivers Early Comedy and Meets Vince Edwards Ben Casey," 1966, YouTube video, accessed February 14, 2020, https://www.youtube.com/watch?v=c-q3Uu32uFY.

25. "Joan Rivers Early Comedy and Meets Vince Edwards Ben Casey."

26. "Joan Rivers Carson Tonight Show 1980," 1980, YouTube video, accessed April 8, 2020, https://www.youtube.com/watch?v=U53v7v2-GKo.

27. Wayne Federman and Andrew Steven, "Ep. 04: The 1980's Comedy Boom," *The History of Standup*, accessed February 21, 2020, https://www.thehistoryofstandup.com.

28. Kohen, *We Killed*, 134.

29. Kohen, *We Killed*, 134–145.

30. Kohen, *We Killed*, 141.

31. Kohen, *We Killed*, 119.

32. "Bio," Elayne Boosler: Official Site of the Comedian, Writer, and Animal Activist, accessed April 8, 2020, https://www.elayneboosler.com/bio/.

33. Elayne Boosler, "Bio."

34. "Comic Relief 'Elayne Boosler' Stand Up Comedy," YouTube video, accessed April 8, 2020, https://www.youtube.com/watch?v=DjDC6Yj2OrQ.

35. "Comic Relief 'Elayne Boosler' Stand Up Comedy."

36. "Comic Relief 'Elayne Boosler' Stand Up Comedy."

37. Kohen, *We Killed*, 121.

38. Kohen, *We Killed*, 147.

39. Kohen, *We Killed*, 120.

40. Kohen, *We Killed*, 181.

41.   Warga, "Joan Rivers–Not Silent, but Deep."

10. A Different Kind of Feminine: How Marilyn Monroe Challenged Expectations of Womanhood

ALICIA AUCOIN

One of the most iconic sex symbols of all time, actress Marilyn Monroe may seem out of place next to the wholesome housewives of the 1950s. Through her paradoxical persona, Monroe challenged gender norms by simultaneously being a working woman and a sex icon. Monroe did not adhere to the expectation of women to be conservatively dressed housewives and mothers. At the same time, many have critiqued Monroe as a caricature of femininity: weak, gentle, and, in her case, submissive to the male-dominated film industry's demands that she take on the image of a dumb-blonde bombshell. Not many people would perceive Monroe as a feminist.

Monroe's story and the complex nature of her sexual persona have captivated scholars and fans alike. As one example, Barbara Leaming's book *Marilyn Monroe* is an in-depth biography of the actress that provides a unique perspective of Monroe as an icon of American sexuality.[1] The American feminist Gloria Steinem also has a prominent voice in Monroe's historical narrative. One of the most outspoken scholars on Marilyn Monroe, Steinem has written various articles on Monroe. Her book *Marilyn* portrays Monroe as a shy woman with a child-like innocence who needed to be saved from the patriarchal world of show business.[2] Steinem's traditional feminist narrative offers another unique interpretation of the actress's life and career.

In more recent years, writers have analyzed Monroe from a more contemporary feminist perspective. Michelle Morgan's *The Girl* looks at how Monroe took control of her life following the making of the film *The Seven Year Itch*, her divorce from baseball legend Joe DiMaggio, and her subsequent marriage to author and playwright Arthur Miller.[3] Amanda Konkle's *Some Kind of Mirror* analyzes Monroe's film performances and how they related to the stereotype of women in the 1950s.[4] These books, along with a number of additional historical studies, provide the backdrop for my research. Each source has a unique perspective on the life of Marilyn Monroe and has helped shape the narrative this chapter seeks to tell.

In this piece, I aim to show how Monroe's paradoxical career made her a feminist in her own right by confronting society's idea of womanhood and female sexuality, as well as challenging the expectations of the film industry. Moreover, I assert that Monroe must be classified as a feminist because of the way she took pride in her image. I do not claim that Monroe would have identified as a feminist herself if she was alive to see the rise of second-wave feminism in the 1970s, but rather that she exemplified characteristics that every strong woman should strive to reach. Ultimately, this chapter will analyze aspects of Monroe's life and career using a twenty-first century feminist lens to show how Monroe was not just a dumb blonde who needed help, but instead, a capable woman whose seemingly "natural" sexuality was her biggest strength and something she should be regarded for rather than pitied.

Pushing the Envelope of Femininity

Marilyn Monroe challenged the expectations of women in the 1950s. During this decade, women were expected to play the role of the socially conservative housewife who found fulfillment in housekeeping and child-rearing. Monroe was the opposite of this: a three-time divorced, working woman who was far from conservative in her image. In her biographical study, *Some Kind of Mirror: Creating Marilyn Monroe*, author Amanda Konkle argues, "Monroe's roles engaged with the issues surrounding being a single woman in postwar culture, because she was simultaneously a sexpot and a star, she subverted some of the repressive ideology around postwar gender roles, marriage, and female sexuality."[5] Although Konkle makes a valid point, it could also be argued that Monroe challenged these expectations, not just because of her occupation and image, but also because of the way she fought to survive as a single woman with no children in a world dominated by the ideal of the patriarchal household and nuclear family.

The end of World War II and the start of the Cold War brought both economic growth and a new cultural norm to the United States. Economically, the country was booming. An increase in jobs paying good wages meant people could afford to marry earlier. According to David Farber in his book *The Age of Great Dreams*, "the average woman married when she was twenty years old, and 70 percent of all women were married by the age of twenty-four."[6] Women married younger, started their families earlier, and had more children. According to historian Susan Ware, by 1957 the average woman was "having close to four children."[7] This economic boom allowed for bigger families, amplifying the need for women to stay at home and raise their children rather than work in a factory to financially support their families. The role of the household breadwinner would typically fall to the male. Economic forces thus played an important role in the creation of these social norms.

Cold War politics also contributed to the expectation of domesticity for women. Following World War II, many of the women who took up jobs in munitions plants and other factories quickly gave them up to returning veterans. As historian Elaine Tyler May makes clear, the existential threat of the Cold War—the combined fears of communism and nuclear disaster—created a framework where society expected women to fulfill their civic duties through domestic work instead of factory labor. According to May, "experts called upon women to embrace domesticity in service to the nation in the same spirit that they had come to the country's aid by taking wartime jobs."[8] Staying home to raise children was quickly cast as a woman's patriotic duty, thus integrally linking the nuclear family to a patriarchal household.

One of the many ways that Monroe challenged this dominant social and cultural expectation was through her identity as a working woman rather than a housewife. Monroe knew that she was never destined to be a housewife or a "kept" woman. In an interview with LIFE magazine in August 1962, when talking about her desire to be an actress, Monroe said, "it was the creative part that kept me going—trying to be an actress ... And I guess I've always had too much fantasy to be a housewife ... I was never kept, to be blunt about it. I always kept myself. I have always had a pride in the fact that I was on my own."[9] For Monroe, to be "kept" meant to be financially supported by a man because of a sexual relationship. Monroe never wanted to be a housewife and she took pride in her financial independence. Ultimately, Monroe challenged the expectation of women to be financially dependent housewives. She showed women that they could be something other than house warmers, husband-kissers, and child-bearers.

In the 1950s people expected that a woman marry only once; however, this was not the case for Monroe. Over the course of her life, Monroe married and divorced three times: the first time to her neighbor's son, James Dougherty, when she was only sixteen; the second time to professional baseball player Joe DiMaggio; and the third time to award-winning playwright Arthur Miller. In an economy dominated by the ideal of the male breadwinner, divorce was an uncommon occurrence. Living in single-income households, many women simply did not have the financial ability to divorce their husbands and go off on their own. But unlike many women of her time, Monroe did not marry for the sake of financial support. She was already doing that herself. Removing the barrier of financial support likely played a role in Marilyn's multiple marriages.

It is speculated that Monroe married not only in search of personal fulfillment, but also to fill a void. Some have interpreted Monroe's multiple marriages as reflecting her deep desire for a male role model in her life. In a 1955 article for the *Washington Post*, "The Mystery of Marilyn Monroe," Zolotow, who had interviewed Monroe on various occasions, wrote that "out of an unconscious yearning for her father she would come to make men the center of her thinking. I believe that what she projects from the screen is this yearning which still remains unsatisfied."[10] Zolotow argued that the sense of yearning Monroe portrayed in her films stemmed from a fatherless childhood. Monroe was raised in foster care, bouncing from home to home with no male role model in her life, which suggests Zolotow's theory rings true. Many believed that Monroe lived her life searching for acceptance from a male figure that she likely did not have growing up.

It is also argued that Monroe used marriage as a source of agency. In an interview, Gloria Steinem critiqued Monroe's multiple marriages, arguing that she "was trying to get her identity through a man, which we were then taught to do, to marry whoever it is we wanted to become; in her case, Joe DiMaggio, an American hero ... Arthur Miller, a serious person, and so on."[11] Monroe wanted to be loved by the public, which meant that she had to be someone the public loved. This seemed to be a focal point in her marriage to Joe DiMaggio. Monroe also fought throughout her entire career to be taken seriously. She often complained about not being cast in a serious role.

Monroe likely thought that she would be taken seriously after marrying a person like Arthur Miller, who had a successful career in show business as a playwright. Being taken seriously was important to Monroe; she wanted to be accepted as more than just a dumb blonde. Overall, in analyzing her last two marriages, it's possible to conclude that Monroe married to expand her reputation.

Monroe's last two high-profile marriages might have created an image for the actress as a serious, hard-working, yet fun-loving American hero. However, it was her image as a "sex goddess" that brought her fame. Monroe challenged society's expectations by portraying femininity as sexual rather than maternal. As mentioned earlier, women of the time were expected to be housewives: symbols of maternalism and femininity. Monroe challenged this idea by showing that femininity could be sexual too. Unlike the typical television series of the time, which portrayed women in maternal and non-sexual roles,[12] the film industry portrayed female stars as sexual beings. Through her roles as a dumb-blonde "sexpot," which will be further discussed later in the chapter, Monroe transformed the status quo for female leads within the film industry. Monroe's image of sexual femininity was largely developed in her career as an actress, but what made her so successful was how she portrayed this image off camera as well.

Monroe embraced her persona as a sex icon, not just on film as characters but in her own life as well. In 1962, for example, Monroe was given the opportunity to sing "Happy Birthday" to President John F. Kennedy. Monroe viewed this opportunity as not just a gig, but a performance. According to Barbara Leaming's biography of the actress, Monroe "sat on the living room floor endlessly tape recording and listening to herself ... Her interpretation grew sexier ... Marilyn insisted it had to be sexy."[13] On the night of her performance,[14] she wore a nude tight-fitting dress studded in rhinestones. With the way the light hit her, she looked like she was naked except for the dazzling rhinestones that adorned her body.[15] According to Broadway columnist Dorothy Killagen, it looked like Monroe was "making love to the president in the direct view of forty million Americans."[16] Through her performances, style, and mannerisms, Monroe fully committed to portraying the role of a sex icon.

Ultimately, Monroe challenged society's expectations of women through her career, her multiple marriages, and her sex appeal. Monroe was a single, self-supporting woman who did not fit the maternal housewife stereotype of femininity; instead, she expressed her femininity through her sexual persona. Monroe embodied the image of a sex icon both on and off the stage, demonstrating that femininity could be both maternal and sexual.

The Film Industry

Marilyn Monroe's public image as a sex icon remains a compelling topic of discussion. An article published in the *Guardian* in 2001, celebrating what would have been Monroe's 75th birthday, discusses how Monroe became an icon among many feminists. Some have argued that Monroe would have identified as a feminist if she lived to see the movement, while others question her significance in the movement at all. For example, the article quotes Nancy Friday, author of *My Mother, Myself* and *The Power of Beauty*, as saying, "I do not understand why the women's movement sees her as significant. She was a woman exploited for her beauty; few admired her acting or cared about her personal feelings. Her role was a sex object. Looking at her life story you can see she is a powerful reminder of why feminism was necessary."[17] Friday degraded Monroe's contribution to the film industry as an actress and disregarded her humanity, labeling Monroe as nothing more than a sex object. Monroe has often been regarded as a reason for feminism, rather than a role model for women.

Although Monroe accomplished a wildly successful career in film, many still remember Monroe as a woman who submitted to the chauvinistic demands of a male-dominated industry. Her first contract with 20th Century Fox studios has often been labeled as controlling and exploitative. The studio regularly cast her as the role of a dumb blonde and paid her a meager salary for all of her hard work, which often received little recognition.[18] In addition, the contract only allowed Monroe to star in Fox's films, thus giving the studio the power to monopolize on her popularity. Although the actress has often been labeled as a woman whose looks and sex appeal were exploited through her contract, Monroe never fully submitted to the industry's demands.

Monroe's first contract with 20th Century Fox did not keep the actress from challenging expectations. She used her sex appeal to attain movie roles and make a name for herself as an actress. Her label became so desired and well-known that the film industry began to revolve around her. When talking about the actress's contribution to the film industry, Amanda Konkle stated, "many of her roles were created specifically for her, and when she failed to report to work, productions shut down. Monroe significantly contributed to the financial success of both Hollywood and the publicity industry in the 1950s."[19] Monroe was the center of attention in Hollywood and much of the film industry's financial success should be credited to her. Monroe challenged the film industry through legal battles, demanding better pay and more artistic freedom. Monroe was not a woman of exploitation. She was a woman with agency.

First, the film industry heavily controlled Monroe's image; however, Monroe used her sexual persona to her own advantage to advance her career and gain popularity among the public. Under her first contract with 20th Century Fox, Monroe was only cast in roles where she was expected to portray a blonde sex icon. Throughout cinematic history, female blondes have been fetishized in American culture as the ultimate sex goddesses.[20] The film industry capitalized on this image, which is why Monroe, along with many other blonde actresses, were able to make a career for themselves. In 1953 Monroe portrayed the air-headed, blonde showgirl engaged to a wealthy man in the film *Gentlemen Prefer Blondes*.[21] Later that year in the film *How to Marry A Millionaire*, Marilyn portrays a dumb-blonde gold digger trying to marry a millionaire.[22] In one of her most iconic roles in the film *The Seven Year Itch*, Monroe portrays a gorgeous, blonde model and neighbor who the main character desires to have an affair with.[23] Monroe was often type-cast into these roles because of her sex appeal. Many have criticized the film industry for exploiting Monroe's looks and sex appeal for their own wealth. Others have also critiqued Monroe for giving in to the demands of the film industry by fulfilling the sexual desires of men, but that was not the case. Monroe's sex appeal was her main tool in dominating the film industry.

Monroe was not exploited for her looks; instead, she used her beauty and sex appeal for her own gain. In her book *The Sex Goddess in American Film*, Jessica Hope Jordan talks about what she calls the "dumb-blonde theory." Jordan describes this theory is the idea "that there is something fundamentally self-contradictory about beautiful, sexy blondes who are also intellectuals, who additionally possess brains enough to capitalize on their looks and sexuality."[24] This theory states that the stereotype of a blonde being anything except for dumb and pretty is self-contradictory. Monroe was a woman who knew how to capitalize on her looks. Although she was forced to portray the role of a dumb-blonde sex icon, she was able to use her image to create a career for herself. Monroe, in other words, was more than just a dumb blonde.

Second, even though Monroe's first contract with 20th Century Fox paid her very little, she took full advantage of her roles in order to establish herself as a powerhouse within the industry. Since Monroe was contractually obligated to work exclusively with 20th Century Fox, she was forced to take whatever jobs they gave her, for whatever price they paid her. Therefore, Monroe was often unfairly compensated for her work. For example, when Monroe filmed *Gentlemen Prefer Blondes*, her co-star Jane Russell was paid $200,000 for the film, while Monroe only made $500 a week.[25] However, in an interview, Monroe explained that she was less upset about her meager pay than she was about not receiving her own trailer. To Monroe, it was not about the money; rather, it was about the experience. Monroe's career was driven by her desire to develop her artistic style as an actress. In 1954, 20th Century Fox offered Monroe a contract with better pay after she turned down roles in the films *How to Be Very Very Popular* and *The Girl in the Red Velvet Swing*. Monroe resisted to take on new roles because she had not been offered a new contract since she was first signed in 1950. To Monroe, "it was not about the money, it was the principle."[26] According to a newspaper article titled "The Mystery of Marilyn Monroe," Monroe stated that she wanted "the right to say whether she liked a story or didn't like it. She wanted to play in serious pictures."[27] Monroe did not mind that she received a small salary for her work because she was more interested in developing her career.

Monroe fought back against the film industry in other ways as well. She refused to star in films, subjecting herself to multiple legal battles with 20th Century Fox. At the end of 1954, after undergoing major surgery and divorcing her second husband, Joe DiMaggio, Monroe set off for the East Coast. Monroe lived with her friend Milton Greene and his wife in Connecticut for a time, penniless after being suspended by the studio, but eventually made her way to New York.[28] Throughout Monroe's entire career, 1955 was one of her most pivotal years. She developed her skills as an actress by attending New York's Actors Studio and she became president of her own film company, Marilyn Monroe Productions, Inc.[29] Gloria Steinem wrote that Monroe created the company only out of fear that she "was being exploited by Hollywood."[30] Despite this claim, Monroe displayed great courage in creating her own production company and standing up against the "big guys" of the film industry to protect herself and her career.

Finally, Monroe fought her legal battle with 20th Century Fox and won. On December 31, 1955, the actress finally signed an improved contract with the film studio.[31] Under this contract, not only would Monroe receive one hundred thousand dollars per film, but she was also only required to film four pictures over the next seven years. Although she was not allowed to approve scripts, which meant she still was still often portrayed as a dumb blonde in her roles, she could finally star in films for other studios.[32] This allowed her the freedom to explore and develop her artistic style in other roles. An industry veteran was even quoted stating that Monroe's new contract was "one of the greatest single triumphs ever won by an actress against a powerfully entrenched studio … Marilyn Monroe may turn out to be not only the sexiest but the smartest blond of our time."[33] Monroe made history through her new contract with 20th Century Fox. She fought for what she deserved and defied the expectations of a woman's role in the film industry.

Ultimately, Monroe's initial contract with 20th Century Fox studios limited her artistically, but she was by no means exploited. Even though she was only cast as a dumb blonde and her salary was small, acting meant more to the actress than just an image and some money. It was her dream. Monroe strategically used her roles as a dumb blonde to become famous. She settled with the small salary because she was doing what she had always dreamed. Once the actress made a name for herself, she took a stand and fought for more artistic freedom in her acting through more serious roles. She also eventually battled her way to a higher salary. Monroe was not a victim of the film industry; she was a victor.

The Secret to Her Sex Appeal

The film industry may have established Monroe's image as a sex symbol, but it was Monroe herself who made that image into something memorable. By the end of her career, Monroe had become one of the most famous sex symbols in the world. Although some might argue that she was forced into her role as a sex icon, Monroe would have never become so famous if she did not take pride in her image. One of Monroe's most powerful qualities was the way she owned her femininity and sexuality.

In the 1950s, femininity and female sexuality were understood to be two very different concepts. In society's eyes, female sexuality was viewed as dangerous and destructive, while femininity represented maternal and domestic duties and desires. A woman's sexuality was regarded as a weapon that could cause destruction. Women known for their sex appeal were even referred to as "bombshells" due to the weapon's destructive capabilities. In the period's film noir genre, female sexuality was portrayed as a "destructive power," although it was not as dangerous if "contained and domesticated."[34] Society demanded the "containment" of female sexuality, almost as if its spread was as dangerous as that of communism. Monroe used her sexuality not as a weapon, but as a tool.

Monroe challenged the idea of femininity and sexuality as opposing concepts. As mentioned earlier, Monroe transformed society's understanding of maternal femininity, showing that femininity and sexuality were not separate from one another, but rather that they worked hand-in-hand. The soft and innocent feminine qualities that the actress evoked in her sex appeal ultimately created this label of sexual femininity. In her sexuality, the actress evoked a sense of innocence that was feminine in nature. They were not opposites of each other, but two sides of the same coin. It was this innocent portrayal of femininity and sexuality that made her famous.

Monroe's audience was attracted to the innocence the actress portrayed in her various roles. In her biography of the star, writer Barbara Leaming argues that Monroe offered a different view of sex to what she characterizes as the puritanical culture of post-WWII America. Leaming writes, "as a symbol, she promises us that sex can be innocent, without danger ... that is why Marilyn remains, even now, the symbol of our secret desires."[35] The actress portrayed sex in a way that made it seem innocent and safe, the opposite of society's understanding of the "dangerous" and "destructive" female sexuality. Scholars like Jessica Hope Jordan alternately describe Monroe's acting and sexual appeal as one of "true helplessness and desperation."[36] These words evoke a feeling of child-like innocence, as if the actress did not understand the extent of her exposure. However, Monroe's portrayal of innocence in her work does not mean that she was weak or "helpless." Arguably, this innocence does not stem from helplessness and desperation, but rather confidence in one's natural beauty. The actress's raw beauty and confidence are what drew so many to her.

An article published in a 1952 edition of LIFE Magazine touches on the idea that Monroe's sex appeal stemmed from her natural beauty. The article states, "Marilyn is naïve and guileless. But she is smart enough to have known how to make a success in the cutthroat world of glamour. She does it by being as wholly natural as the world will allow."[37] This article mentions Monroe's sense of naïveté, a quality often associated with children, but also states that Monroe knew how to use her sex appeal to her advantage. Monroe's secret was to just be herself.

Monroe was a believer in natural beauty. In her 1962 interview with LIFE magazine, she not only owned her role as a sex icon, but also spoke about her own understanding of beauty and femininity. In the interview she stated:

> I don't mind being burdened with being glamorous and sexual ... I feel that beauty and femininity are ageless and cannot be contrived, and glamour—although the manufacturers won't like this—cannot be manufactured ... I think that sexuality is only attractive when it's natural and spontaneous ... We are all born sexual creatures, thank God; but it's a pity so many people despise and crush this natural gift. Art, real art, comes from it—everything.[38]

Monroe viewed sexuality as something that went hand-in-hand with natural beauty and femininity. She saw it as a natural gift and the root of all art. Monroe's confidence and warmth in her tone of voice when talking about this subject showed that her sex appeal did not stem from a sense of helplessness and desperation, but from a belief in her own natural beauty and femininity.

This sense of confidence in her own sexuality can be seen in many of her photographs. Gloria Steinem uses photographs taken by George Barris in her book *Marilyn*. Many of these pictures showcase Monroe's natural, raw beauty.[39] In the photo on the second page of the book, the sun is setting and Monroe is kneeling on the beach. The actress is almost completely nude with only a green towel wrapped around her waist. With her hair blowing in the wind, Monroe gives off a sensual, relaxed smile. Her poses look natural and relaxed. Only a person who was confident in their own skin could pose nude on a beach and take a photograph like this so effortlessly. Monroe's sexuality was not hyper-feminine, overly seductive, or forced. The raw beauty and confidence that Monroe radiated are what she should really be known for. That was the real beauty of Marilyn Monroe.

Monroe's confidence glows most elegantly in the photographs from her last photo shoot. Shortly after Monroe's death, *Eros* magazine dedicated a spread to her. Using images from her last photo shoot meant to be published in *Vogue*, *Eros* put together a beautiful tribute. At the beginning of the portfolio was a quote from Monroe herself stating, "I never quite understood it, this sex symbol. But if I'm going to be a symbol for something, I'd rather have it sex than some of the other things they've got symbols for."[40] Although this quote somewhat shows the innocence in Monroe's sexuality, it also shows just how natural it was for her, as well as the way that she owned her image as a sex symbol.

The tribute goes on to talk about Monroe and the way that she effortlessly posed for the pictures, but the true magic was in her nude photographs. As the article chronicles:

> One night, Marilyn seemed to tire of posing in all the chic clothes from New York. She grabbed a flimsy bed jacket and whisked it away to the bedroom. When she emerged, she was a different woman. While she laughed and relaxed and had a marvelous time, Stern went on to take the pictures that appear in this issue.[41]

The innocence that Monroe brought to her sexuality is what made her so captivating. People were drawn to her because of the way that she so easily and confidently portrayed her sexuality and her femininity.

Marilyn Monroe's unique sexuality is what made her a sex symbol. She challenged the idea that sexuality and femininity were separate identities. What made her unique was her ability to so effortlessly portray a sense of innocence in her work. This innocence did not stem from a place of helplessness or desperation, but rather stemmed from her inner sense of beauty and femininity. As Leaming argues, Monroe made sex seem innocent and safe to a society that viewed it as a sin. Monroe's philosophy of inner beauty and the way that she embraced her sexuality set an example for how all women should view themselves. Monroe is an inspiration for women to view sexuality and femininity differently. This is what makes her a feminist.

Conclusion

Marilyn Monroe was an actress, a sex symbol, and an American icon. Monroe lived a paradoxical life in the way she challenged societal expectations of the 1950s. The actress was a three-time divorced, working woman who made a living for herself through personifying her sex appeal both on and off camera. She lived a life in stark contrast to the dominant expectations of women to be financially dependent housewives and mothers. Monroe did not challenge these expectations with intent to send a message, but instead out of necessity to survive in the harsh realities of post-war America. Her admirability is not only in the fact that she challenged these societal expectations, but also that she fought to make something of herself in an era that was not structured for women to succeed outside of the boundaries of a patriarchal, nuclear family.

Many feminists have labeled Monroe a sex symbol who was exploited by the chauvinistic demands of the male-dominated film industry. Although Monroe tolerated these demands at first, she only did so in order to fulfill her dream of becoming an actress. After rising to stardom, the actress challenged the film industry's sexist demands and standards, eventually winning a revised contract with 20th Century Fox. She portrayed the stereotype of a dumb blonde in her roles, but at the same time, she broke this stereotype in her own life by using show business to create a profitable career. Her business and acting skills led her to create her own production company where she could freely develop her artistic direction as an actress. Overall, Monroe's work helped to pave a way for future women in cinema.

One of the most complex aspects of Monroe was the way she embraced her femininity and sexuality. Monroe challenged society's idea of womanhood by representing a sexual femininity that went against society's understanding of femininity as maternal. Her innocent, confident, and natural portrayal of sexuality challenged the idea that femininity and sexuality must be separate. She owned her image as sex icon in a way that was respectable and she exemplified what natural beauty and sexual femininity could look like. Ultimately, this was Monroe's greatest strength.

In the standard historical narrative of Monroe's life, many scholars portray her as a woman who needed saving from her own past and the hardships of show business. However, what they fail to see is her inner feminist. Monroe possessed the strength to challenge societal expectations, the intellect to challenge the film industry, and the confidence to embrace her sexuality. These are all tools that people should learn from and use in their own lives. Monroe is not a Hollywood sob story or a victim of society; therefore, we should stop regarding as her such. Although her life ended sooner than many expected, she lived long enough to make her mark on the world. Marilyn Monroe was unique. She was innocent and she was sexy. She was a different kind of feminine.

Notes

1. Barbara Leaming, *Marilyn Monroe* (New York: Crown, 1998), 431.
2. Gloria Steinem and George Barris, *Marilyn* (New York: Henry Holt Company, 1986).
3. Michelle Morgan, *The Girl: Marilyn Monroe, The Seven Year Itch, and the Birth of an Unlikely Feminist* (Philadelphia: Running Press, 2018).
4. Amanda Konkle, *Some Kind of Mirror: Creating Marilyn Monroe* (New Brunswick, Camden, and Newark, New Jersey: Rutgers University Press, 2019).
5. Konkle, *Some Kind of Mirror*, 20.
6. David Farber, *The Age of Great Dreams: America in the 1960s* (New York: Farrar, Straus, and Giroux, 1994), 11-12.
7. Susan Ware, *American Women's History: A Very Short Introduction* (New York: Oxford University Press, 2015), 100.
8. Elaine Tyler May, "Explosive Issues: Sex, Women, and the Bomb," in *Homeward Bound: American Families in the Cold War Era* (New York: Basic Books, 2008), 159.
9. "Fame May Go by And-so Long, I've Had You," *Life Magazine*, 1962.
10. Maurice Zolotow, "The Mystery of Marilyn Monroe," *The Washington Post and Times Herald*, September 25, 1955.
11. Women's Media Center, "Gloria Steinem on Marilyn Monroe," YouTube video, 27:04, March 5, https://www.youtube.com/watch?v=xp3_wc8_Tmk.
12. Ware, *American Women's History*, 99-100.
13. Leaming, *Marilyn Monroe*, 408.
14. David Thomson, "Happy Birthday, Mr. President: The Story of Marilyn Monroe and That Dress," *The Guardian*, November 3, 2016, https://www.theguardian.com/film/2016/nov/03/happy-birthday-mr-president-the-story-of-marilyn-monroe-and-that-dress.
15. Missmalevolent, "Marilyn Monroe-Happy Birthday Mr. President," YouTube video, 3:51, November 26, 2007, https://www.youtube.com/watch?v=EqolSvoWNck

16. Leaming, *Marilyn Monroe*, 409.

17. Sharon Krum, "Happy Birthday Marilyn," *The Guardian*, May 29, 2001, https://www.theguardian.com/film/features/featurepages/0,,498050,00.html.

18. "Fame May Go by And-so Long, I've Had You," *Life Magazine*, 1962, 34.

19. Konkle, *Some Kind of Mirror*, 13.

20. Jessica Hope Jordan, *The Sex Goddess in American Film, 1930-1965: Jean Harlow, Mae West, Lana Turner, and Jayne Mansfield* (Amherst, New York: Cambria Press, 2009), 3-9.

21. Howard Hawks, dir., *Gentlemen Prefer Blondes* (California: 20th Century Fox, 1953), Amazon Prime video.

22. Jean Negulesco, *How to Marry A Millionaire* (California: 20th Century Fox, 1953), Amazon Prime Video.

23. Bill Wilder, *The Seven Year Itch* (California: 20th Century Fox, 1955), Amazon Prime video.

24. Jordan, *The Sex Goddess in American Film, 1930-1965*, 37.

25. "Fame May Go by And-so Long, I've Had You." *Life Magazine*, 34.

26. Zolotow, "The Mystery of Marilyn Monroe."

27. Ibid.

28. Maurice Zolotow, "Who Runs Marilyn Monroe?," *Washington Post* and *Times Herald*, December 16, 1956.

29. Morgan, *The Girl*, 10.

30. Steinem and Barris, *Marilyn*, 63.

31. Konkle, *Some Kind of Mirror*, 148.

32. Konkle, *Some Kind of Mirror*, 148. Also see Leaming, *Marilyn Monroe*, 192.

33. Dorothy Manning, "The Woman and the Legend," *Photoplay*, October 1956, 96.

34. Elaine Tyler May, "Explosive Issues: Sex, Women, and the Bomb," in *Homeward Bound: American Families in the Cold War Era* (New York: Basic Books, 2008), 165.

35. Leaming, *Marilyn Monroe*, 431.

36. Jordan, *The Sex Goddess in American Film, 1930-1965*, 157.

37. "Hollywood Topic A-Plus," *Life Magazine*, April 1952, 104.

38. "Fame May Go by And-so Long, I've Had You." *Life Magazine*, 36.

39. Steinem and Barris, *Marilyn*, ii.

40. "Eros," *Eros Magazine Vol. 3*, 1962, 2.

41. "Eros," *Eros Magazine Vol. 3*, 1962, 5.

11. Mary Tyler Moore: The Unlikely Feminist

GRACE BARTH

If there is one word to describe women's roles on television in the 1960s and 1970s, it would be "housewife." Housewives were the feature role for women in television, like Florence Henderson in *The Brady Bunch*, Mary Tyler Moore in *The Dick Van Dyke Show*, and Jean Stapleton from *All in the Family*. Over the course of many decades, acting roles for women on television have come to include almost every occupation, such as Claire Danes, a CIA agent in *Homeland*; Rachel Brosnahan, a sharp-witted female comedian in *The Marvelous Mrs. Maisel*; and Elisabeth Moss, a secretary who works her way to become the creative director of a major advertising agency in *Mad Men*. How did television evolve to break down stereotypical roles for women? Who or what was the catalyst for this change? Enter Mary Tyler Moore, the lead in *The Mary Tyler Moore Show*.

The Mary Tyler Moore Show focused on Mary Richards, the main character played by Moore, a modern woman who just dumped her long-term boyfriend after realizing he would never marry. Mary Richards then made the bold decision to move to the big city of Minneapolis, Minnesota. At first, Mary Richards landed a job as a secretary at WJM-TV, a fictional television station. After speaking with her boss Lou Grant, however, she was instead hired as an associate producer and later in the show's plot, became WJM-TV's news producer. *The Mary Tyler Moore Show* broadcasted a different message than any other typical American sitcom that aired in the 1970s. Rather than relying on traditional themes in American sitcoms that revolved around the happy-go-lucky suburban family, independence and freedom of mind are strong themes within the show.

Scholarship in recent years has largely related Moore's character to the feminist movement of the 1970s. Scholar Allyson Jule described Moore's character as presenting a new attitude in the 1970s: that a woman could be single and still be a whole person.[1] As Allyson Jule argued, Mary Richards is a combination of girl-next-door sweetness and "old-fashioned" honesty and integrity, but on the other hand, is a spunky new woman of the 1970s.[2] Professor Marc Shapiro argued that the trajectory of Moore's career paralleled the trajectory of changes in women's roles and rights over the course of the 1960s and 1970s. Moore starts off as a housewife on *The Dick Van Dyke Show*, playing along with Hollywood's traditional stereotypical roles for actresses, and eventually becoming an independent associate producer for a television news station on *The Mary Tyler Moore Show*.[3] My research on Moore's trailblazing show contributes to existing scholarship on how the actress embraced feminist ideals for her character on television and in her own life.

In this chapter, I will examine elements of *The Mary Tyler Moore Show* that make it a feminist teaching tool, looking at scholarly work and combing through memorable episodes and elements from the show itself. *The Mary Tyler Moore Show* is truly groundbreaking in demolishing traditional roles for actresses at the time and in representing women as more than just housewives. However, there are some elements of the show that are rooted in traditionally gendered, homey aspects of television in the 1970s. Nonetheless, it is important to illustrate the show's successes as well as its limitations. In this chapter, I argue that *The Mary Tyler Moore Show* supported not only the concept of the newly liberated "working woman" but feminist ideals and beliefs such as equal pay, independence, and reproductive rights.

The Fight for Equal Pay

Second-wave feminism, in many ways, represented the discontent of white middle-class women who were fed up with being treated as second-class citizens. Their voices first emerged in 1963 when writer Betty Friedan published *The Feminine Mystique, a* widely popular book on feminist culture. Friedan accurately pinpointed what was "wrong" with so many middle-class American women: domesticity. After publication, *The Feminine Mystique* helped fuel growing dissatisfaction among American women, which spurred the second-wave feminist movement of the 1960s and 1970s.[4] In fact, in 1966, a group of women led by Friedan formed the National Organization for Women (NOW) which styled itself as a civil rights organization for women.[5] The mission of the NOW was to "take action to bring women into full participation in the mainstream of American society, assuming all the privileges and responsibilities thereof in truly equal partnership with men."[6] Soon it was the largest feminist organization in the country.[7]

Between January and March of 1970, substantial stories on the women's liberation movement appeared in virtually every major journal and broadcast network.[8] With greater access to the media, second-wave feminism received tremendous coverage on events such as the Women's Strike for Equality, the congressional passage of the Equal Rights Amendment in 1972, the congressional passage of Title IX of the Education Act of 1972, and the 1973 Supreme Court case *Roe v. Wade*.[9] Women's rights were once again on the national agenda. A mammoth media event that perfectly sums up feminism in the 1970s was "The Battle of the Sexes." "Battle of the Sexes" was a tennis match between the legendary Bobby Riggs, a 1939 Wimbledon winner and a known defender of manhood, against tennis sensation Billie Jean King on September 20, 1973.[10] Riggs hustled the media with taunts against King's campaign for more opportunities and more money for professional women's tennis players.[11] Although the odds were in Riggs's favor, King won three sets with ease, scoring 6–4, 6–3, and 6–3. "The Battle of the Sexes" sparked many debates, along with female pride in households and workplaces across the country.[12]

As the second wave of feminism rolled through the United States in the 1970s, the power of television helped bring feminist ideals to light and converted the public to the cause. The media, however, did not hold positive thoughts about women involved in the movement. According to Andi Zeilser, news organizations reporting on women's liberation described feminists with terminology that alternated between condescending ("libbers") and fear-mongering (women described as "militants"; the movement itself called a "contagion"). They spent the same amount of time reporting on the dress and hairstyles of feminist women as they did on actual actions and concerns.[13]

By the early part of the 1970s, television critics and academics pointed out that television did not give women their proper due.[14] Zeilser noted that the normally apolitical *TV Guide* repeatedly wagged its finger at the industry for refusing to rise above the characterization of women as pretty, skinny, dopey, hapless housewives, both on network shows and in the commercials that supported them.[15] *The Mary Tyler Moore Show* was thus a breath of fresh air. For seven years, the central figure of *The Mary Tyler Moore Show* served as a wholly original and pathbreaking sitcom, the first in history to introduce a female character whose primary relationship was neither with her family nor her male love interest, but instead her friends and co-workers.[16]

Moore's role radiated new and daring characteristics that embodied the idea of the "new" woman of the 1970s. Moore's character combined a girl-next-door demeanor with a certain "spunk" that characterized the real feminists involved in the movement. As described by Zeilser, she is the "strawberry shortcake of TV feminism" that was palatable to viewers.[17] "A Darkened Star," an article written in the *National Review*, illustrated how Mary Richards shared the preoccupations of many educated career girls during the 1970s: the need to be successful and well-liked and the reluctance to be either fawning or dominating.[18] Mary Richards needed to portray the perfect combination of an independent woman that also resembled real-life women of the 1970s, with a slight tone of conventionality so as not to scare viewers away.

One of the many issues feminists advocated for in the 1970s was equal pay. *The Mary Tyler Moore Show* did not shy away from introducing this fight to its viewing audience. In an episode titled "The Good-Time News," Mary Richards realized that she was earning fifty dollars less than a former male colleague. Utterly shocked, Mary goes to her boss Lou Grant's office to talk about this issue. Mary walked into his office and asked why she was earning fifty dollars less than her male colleague who worked the same job. To Mary's surprise, her boss responded, "it's because he had a family to feed."[19] Shocked, Mary walked out of the room. At the conclusion of the episode, Mary and Lou discussed the matter and Lou agreed to pay Mary an additional fifty dollars, a solution both Mary and real-life feminists were happy to see.

Another revolutionary concept that *The Mary Tyler Moore Show* addressed was Mary Richards' occupation. If a woman was on television in the 1950s and 1960s, her character's occupation would have likely been a nurse or a teacher, which were considered suitable jobs for a woman at the time. The 1970 *Life* magazine article, "The Subversive Mary Tyler Moore: Women's Role on TV," argued that "if women have a profession it's usually nursing, where they minister to men. If they are superior to men, it's because they have magical powers. If they are over thirty years old, they've got to be widows, almost always with children, so that they can't run around enjoying themselves like real people."[20] Mary Richards was neither a nurse nor a teacher, she was not a widow, and she did not have children. Instead, Mary Richards was an accomplished career woman in a male-dominated field.

In real-life, Moore was also inclined to feminist ideals. In a letter written by the actress to the National Assembly on the Future of the Family, Moore stated that "women desperately need more economic security for their old age, more recognition for the work they do both inside and outside the home, more child care options, more opportunity, more justice. And less hassling by age-old patterns of discrimination."[21] In 1975, Moore was awarded the *Los Angeles Times'* Woman of the Year award. Speaking with the *Los Angeles Times*, Moore said, "I like that kind of work. Hard work is very relaxing for me."[22] Moore did not just bring feminist ideals to the television screen; she also integrated them into her own life.

Mary Richards in *The Mary Tyler Moore Show* was unabashed in demonstrating feminist ideals that have been historically shunned away. Mary Richards was unafraid to discuss equal pay with her boss, and she was rewarded for it. Mary Richards also had a job that was not typical or traditional for women. *The Mary Tyler Moore Show* was bold in tackling feminist ideals about women in the workplace, and in doing so, reached a large television audience.

Challenging Stereotypical Roles for Women

When Moore was on *The Dick Van Dyke Show*, her character symbolized the typical housewife, a woman who cleaned, washed, and completed chores in nothing other than a dress and heels. However, Moore was unimpressed with this character. From her autobiography, *After All*, Moore explained her decision to break tremendous ground for women on television:

> Everyone I talked to agreed that it was appropriate—that's what their wives wore [pants]. But here again, television hadn't quite caught up with the times. And so it was, at my own suggestion, that in a long line of situation-comedy wives, I would be the first to disdain the costume of old and opt for what was then called capri pants and flats.[23]

Moore told *Variety* magazine that wearing pants was much more realistic than wearing a skirt: "Wearing pants is what I do in real life, it's what my friends do in real life and that's being a realistic wife who wears pants and does not care how she looks."[24]

Moore revolutionized television as her character on *The Dick Van Dyke Show* and continued to pave the way for modern women on television as her character Mary Richards on *The Mary Tyler Moore Show*. Mary Richards broke ground by landing a job in a male-dominated workplace, remaining single without serious relationship commitments throughout the show, departing from the "good wife" character that dominated TV, wearing pants, and talking about the taboo subject of birth control.

Debra Baker Beck argues that before *The Mary Tyler Moore* Show, the mass media illustrated what she labels "Western codes." Beck explained that when the world is viewed as series of dualisms, those who do not fit the "good" qualifications—generally male, white, middle-class, and Christian—are automatically cast as "bad."[25] For feminists, being cast as outsiders, troublemakers, and even evil was inevitable since they challenged the very basis of a patriarchal society.[26] *The Mary Tyler Moore Show* took on the daunting task of not taking to heart the Western codes that mass media previously illustrated. Instead, they highlighted an independent woman with no husband and no kids.

Andrea Press suggested that Moore is considered the pioneer of television's "career woman" and did so without a man. Moore left a broken engagement to "make it on her own," as the theme song tells us presumably because a woman without a husband or family was so unusual as to be worthy of prime-time television of the 1970s.[27] Early television offered a rather restricted image of women, confining them to the home and family setting. The increase in the number of working women in the 1960s and 1970s precipitated a rise in television depictions of working women and women living in nontraditional family lives.[28] In the wake of *The Mary Tyler Moore Show*, television series started to more accurately represent the American family. In a new turn toward relevance, television of the 1970s and 1980s began to feature the single mother, an ensemble of mothers, or combined families.[29] In fact, in the last episode of *The Mary Tyler Moore Show*, Mary Richards remains uninvolved in a serious relationship and without children.[30]

The women's movement also helped diversify American television. Many programs in the 1970s featured older women, African American women, divorced women, single mothers, and working-class women. They even covered controversial issues such as rape, equal employment opportunities, abortion, and racial and sexual discrimination.[31] The Mary Tyler Moore Show continuously pushed the envelope of propriety for formal networks in addressing these controversial issues. Samuel Austerlitz explained one of the most groundbreaking moments to occur on the show was an encounter between Mary Richards and her mother. In an episode titled "Just Around the Corner / You've Got a Friend," while visiting her apartment, Mary's mother said, "don't forget to take your pill," to which both Mary and her father responded with "I won't." Mary's father looked askance at her, but a point had been scored in favor of honesty on television. [32] During the same episode, Mary decided to go out that night, and when her mom asked, "when will you back, dear?" Mary responded, "jee I don't know."[33]

In an episode titled "Divorce Isn't Everything," the characters discussed social life after divorce. After Mary Richards found an ad for a "divorced peoples club" in the paper, she was intrigued. Mary then told her friend Rhoda about the club as well as the fact that the club takes a trip to Paris, which made Rhoda want to join Mary even though she was not divorced. Throughout the show, Mary and Rhoda discussed how being a divorced person was not the end of the world, an idea that many Americans disregarded during the time. Back in the 1970s, and especially during the 1950s, it was rare for a woman to be divorced, akin to social suicide. However, The Mary Tyler Moore Show revolutionized the idea that divorced people deserved the same respect as anyone else.[34]

The 1978 article "Looking for America" featured in Moving On asserted the transition of television during the 1970s towards a more respectful direction in terms of the recognition of women's struggles:

> The television sitcoms have a long way to go before they could be considered an accurate reflection of the lives of American women. But the growing trend toward greater respect for the intelligence of women and identification with their problems means that these shows can at least sometimes be watched without humiliation or anger.[35]

Although many sitcoms of the 1970s still harnessed the past, *The Mary Tyler Moore Show* remolded traditional stereotypes about taboo subjects and reflected a better representation of the more complicated dimensions of American life.

Moore broke numerous traditions for how women should be portrayed on television. According to writer Bonnie Dow, Moore can be viewed as disrupting hegemonic practices of female representation on television in at least two ways: She departed from the "good wife" character type, which dominated popular domestic sitcoms from the beginning of television. She also expanded the limited parameters of the single adult woman comedy, which, although existent since the beginning of television, was hardly a dominant form in the way that domestic sitcom was.[36]

Critiques of *The Mary Tyler Moore Show*

The Mary Tyler Moore Show was truly groundbreaking. However, did the show go far enough to address feminist ideals and truly separate itself from the restraints of traditional television roots? The author of *Prime-Time Feminism: Television, Media Culture, and the Women's Movement since 1970*, Bonnie J. Dow, illustrated that *The Mary Tyler Moore Show* was the first sitcom to draw upon feminist consciousness-raising as a contextual frame. The show offered a very qualified feminist vision that blended discourses of the "new woman," working and living on her own outside of the confines of past domestic sitcoms with traditional female roles.[37] Dow argued that, at the same time, the show produced a vision of feminism that was a selection, deflection, and reflection of various available discourses. The construction of Mary Richards as an essentially passive character was just one of the strategies towards Moore's finely tuned negotiation of tradition and change.[38] Because Mary Richards was not married, this allowed producers to reconstruct a new "home life" structure, one that existed in Mary Richards' office rather than in a traditional suburban home. In the public sphere of the workplace she functioned akin to the more familiar relational patterns of female domestic characters situated within patriarchal families.[39]

Another aspect of the show that questioned feminist ideals was Mary Richards' relationship with her boss, Lou Grant. Dow argued that their relationship was a paternal one. Mary Richards consistently sought Lou

Grant's approval and advice, and he guided and protected her.[40] However, while Mary Richards acted as Lou's dutiful daughter, she also acted as a nurturing wife and mother to Lou and to other characters. It was her general responsibility to maintain interpersonal relations and she does so through personal advice, support, and mediation of conflict.[41] Mary Richards' isolation as the sole woman in the newsroom and her portrayal as the only reasonably successful and fulfilled woman in *The Mary Tyler Moore Show* demonstrated her tokenism. Mary Richards succeeded in the public realm only by succumbing to male expectations that she fulfill traditional female roles.[42] Going back to the episode where Mary Richards brought up the fifty dollar difference between herself and a former male colleague with her boss Lou, she was rewarded with a raise—not so much because she argued the point with Lou Grant, but because she constantly proved herself to be "one of the guys."[43]

The Mary Tyler Moore Show was different from other sitcoms at the time. Mary Richards remained single throughout the show, she discreetly referenced birth control, and she maintained a career as an associate producer instead of a secretary, nurse, or teacher. However, the show was still rooted in traditional aspects of sitcom television. Mary Richards was seen as a daughter to her boss who needed protection and guidance, someone who still exhibited a sweet, girl-next-door attitude and was viewed as the "caretaker" of the workplace. However, even with all these critiques, *The Mary Tyler Moore Show* was still considered one of the first revolutionary sitcoms in American television that challenged stereotypical, traditional roles for women.

Mary Tyler Moore: The Feminist

Moore was held in high regard during the growing women's movement at the time and was considered the standard-bearer for voices that demanded to be heard. Even though Moore did not think much of it, she became a poster child for the feminist movement of the 1970s. When the Equal Rights Amendment was debated in Congress, Moore was in the midst of the fight for ratification, along with other notable feminist leaders such as Bella Abzug, Shirley Chisholm, and Gloria Steinem. A few years later, on February 4, 1981, around 3,500 women converged on Capitol Hill as part of the "Women's Rights Day in Congress" to lobby, rally, and testify before Congress for equal rights, reproductive rights, and economic rights. [44] There was a rally with speakers including Bella Abzug, Shirley Chisholm, Barbara Mikulski, Gloria Steinem, and Mary Tyler Moore.[45]

Moore kept an interesting relationship with Steinem. Telling *Cosmopolitan*, "I'm very interested in women's rights. I read Betty Friedan's book 15 years ago, and I'm a big fan of Gloria Steinem, and I know marriage ought to be an equal partnership, but I'm content to have it 75–25."[46] Often times, Steinem encouraged Moore to become more involved in the feminist movement, to which Moore reluctantly agreed. In her autobiography, *After All*, Moore recounted her experience on Capitol Hill to support the passage of the Equal Rights Amendment, not afraid to step into the public light and face tremendous scrutiny:

> When Gloria asked me to fly to Washington, DC, with her to attend a rally to support passage of the Equal Rights Amendment, I reluctantly agreed. The reason for my reticence was my perennial sweaty-palmed, knee-shaking fear of standing at a microphone and speaking right to people's faces who are staring back at me. It doesn't matter whether it's ad-lib or a prepared text. It doesn't matter whether it is before ten people or two thousand, it is terrifying. I became Mary, the person who, without a role to play, might finally be seen naked and judged to be the fake she is.[47]

Afterward, Moore was glad to be a part of a larger movement:

> It wasn't a wasted experience. Afterward, I went through the room-to-room process of lobbying congressmen to listen to our pleas for funding day-care centers, equal pay for equal work, all part of the process that makes this country of and by the people. Gloria was off to points elsewhere and I took the train back to New York alone. I was pleased that my little speech was well received. And even though I had missed the date with frog number ten, who could have turned into a prince, so what? I was a member of a group who fought for equality and was proud of myself for making a contribution to that goal.[48]

Rather than just portray her character as a new woman of the 1970s on television, Moore took her character to heart and fought to ratify the Equal Rights Amendment alongside feminist icons such as Chisholm and Steinem.

Conclusion

The Mary Tyler Moore Show was courageous to bring taboo subjects to television and to challenge the patriarchy within sitcom television. The show was unashamed in bringing birth control, equal pay, divorce, and late-night partying to light. CBS, the television station which aired the show, used their platform as a major broadcasting station to transgress the status quo of women in television. Moore was unashamed in using her platform as a means of resistance against stereotypical roles for women in television.

The Mary Tyler Moore Show should be highly recognized when studying feminism in pop culture. If it was not for the show, we might still have women on television wearing dresses and heels while vacuuming. *The Mary Tyler Moore Show* departed from traditional sitcoms of the 1970s and was truly innovative in that it sought to dismantle stereotypical roles for actresses of the time. Familial structures on television today represent a more diverse America: biracial families, gay couples adopting children, women who do not have or want families, and women in a wide range of occupations. Television today is something to truly celebrate.

Notes

1. Allyson Jule, "Using *The Mary Tyler Moore Show* as a Feminist Teaching Tool," *Gender and Education* 22, no. 1 (January 2010): 128, https://doi.org/10.1080/09540250902769446.
2. Jule, "Using *The Mary Tyler Moore Show*," 128.
3. Marc Shapiro, *You're Gonna Make It After All: The Life, Times and Influence of Mary Tyler Moore* (Riverdale, NY: Riverdale Avenue Books, 2017), 1.
4. Debra Baker Beck, "The 'F' Word: How the Media Frame Feminism," NWSA *Journal* 10, no. 1 (Spring 1998): 145.
5. Susan Ware, *American Women's History: A Very Short Introduction* (Oxford: Oxford University Press, 2015), 103.
6. Sara M. Evans, *Born for Liberty: A History of Women in America* (New York: Free Press Paperback, 1989), 277.

7. Ware, *American Women's History*, 104.

8. Evans, *Born for Liberty*, 287.

9. Ware, *American Women's History*, 104–105.

10. Evans, *Born for Liberty*, 289.

11. Evans, *Born for Liberty*, 289.

12. Evans, *Born for Liberty*, 289.

13. Andi Zeilser, *Feminism and Pop Culture* (Berkeley, CA: Sea Press, 2008), 60.

14. Zeilser, *Feminism and Pop Culture*, 75.

15. Zeilser, *Feminism and Pop Culture*, 75.

16. Zeilser, *Feminism and Pop Culture*, 76.

17. Zeilser, *Feminism and Pop Culture*, 76.

18. Richard Corliss, "A Darkened Star," *National Review* 29, no. 14 (April 15, 1977): 448.

19. *The Mary Tyler Moore Show*, "The Good-Time News," directed by Hal Cooper, written by James L. Brooks and Allan Burns, CBS, September 16, 1972.

20. John Leonard, "The Subversive Mary Tyler Moore," *Life* 69, no. 25 (December 18, 1970): 8.

21. Gay, Lesbian, Bisexual, and Transgender Historical Society, "Future of the Family," September 27, 1976–December 6, 1979.

22. Wayne Warga, "Mary Tyler Moore has it all Working," *The Atlanta Constitution (1946–1984)*, April 27, 1975, 14F.

23. Mary Tyler Moore, *After All* (New York: G.P. Putnam's Sons, 1995), 86.

24. Marc Shapiro, *You're Gonna Make It After All*, 2.

25. Beck, "The 'F' Word: How the Media Frame Feminism," 140.

26. Beck, "The 'F' Word: How the Media Frame Feminism," 140.

27. Andrea Press, "Gender and Family in Televisions Golden Age and Beyond," *The Annals of the American Academy of Political and Social Science* 625, (September 2009): 142.

28. Press, "Gender and Family in Televisions Golden Age and Beyond," 148.

29. Press, "Gender and Family in Televisions Golden Age and Beyond," 143.

30. *The Mary Tyler Moore Show*, "The Last Show," directed by Jay Sandrich, written by James L. Brooks, Allan Burns, Ed. Weinberger, Stan Daniels, David Lloyd, and Bob Ellison, CBS, March 19, 1977.

31. Beck, "The 'F' Word: How the Media Frame Feminism," 146.

32. Saul Austerlitz, *Sitcom: A History in 24 Episodes from I Love Lucy to Community* (Chicago: Chicago Review Press, 2014), 103.

33. Austerlitz, *Sitcom*, 103.

34. *The Mary Tyler Moore Show*, "Divorce Isn't Everything," directed by Alan Rafkin, written by James L. Brooks, Allan Burns, and Treva Silverman, CBS, October 10, 1970.

35. Jane Melnick, "Looking for America," *Moving On* 2, no. 2 (April 1978): 15.

36. Bonnie J. Dow, *Prime-Time Feminism: Television, Media Culture, and the Women's Movement Since 1970*, (Philadelphia: University of Pennsylvania Press, 1996), 34.

37. Dow, *Prime-Time Feminism*, 25.

38. Dow, *Prime-Time Feminism*, 50.

39. Dow, *Prime-Time Feminism*, 50.

40. Bonnie J. Dow, "Hegemony, Feminist Criticism and *The Mary Tyler Moore Show*," *Critical Studies in Mass Communication* 7 (1990): 265.

41. Dow, "Hegemony, Feminist Criticism and *The Mary Tyler Moore Show*," 266.

42. Dow, "Hegemony, Feminist Criticism and *The Mary Tyler Moore Show*," 269.

43. Anita Diamant, "The Limits of Growth," *Equal Times*, June 5, 1978.

44. Chris Guilfoy, "3500 Lobby U. S. Congress on 'Women's Rights Day,'" *Gay Community News* 8, no. 30 (1981), 3.

45. Guilfoy, "3500 Lobby U.S. Congress on 'Women's Rights Day."

46. Christopher Bryars, "Mary Tyler Moore: How Her Spirit Ignited a Star," *Chicago Tribune*, 23 Jan 1977, d1.

47. Moore, *After All*, 224.

48. Moore, *After All*, 226.

12. A Tight White Super Suit: How Women's Underground Comics Came to Be

TRENTON SPILMAN

> *When the character [Power Girl] was created Wally Wood was the artist that drew Power Girl, and he was convinced that the editors were not paying attention to anything he did. So, his inker said every issue I'm going to draw the tits bigger until they notice it.*[1] – *Jimmy Palmiotti*

Men dominated as the leading comic book publishers of the 1970s and 1980s, both as the creative minds behind the characters and as the characters themselves.[2] When a female superhero did appear in an issue, she did not often represent a strong or independent woman. Unrealistic body standards, sexualized costumes, and a reliance on a male counterpart controlled the narratives of female superheroes across DC and Marvel comics. In 1976, Wally Wood created DC Comic's newest superhero, Power Girl. Instead of being inspired by a powerful physique like her older cousin Superman, Power Girl wore an all-white leotard adorned with a red cape and a keyhole neckline exposing her cleavage.[3] Likewise, Marvel Comics presented Ms. Marvel in 1977. Despite being gifted with strong superpowers, Ms. Marvel was portrayed as dependent on male heroes to defeat villains. In 1970, a group of independent women came together to write *It Ain't Me, Babe*, the first comic completely written and drawn by women.[4] Like *It Ain't Me, Babe*, *Wimmen's Comix* rose as a response to second-wave feminism—the increase of feminism throughout the civil rights movements of the 1970s.[5] *Wimmen's Comix*, an independent publishing company made up of an inspired group of women, sought to challenge sexist representations of female superheroes by creating accurate portrayals of women.[6]

The rise of scholarly investigations in women's comics parallels the increasingly mainstream popularity of comic books in modern culture. For example, Nathan Miczo published an anthology in 2014 discussing female stereotypes in comics.[7] Comic books stereotypically represent the perfect female body. *Superhero Bodies: Identity, Materiality, Transformation*, edited by Wendy Haslem, details how the ideal superhero body distorts the reader's perception of a normal body type.[8] Sherrie Inness also wrote a book discussing how unrealistic depictions of women affect readers.[9]

This chapter will explore how comic book publishers and artists in the 1970s and 1980s portrayed women in their work. Why did men working in the comic book industry create female characters that did not accurately portray women? How did female writers overcome the inequality of the comic book industry? Using historical magazines, comic books, graphic novels, books, journal articles, and pictures drawn by comic book artists as my evidence base, I argue that from 1970 to 1989 mainstream publishers and artists exploited the portrayal of women in comic books, which urged women working in the comic book industry to produce more gender accurate underground comics.

A Man's Eye for Superheroes

The bittersweet rise of empowered female characters in comics demonstrates both the oppressive and liberating sides of popular culture.[10] The empowerment of new female characters fell short because of the need to over-sexualize women to appease male preferred beauty standards.[11] However, comics in popular culture also "challenged traditional gender roles" and "encouraged the embrace of new behaviors" in the fight to liberate women.[12]

The Bronze Age of comic books took place during the 1970s when the women's liberation movement resonated a new independence for female characters.[13] Female characters in comic books during the 1970s evolved from being supporting characters, like Spiderman's girlfriend Mary Jane, to independent representations of women.[14] However, introducing stronger female characters hardly achieved equality for women.[15] Instead, "the tone of these stories suggested that the male writers didn't take women's liberation seriously,"[16] mocking feminism and creating over-sexualized female characters, such as Power Girl and Ms. Marvel.

Power Girl, DC Comic's most sexualized female super hero, is Superman's younger Kryptonian cousin from Earth one.[17] In 1976, artist Wally Wood drew Power Girl's breasts larger in each new issue to see if editors would notice.[18] DC Comics published seven issues before the editors caught on to Power Girl's breast size. [19] While male superheroes are known for their superhuman abilities, Power Girl's breasts became one of the character's most popular traits. Despite the efforts of writers and editors to validate her appearance, Power Girl stood as a sexualized character who did not meet her full potential until the start of modern comics.

Despite having the same powers as Superman—super strength, flight, and bullet immunity—DC comics wrote Power Girl as a lesser version of Superman, the strongest superhero and leader of the Justice League. For the longest time, Superman hid Power Girl away from the world after arriving to Earth on a spaceship, the same way he arrived.[20] The intention behind Superman's action was to protect Power Girl from getting hurt by society, however, his actions instead impeded on Power Girl's development of her powers and confidence. Power Girl frequently received references as "Superman's cousin," demeaning her individuality and forcing her identity to live in the shadow of Superman, a powerful and beloved male hero.[21] Power Girl and Superman's dynamic exemplifies societal gender roles during the 1970s and 1980s[22] and clearly demonstrates the male backlash towards second-wave feminism. The identity created for Power Girl perpetrated female inequality and submission to male authority.

The sexual depiction of Power Girl hindered the character's ability to symbolize female empowerment. A combination of dialogue, plot, and art gives comic book creators the freedom to create a character exactly how they picture them. Power Girl's creators pictured an all-white super suit, accompanied by a red cape and keyhole neckline, revealing her cleavage.[23] Power girl's exposed cleavage became the trademark of her costume, like Superman's S or Batman's bat. Despite her costume, the artist attempted to empower Power Girl as a woman. Star Spangled Kid hands a red crest, like Superman's, to Power Girl as a token of acceptance into the Justice Society. Power Girl immediately crushes the crest to show her independence from Superman.[24] Power Girl's independence strengthened the women's movement in the late 1970s, but at the same time, her sexualization hurt the women's movement. According to pop-culture author and comic book historian Mike Madrid, in the 1970s, "feminism and sexual freedom didn't always mesh up well."[25] Power Girl took a dignified stance for her suit by destroying the red crest and signifying her independence from Superman. However, the male creators did not change the sexual nature of the character and instead embraced it as Power Girl's symbol, demonstrating a push for sexual content.

Ms. Marvel provides another example of publishers attempting to create a powerful female superhero. Ms. Marvel, alternatively known as Carol Danvers, is an intergalactic superhero. Ms. Marvel unknowingly gained her powers from mixing her DNA with the superhero Mar-Vell after an explosion.[26] Carol Danvers emerges from the explosion as with the ability of super strength and flight.[27] Carol Danvers works as a writer for the fictional *Women's Magazine* at the *Daily Bugle*.[28] To turn into Ms. Marvel, Carol Danvers faints and resurfaces as her alter ego.[29] The character's first comic book run lasted over twenty issues, featured as a reoccurring character in the XMEN and Avengers comics.[30]

Marvel Comics attempted to create the "iconic female character" with Ms. Marvel, the female version of a hero like Captain America.[31] However, Marvel repeatedly established Ms. Marvel as a weak and dependent character. Ms. Marvel depended on others in physical battle and easily succumbed to manipulation by villains. For example, a scene from issue eight of *Ms. Marvel* shows Carol Danvers washed up on shore after a battle with the villain Grotesk, only to be saved by a normal man.[32] Further, Ms. Marvel's story line focused more on emotional and mental fights rather than physical fights.[33] In the first issue of *Ms. Marvel*, Carol Danvers' mind is erased after the explosion with Mar-Vell.[34] Carol Danvers does not become aware of her alter ego as Ms. Marvel until issue three,[35] when she goes to a therapist who finds out about her dual personality.[36] The therapist quickly proceeds to manipulate Carol Danvers into thinking she is delusional, which created a loss of self-assurance and self-identity.[37] Nathan Miczo, a scholar who wrote about the comparison between Ms. Marvel and gender stereotypes in literature, argues that "rather than her superpowers being an extension and reflection of Carol's inner self, this bold new superheroine's powers were literally alien to her and entailed a loss of self for their manifestation."[38] While it is not uncommon for superheroes to be manipulated, as male heroes can be manipulated to destroy cities, Ms. Marvel was manipulated to be a dependent female relying on male characters to regain her own identity.[39]

A defeated and dependent woman is the first impression readers get from Marvel's first iconic female character.

Marvel's artists and editors created each cover page to depict a struggling and defeated Ms. Marvel. For example, the cover of issue six shows Ms. Marvel unconscious, being lifted above a fiery landscape by the villain Grotesk.[40] An unconscious woman being lifted in front of a burning city persuades readers that Ms. Marvel is weak and too incompetent to defeat her villains. Male characters, on the other hand, are drawn as powerful figures. Superman is regularly seen lifting cars to save citizens, symbolizing the male hero as strong and charismatic.[41] The cover of a comic book is an impactful representation of the story and its characters and is therefore critical to creating an initial interest for readers.

Women were often unrealistically portrayed in mainstream comics. Publishers like DC Comics and Marvel Comics sexualized their characters and wrote stories based on the emotionally dependent female stereotype. Power Girl had the potential to embody the ideals of independence and feminism but was ultimately submitted to over-sexualization by DC creators. Ms. Marvel, the "iconic female character," lacked independence in the Marvel universe.[42] Mainstream publishers created comic book characters that did not accurately portray women, making them appeal to the male fantasy rather than making the character relatable to female readers.

Marginalized by the Comic Book Industry

Going into the 1970s, women continued to fight marginalization in many aspects of life: creatively, professionally, politically, and through labor unions.[43] Women endured stereotypical feminine careers "such as teaching, nursing, clerical and sales work, and personal service" while also receiving unequal opportunities for higher positions.[44] Administration level positions favored men who feared working with women, and the comic book industry was no different.[45] During the 1970s and 1980s, women struggled in the workforce due to systematic inequalities.

Comic book publishing companies wrote off women trying to publish their own stories.[46] Magazines, newspapers, and comic book stores rejected female driven stories that expressed the female fantasy.[47] In an interview with Trina Robbins, the head editor of *Wimmen's Comix*, when discussing the right to equally express female fantasies, she writes:

> You know there's a printer in the Midwest who didn't believe we *should* have that right. This guy has printed comics as gross as *Bizarre Sex* (check it out and you'll see what I mean) but the difference was that those comics were all done by men. When *Wet Satin* came to him to print he wouldn't touch it. Called it pornographic. Draw your own conclusions.[48]

Surprisingly, female publishers for women's magazines also failed to publish women's work. According to Lee Marrs, an editor for *Wimmen's Comix*, publishers would not take satire.[49] Women's magazines feared making fun of ideas and people involved with the feminist movement, a topic commonly submitted to publishers because women in the 1970s and 1980s actively protested for independence and equal rights.[50] Female artists and writers struggled to have their work published in the comic book industry due to prejudice and lack of interest for controversial topics.

The comic industry preferred male writers and artists, demonstrating an unwillingness to expand into diverse varieties of comic book stories.[51] Unlike men, women wanted superhero stories to reflect female political, social, and sexual movements of the 1970s and 1980s, but publishers believed diversifying from consumable narratives and styles would lead to a decrease in sales.[52] In an interview with comic book artist Terre Richards, she argued, "The undergrounds were a reaction to the shackles of the Eastern Establishment—the industry of Marvel, D.C. and Warren Publications—and the daily syndicates, both of which promoted politically irrelevant, boring, 'assembly line' comics and strips."[53] Traditional "assembly line" comics entail the cliché of overly muscular male heroes saving cities from mayhem. The hero receives universal praise and goes home to a docile, slender girl congratulating the hero for his strength and bravery. Tailoring comic books to men reinforced a specific art and story style that prevented women from working as head artists and writers in mainstream comic industries.

A lack of female-centric stories and accurate portrayals of women in mainstream comics served to enhance the male fantasy and marginalization of women. This ultimately paved the way towards underground comics for women.

The Rise of Underground "Comix"

Despite being marginalized, women proceeded to fight for equality and independence. At the start of the 1970s, the women's movements sparked some division among various groups of women. Women with different ideas regarding equality and independence disagreed and split into different movements fighting for different ideals.[54] However, most radical feminists agreed that they did not fight to be treated equal to men, they wanted to be independent of them.[55] And many feminists came together to fight for abortion and sex rights.[56]

The 1970s witnessed second-wave feminism, broadening the fight for female independence and equality. Women in the comic book industry demanded stronger representation of female characters and the right to represent themselves creatively. Comic book historian Mike Madrid wrote, "The heroine of the 1970s was no longer content to be the devoted but ineffectual girlfriend or assistant, making coffee or sewing costumes for her male teammate. The era of the emancipated superheroine had arrived."[57] The ideology of the 1970s women's movement paved the way for liberated female characters to rise in comic books. Women in the comic book industry took advantage of every opportunity to create feminist inspired stories, but the male dominated industry continued discriminatory practices. The development of women-run underground comics emerged as the solution to discrimination. Underground comics combated the lack of opportunities in mainstream comics and allowed women to create accurate and strong female stories.

The 1970 comic book It Ain't Me, Babe by Trina Robbins paved the way for women's underground comics.[58] It Ain't Me, Babe established female-centric stories by creating new variations of already iconic characters. For example, an arc of It Ain't Me, Babe tells the satirical story of a female Tarzan freeing women chained from the oppression of men.[59] The witty comic comments on societal norms in the 1970s, where women experienced unequal social and political treatment. The popularity of It Ain't Me, Babe encouraged the growth of underground comics.

Underground comics gave women creative freedom over their comic book stories. Two years after the publication of It Ain't Me, Babe, the women's underground comic book, Wimmen's Comix, hit the shelves. Wimmen's

Comix ran for seventeen issues, from 1972 until it ended in 1992.[60] Like *It Ain't Me, Babe*, *Wimmen's Comix* centered around the female fantasy, battling the media's misogyny.[61] The stories in *Wimmen's Comix* involved gender swapping, straight and gay sex, abortion, and superheroes.[62] The creative freedom experienced by women working for *Wimmen's Comix* permitted the variety of subjects represented across all seventeen comic book issues.[63]

Unfortunately, marginalization even continued within underground comics. Female publishers also rejected *Wimmen's Comix* that did not contain messages about the women's liberation movement. Female publishers desired the representation of the feminist agenda in *Wimmen's Comix* and male publishers lacked interest in the variety of topics expressed in the comic.[64] Outside of *It Ain't Me, Babe* and *Wimmen's Comix*, women creating underground comics were not successful.[65] Artists and writers of *Wimmen's Comics* believed the lack of comedic appreciation in the early 1970s explained why magazines did not support women's independent comic books.[66] In an interview with the comic book artist Lee Marrs, she states:

> The fact that in *Wimmen's Comix* we have a variety of outlooks, that we poked fun at all kinds of people and places, really freak them out. We got irate letters, we got threats, people just didn't like us at all. Also we were fighting against a general prejudice against comics books per se.[67]

The *Wimmen's Comix* satirical style of storytelling confused magazines. *Ms. Magazine* wanted comic book submissions about the perfect female hero, but because they received an accurate portrayal of women from *Wimmen's Comix*, they believed men posed as women to profit off the women's movement.[68] Feminist bookstores wanted to publish stories that portrayed women as perfect, independent characters in order to combat the perfect male superhero trope. *Wimmen's Comix* wrote stories about "women coping with the weaknesses and confusions" of daily life, resulting in rejections because publishers found the stories to be inappropriate.[69] Female creators resorted to publishing wherever they could get accepted. Trina Robbins, for example, published in *Playboy* after receiving rejections from feminist magazines: "If my sisters treat me like shit, I'll go where I'm accepted as an equal human being."[70] Unfortunately, *Wimmen's Comix* writers and artists suffered publication rejections by both misogynists and feminists.

Many readers accepted the sexualized characters created by DC and Marvel Comics, but also criticized women creators for depicting characters with sexual appeal. Trina Robbins, head editor for *Wimmen's Comix*, said, "I have been criticized on the grounds that the women I draw are beautiful and therefore 'sex objects,'" to which she answers that all women are beautiful.[71] *Wimmen's Comix* even received criticism because the comics were written by women. Men include over-sexualized female characters in their comics regularly and receive significant commercial gain, while women are denied the right to publish explicit fantasies. Trina Robbins expressed the need for equality of creative expression, stating:

> These are definitely our own fantasies. If some are frighteningly violent, that's because women can sometimes be as violent as men. We're not trying to say that women are saints, that women are better than men, or that a world ruled by women would have no war. I think that's bullshit. Sometimes being equal to any man includes being as fucked up as any man, and we have the right to express that.[72]

Trina Robbins expressed that the women's movement wanted equality as well as independence from men. Trina Robbins wanted the right to equally express explicit female fantasies. The cover for issue seven depicts three armed women huddled over a man as the world burns behind them.[73] Although not without receiving criticism and rejection, *Wimmen's Comix* fought for the right to have creative freedom over their content.

Wimmen's Comix wrote and illustrated satirical stories portraying the problems women faced every day. The content in *Wimmen's Comix* resulted in feminist magazines rejecting their publication because the stories did not fit the perfect female superhero ideology.[74] The edgy stories, however, found a home wherever accepted.[75] Women conquered the marginalized, male-dominated comic book industry by creating their own female-run comic books where they could share more accurate fantasies and portrayals of female characters.

Conclusion

Along with the interviews from Lee Marrs, Terre Richards, and Trina Robbins, this chapter clarifies how the comic book industry oppressed women attempting to break into the field. It is important to note that this chapter furthers previous scholars' research by illustrating how women were unfairly treated in the comic book industry and how women overcame marginalization. Further research should investigate similar characteristics between mainstream comics and underground comics to uncover how both sides of the comic book industry exploited the same female stereotypes. This research would further clarify evidence of inequality from every angle, rather than just mainstream comics versus women's comic books.

This chapter argued that from the 1970s to the end of the 1980s, mainstream publishers and artists exploited the portrayal of women in comic books, pushing women in the industry to produce gender accurate underground comics. Rather than attempting to break into mainstream comic book publishing, like DC Comics or Marvel Comics, women acted against the male-dominated industry by writing and illustrating female centric comic books like *It Ain't Me, Babe* and *Wimmen's Comix*.

Notes

1. Jimmy Palmiotti, "Jimmy Palmiotti: Time Bomb and Power Girl – the Breasts of Friends?" interview by Karyn Pinter, *Comics Bulletin*, Sept 15, 2010, http://comicsbulletin.com/jimmy-palmiotti-time-bomb-and-power-girl-breast-friends/.
2. Trina Robbins, "Interviews with Women Comic Artists: Trina Robbins," *Cultural Correspondence: Sex Roles & Humor*, no. 9 (Spring 1979): 10, https://library.brown.edu/cds/catalog/catalog.php?verb=render&id=1123700110226457&colid=21.
3. Gerry Conway, *All-Star Comics* #58 (Burbank, CA: DC Comics), 1976.
4. Jill S. Katz, "Women and Mainstream Comic Books," *International Journal of Comic Art* 10, no. 2 (2008): 105.
5. Susan Ware, *American Women's History: A Very Short Introduction* (New York: Oxford University Press, 2015), 103.
6. Leah Misemer, "Serial critique: The Counterpublic of Wimmen's Comix," *Inks: The Journal of the Comics Studies Society* 3, no. 1 (June 20, 2019), 7, https://doi.org/10.1353/ink.2019.0001.
7. Maja Bajac-Carter et al., *Heroines of Comic Books and Literature: Portrayals in Popular Culture* (Blue Ridge Summit, MD: Rowman & Littlefield Publishers, 2014), http://ebookcentral.proquest.com/lib/vt/detail.action?docID=1655587.
8. Wendy Haslem et al., *Superhero Bodies: Identity, Materiality, Transformation* (New York: Routledge, 2018), https://doi.org/10.4324/9780429022289.
9. Sherrie A. Inness, *Action Chicks: New Images of Tough Women in Popular Culture*,

1st ed. (New York: Palgrave Macmillan, 2004), http://catdir.loc.gov/catdir/toc/hol041/2003050906.html.

10. Ware, *American Women's History*, 113.

11. Ware, *American Women's History*, 113.

12. Ware, *American Women's History*, 113.

13. Mike Madrid, *The Supergirls: Fashion, Feminism, Fantasy, and the History of Comic Book Heroines* (Oregon: Exterminating Angel Press, 2016), 156–157.

14. Madrid, *The Supergirls*, 156.

15. Madrid, *The Supergirls*, 157.

16. Madrid, *The Supergirls*, 157.

17. Gerry Conway, *All-Star Comics* # 58, 17.

18. Palmiotti, *Jimmy Palmiotti*, 2010.

19. Palmiotti, *Jimmy Palmiotti*, 2010.

20. Madrid, *The Supergirls*, 149.

21. Gerry Conway, *All-Star Comics* # 63 (Burbank, CA: DC Comics), 1977, 7.

22. Ware, *American Women's History*.

23. Gerry Conway, *All-Star Comics* # 60 (Burbank, CA: DC Comics), 1976, 2.

24. Gerry Conway, *All-Star Comics* # 64 (Burbank, CA: DC Comics), 1977, 3; Madrid, *The Supergirls*, 150.

25. Madrid, *The Supergirls*, 172.

26. Gene Colan, *Captain Marvel* #1 (New York: Marvel Characters Inc), 1968, 18-22.

27. Gene Colan, *Captain Marvel* #1, 18-22.

28. Gene Colan, *Captain Marvel* #1.

29. Gene Colan, *Captain Marvel* #1.

30. Maja Bajac-Carter et al., *Heroines of Comic Books and Literature*, 166.

31. Madrid, *The Supergirls*, 181.

32. Gerry Conway, *Ms. Marvel* # 8 (New York: Marvel Characters, Inc), 1977, 18.

33. Maja Bajac-Carter et al., *Heroines of Comic Books and Literature*, 167.

34. Gene Colan, *Captain Marvel* #1.

35. Gerry Conway, *Ms. Marvel* #3 (New York: Marvel Characters, Inc), 1977.

36. Gerry Conway, *Ms. Marvel* (New York: Marvel Characters, Inc), 1977.

37. Maja Bajac-Carter et al., *Heroines of Comic Books and Literature*, 167.

38. Maja Bajac-Carter et al., *Heroines of Comic Books and Literature*, 167.

39. Maja Bajac-Carter et al., *Heroines of Comic Books and Literature*, 167.

40. Gerry Conway, *Ms. Marvel* #6 (New York: Marvel Characters, Inc), 1978, 1.

41. Jerry Siegel, *Action Comics* #1 (Burbank, CA: DC Comics), 1938.

42. Madrid, *The Supergirls*, 181.

43. Ware, *American Women's History*, 103.

44. Ware, *American Women's History*, 112–114.

45. Lee Marrs, "Interviews with Women Comic Artists: Lee Marrs," *Cultural Correspondence: Sex Roles & Humor*, no. 9 (Spring 1979), 25.

46. Robbins, "Interviews with Women Comic Artists: Trina Robbins," 10.

47. Marrs, "Interviews with Women Comic Artists: Lee Marrs," 24.

48. Robbins, "Interviews with Women Comic Artists: Trina Robbins," 10.

49. Marrs, "Interviews with Women Comic Artists: Lee Marrs," 24.

50. Marrs, "Interviews with Women Comic Artists: Lee Marrs," 24.

51. Terre Richards, "Interviews with Women Comic Artists: Terre Richards," *Cultural Correspondence: Sex Roles & Humor*, no. 9 (Spring 1979).

52. Richards, "Interviews with Women Comic Artists: Terre Richards," 21; Robbins, "Interviews with Women Comic Artists: Trina Robbins," 10.

53. Richards, "Interviews with Women Comic Artists: Terre Richards," 21.

54. William H. Chafe, "The Road to Equality," in *No Small Course: A History of Women in the United States*, ed. Nancy F. Cott (New York: Oxford University Press, 2000), 554.

55. Chafe, "The Road to Equality," 556.

56. Chafe, "The Road to Equality," 575.

57. Madrid, *The Supergirls*, 156.

58. Rita D. Jacobs, "Review of The Complete Wimmen's Comix," *World Literature Today* 90, no. 2 (2016): 73, https://doi.org/10.7588/worllitetoda.90.2.0072.

59. Trina Robbins, Barbara Mendes, Lisa Lyons, Meredith Kurtzman, Nancy Burton, Carole Kalish, and Michele Brand, *It Ain't Me, Babe* (CA: Last Gasp, 1970), 9.

60. Jacobs, "Review of The Complete Wimmen's Comix," 73.

61. Marth Cornog, "The Complete Wimmen's Comix," *Library Journal* 141, no. 9 (May 15, 2016): 59; Misemer, "Serial critique: The Counterpublic of Wimmen's Comix," 7.

62. Cornog, "The Complete Wimmen's Comix," 59.

63. Misemer, "Serial critique: The Counterpublic of Wimmen's Comix," 7.

64. Robbins, "Interviews with Women Comic Artists: Trina Robbins," 10 and 12.

65. Marrs, "Interviews with Women Comic Artists: Lee Marrs," 24.

66. Marrs, "Interviews with Women Comic Artists: Lee Marrs," 24.

67. Marrs, "Interviews with Women Comic Artists: Lee Marrs," 24.

68. Marrs, "Interviews with Women Comic Artists: Lee Marrs," 24.

69. Marrs, "Interviews with Women Comic Artists: Lee Marrs," 24.

70. Robbins, "Interviews with Women Comic Artists: Trina Robbins," 11.

71. Robbins, "Interviews with Women Comic Artists: Trina Robbins," 10.

72. Robbins, "Interviews with Women Comic Artists: Trina Robbins," 10.

73. Trina Robbins et al., *Wimmen's Comix #7* (CA: Last Gasp, 1976).

74. Marrs, "Interviews with Women Comic Artists: Lee Marrs," 24.

75. Robbins, "Interviews with Women Comic Artists: Trina Robbins," 11.

13. Dolly Parton: The Appalachian Advocate, Wild Wife, and Sexualized Singer

BETHANY STEWART

One night while filming 9 to 5, famous country singer Dolly Parton stripped down naked and paraded around to her male and female friends.[1] Later, a group of her friends and her "girlfriend, Judy [Ogle]," went to dinner and had a few drinks.[2] While in separate cars, Ogle and Parton began competing back and forth against one another.[3] The game started with flipping one another off and then progressed to mooning and flashing their bare chests.[4] To win the game, Parton asked Gregg, the driver, to not look while she undressed.[5] She waited until a stop sign, got out of the car, and walked around completely naked.[6] Parton said, "I was so embarrassed, but feelin' so proud that I had done it."[7] Parton's act of exposing herself topped anything that her friend did and definitely won her the game. The wild and lively Parton clearly did not worry about what others thought of her.

Parton's fierce and independent spirit was rooted in her childhood and early career. During her childhood, Parton's family faced extreme poverty.[8] Born in 1946 in eastern Tennessee, she grew up in a two-room shack as the fourth child among twelve brothers and sisters.[9] Parton slept in a bed with five of her siblings. Additionally, Parton's family did not have electricity, a telephone, or running water.[10] Her mother made her winter coat out of patches and scraps of material, while other school kids made fun of her for wearing the unique jacket.[11] The day after Parton became the first in her family to graduate high school, she moved to Nashville to live out her lifelong dream of singing.[12] Parton moved to find a better life and escape her family's poverty.

Parton's music career helped her live out the American Dream. She first worked with Porter Wagoner, a popular country music star, as his singing partner beginning in 1967.[13] After a seven-year partnership, Parton left Wagoner to assemble a group of her own.[14] Her band, The Travlin' Family Band, included four of her brothers and sisters, an uncle, and a cousin.[15]

As her popularity grew, she crossed over from country music to pop and rock genres and started a new acting career in Hollywood.[16] Parton played roles in the iconic films, such as 9 to 5 and *The Best Little Whorehouse in Texas*.[17] Reflecting back on her career, Parton considered herself rich when she wrote a song about that patched winter jacket, "Coat of Many Colors," that hundreds of thousands of people paid to hear her sing.[18] Her life, a true "rags to riches" story, exemplifies the American Dream.

This chapter contributes to an extensive literature that analyzes Parton's life and persona through the lens of women's and feminist theory, Southern cultural history, and the history of country music. Previous authors focus on how Parton's Southern roots, sexuality, and economic class, molded her identity.[19] Graham Hoppe's "Icon and Identity" argues that Parton's eastern Tennessee roots motivated her.[20] Nadine Hubbs' "'Jolene,' Genre, and the Everyday Homoerotics of Country Music" describes Parton as homosexual.[21] Pamela Wilson's "Mountains of Contradictions: Gender, Class, and Region in the Star Image of Dolly Parton" argues that Parton's economic class affected her as a celebrity.[22] This chapter contributes to the already established but growing historiographies that examine Parton's multifaceted life and career.

Graham Hoppe's "Icon and Identity" demonstrates how Parton's "hillbilly" background shaped her as a celebrity.[23] Hoppe researched Parton's career and association with her home: eastern Tennessee.[24] Hoppe describes Parton as "hillbilly."[25] The article describes the building of Dollywood, Parton's theme park, as part of her connection to her home.[26] Hoppe argues that Parton used to be embarrassed about her background in her early career, but as she found her footing, she embraced her roots.[27] Hoppe also argues that Parton embraced the hillbilly stereotype to create her own persona.[28] Hoppe's work shows how Parton interacted with her hometown throughout her career.[29]

Nadine Hubbs' "'Jolene,' Genre, and the Everyday Homoerotics of Country Music" addresses Parton's iconic song "Jolene" and Parton's sexuality.[30] Hubbs analyzes why Parton did not display hatred for the "other woman."[31] Hubbs argues "Jolene" to be a gender-bending song that raised questions about Parton's sexuality.[32] This connection is problematic because no matter how much "proof" the author has, the roots are speculation. Parton is the only person who can truly define her sexuality. This argument signified that, because of internalized sexism, both men and women expect women to behave vengefully and outwardly cruel when threatened. Hubbs also argues that Parton's appearance could be viewed as drag.[33] Despite this speculation, this work is notable due to the fact that the author analyzes several aspects of Parton's life that defied heteronormative culture, for example, how she toured with her best friend instead of her husband.[34] Hubbs' problematic argument labels Parton to be homosexual because of her song "Jolene."[35]

Pamela Wilson's "Mountains of Contradictions: Gender, Class, and Region in the Star Image of Dolly Parton" argues that Parton's childhood poverty kept her from becoming materialistic.[36] Wilson argues that Parton's social and economic classes influenced the type of celebrity that she was.[37] A child of poverty, Parton had a deep appreciation for generosity and service. Even after she grew famous, she gave back to her community instead of stockpiling her money.[38] Wilson argues that Parton's image contradicted society's norms of class.[39]

Contrary to previous literature, my research contributes to this scholarly conversation by looking at how Parton both challenged and exemplified feminine norms, particularly those linked to ideas about Southern and Appalachian womanhood. I will explore my topic by answering a series of questions: How did Parton reinforce expected norms of behavior and images for Southern women? How did Parton's home life challenge society's understanding of family and women's roles within the family? How did society view Parton's expression of her sexuality? Using historical newspaper and magazine articles about Parton, as well as interviews with Parton herself, this chapter will reveal how Parton's public image reinforced and challenged society's accepted notions of Southern white womanhood by combining the wholesome persona of an Appalachian woman with an atypical home life and open expressions of her sexuality.

Society expected Southern white women during the 1970s and the 1980s to submit to the dominance of white men.[40] Culturally, society defined Southern womanhood as passive, genteel, and white.[41] According to Florence King, "Southern ladies" grew up learning "to please their husbands, attend to their physical needs, cover up their indiscretions, and give them no cause for worry."[42] Marilyn Schwartz stated that society would not allow Southern women to desire anything "more than a debutante ball, a beauty queen crown, a good sorority placement, and a good china and silver pattern for their wedding registry."[43] Politically, Southern states did not support equal rights.[44] In 1972, the only Southern states to ratify the Equal Rights Amendment included Texas, Tennessee, Kentucky, and Maryland.[45] In a religious context, Christian beliefs supported women's subordination to their husbands. Women who failed to obey their patriarchs threatened the power of white men. The public conceptions of white Southern womanhood specifically included not challenging the established patriarchy.

College-educated, white, middle-class mothers spearheaded second-wave feminism based on inequality in the workplace in the 1960s through the 1980s.[46] The Equal Pay Act of 1963 and the Civil Rights Act of 1964 prohibited employers from discriminating based on someone's sex, but feminists still advocated for more.[47] Employers tended to restrict job opportunities for women to careers as teachers, nurses, or secretaries.[48] Eleanor Roosevelt led the President's Commission on the Status of Women which supported the nuclear family but also called for equal pay, equal job opportunities, access to education, maternity leave, and more childcare.[49] The nuclear family included the traditional picture of a father and a mother living with their children. However, the second wave of feminism did not address women of other races or classes.[50] Second-wave feminism supported the traditional understanding of the family but called for more equality among middle-class white women.[51]

A Woman of the Rural Smoky Mountains

"If you don't like the road you're walking, start paving another one!"[52]

Parton's connection to the Smoky Mountains of eastern Tennessee and independence reinforced and challenged the public understanding of Southern womanhood. She overcame her family's past by escaping the poverty cycle that trapped most people in the area. Parton's strong faith in Christianity stemmed from her childhood, but she did not follow all beliefs. After she established her career outside of eastern Tennessee, she made sure to go back and help those people through economic stimulation and educational programs. She also did not have any interest in politics and represented women's confinement to the private sphere of life at home. Parton's ties to her hometown aligned and defied Southern womanhood.[53]

The Parton family faced extreme poverty and did not represent a stable nuclear family. Her parents, Avie and Robert, raised twelve children in a two-room home. Parton's parents paid the doctor who delivered her with a sack of flour.[54] Parton's father worked as a seasonal farmer, and according to reporter Bruce Cook, "could never be sure he would be kept on his job through the winter."[55] That large family barely scraped by; they survived on one unstable and small income.[56] Families in eastern Tennessee regularly struggled monetarily and did not align with aspirations for stability. For the impoverished Parton family, life was soon to change.

Parton's independence shined when she overcame her family's poverty. According to reporter Barbara Frit Harrison, "she would never have become a singer or a writer if she had not inherited talent and received encouragement from her parents."[57] Parton did not hold resentment towards her family; she knew that her parents did the best that they could with the cards they had been dealt. Although her devotion to her family aligned with Southern femininity, her successful career shows her ambition and independence. Parton grew from her childhood poverty. By overcoming her difficult past, Parton exemplified an independent woman.

Parton's sense of home for eastern Tennessee reinforced the belief that women belonged in the home. Parton stated, "anybody with any sense would know that I didn't have to go home to record. The sound I was lookin' for was a sound that lives in Nashville."[58] Writer Connie Berman wrote, "though she loves to travel she says her home will always be in Tennessee where 'I get my inspiration.'"[59] Parton did not have to go back to Tennessee to further her career, but she wanted to go back.[60] Her longing for home compared to how women were tied to the home without careers of their own. Typically speaking, people expected men to go out into the public world but expected women to stay at home in the private sphere. No matter how far away Parton explored out of the area, she always returned. Parton's desire to always return to home fell in line with the private sphere confinement that women faced.

Parton reinforced Southern womanhood through her strong belief in Christianity. Parton's parents brought her and her siblings up as fundamentalist members of the Church of God.[61] According to Parton, "my strength comes from God. What shines in me is the love of God."[62] Parton superfan, John Skinner, echoed this same theme.[63] Skinner talked of how Parton always included a couple of religious songs in her concerts, and then stated, "she is a born leader. Her mother believes that Parton is going to bring millions of people to God, and I think that may be so."[64] Parton clearly used her fame as a way to spread the love of God to her fans, thus providing society with a strong example of a good Christian woman.

Although Parton placed a lot of faith in religion, she also showed independence through disregarding specific church beliefs. Parton told reporter Barbara Frit Harrison that she had left behind the church's strictness on "makeup and hair and sex and stuff."[65] Parton dressed in tight clothes accessorized with large hair and bold makeup. Contrastingly, Christianity supported a more reserved and conservative style for women. Christianity advocated against sex between anyone other than a husband and wife; churches taught pre-marital sex to be sinful. Parton did not try to live a life strictly avoiding sin. Parton's beliefs and independence defied established Christian norms.

Parton used her platform for the subordinate women who could not speak up for themselves. Parton stated, "I give them a way to say what they can't express: A wife can sing a country song–'Don't come home a-drinkin' with lovin' on your mind'–and give her husband a message he'd beat her for if she wasn't singing it; I say it for her."[66] She spoke the thoughts and feelings of subordinate women, who did not possess the agency to speak for themselves. Southern society expected women to not speak against men or to challenge them, but those women could sing along to Parton's song to express a message without fear of retaliation. Parton's outspoken nature differed from traditional Southern women.

Parton's desire to help her hometown exemplified that women took responsibility for the household. As the journalist Harrison observed about Parton, "sometimes, talking to her, you get the impression that she believed that, when she's happy, everybody in the Smokies is happy."[67] Parton placed an enormous amount of pressure on herself, but she felt like she needed to help the people from her hometown.[68] Parton put herself in charge of the welfare of eastern Tennessee: her home and her family. Parton's maternal instinct for her hometown reinforced that society believed women should take care of the home.

Parton's efforts to improve her hometown's poverty level complicated her image because she took care of her home, but she also showed her ambition.

Profits from the theme park, Dollywood, benefited the Dollywood Foundation.[69] Parton stated that "Dollywood is to see to the health of Sevier County, Tennessee, where I grew up, and is not only stimulatin' the economy but makin' sure the babies get born, the burn centers endowed."[70] Parton built a major tourist attraction in order to help the prosperity of her hometown, which complicated her womanhood. Her ambition and career boosted the economy and helped with the poverty numbers of her home. Parton's efforts to stimulate the economy provided society with an example of an ambitious woman but also a woman who took care of her home.

Parton's work on increasing literacy paralleled a common social norm, where women served as teachers. Parton's father could not read or write.[71] She also was the first in her family to graduate high school.[72] In order to entice the students to remain in school, The Dolly Parton Foundation made deals with eighth and ninth graders to team up in a buddy system. If they both graduate, each high school student receives one thousand dollars toward college.[73] Students could also reach out to the program hotline for support and encouragement during hard times.[74] Parton's advocacy decreased the dropout rate. Society considered teaching to be "pink collar" and woman's work. While not to diminish the importance of her philanthropic efforts, her choice to support literacy added to the idea that women should remain confined to specific careers.

Parton's lack of interest in politics supported the idea that politics were too dirty for women to be involved in. Parton stated, "I don't get involved in politics, unless it's to walk up to the governor and tell him we need a new road up to the hospital. I'm fulla shit enough without tryin' to get involved in politics."[75] Parton did not want to get twisted up in politics.[76] Connecting back to the private and public spheres, Parton stayed out of the political public sphere. Society expected women to stay in the private sphere in order to remain pure and to cleanse their husbands when they returned from the dirty public sphere. Parton just wanted to make sure that her home was taken care of. Parton's distaste for politics embodied pure women in the private sphere.

Parton's association with her hometown and her sense of independence reinforced and challenged Southern womanhood. Her independence shined when she overcame her family's past and helped others escape the poverty cycle that trapped people in the area. Parton's strong faith in Christianity stemmed from her childhood, but she made the religion into what she wanted. Her religious practices complicated her womanhood. Parton's advocacy for educational programs helped the literacy rate of eastern Tennessee but also fell in line with the belief that women needed to be confined to specific "pink-collar" jobs. Parton did not have any interest in going into the public sphere of politics as long as the government took care of her home. Parton's ties to her hometown, combined with her independent spirit, aligned and defied notions of Southern womanhood.

Anti-nuclear Homelife

"I think everybody should be allowed to be who they are and to love who they love."[77]

Parton's marriage to Carl Dean did not align with the ideal nuclear family. The nuclear family stood on the ideal that a man and a wife need to live together with their children all under one roof. Parton and Dean met on Parton's first day in Nashville at a laundromat. [78] Dean drove by to warn Parton that she would get sunburned standing outside for too long.[79] The couple married two years after the Army gave Dean a stint.[80] As time went on, he built a twenty-three-room house in Nashville and started his own asphalt paving company. Dean did not actively support his wife through public appearances or attending live shows, discouraging her independence. That discouragement did not discourage Parton from openly talking about her husband's feelings or private home matters. As Parton's career progressed, the two did not spend time together physically; Parton did not live with her husband on a regular basis. She and her husband did not want children, which challenged notions of women as child-bearers. Her independence did not hinder the monogamy of her marriage. Parton's independence challenged the patriarchal society that was in place. Parton's atypical marriage challenged the nuclear family.

Dean's lack of public support for his wife's career aligned with the typical rural Southern husband discouraging independence. According to Harrison, Parton's husband "has never been photographed with his famous wife and … has rarely seen her perform."[81] Furthermore, Dean did not like country music; he listened to hard rock, blues, and bluegrass.[82] In relation to Parton's acting career, she stated that Dean is "not a fan of mine. He respects me, but he's never liked any o' my movies."[83] Dean's lack of interest in Parton's career shows that he did not support her ambition or independence. He did not seem to be supportive of Parton's career. Dean, a rural Southern husband, disapproved of his wife's independence and career because Southern society defined womanhood as women's subordination to their husbands.

Parton was not afraid to discuss her private matters publicly, which demonstrated her independence. Parton described her husband as a little boy, who she loves to baby.[84] Parton then continued the conversation, "my husband knows it's okay to cry with me."[85] Parton did not speak in a reserved manner about her husband or their private life; she spoke openly and honestly. Men expected women to tolerate their emotional unavailability because of their dominance over them. Traditional Southern women tried not to give their husbands any trouble; they wanted to please people and not cause ripples. Parton did not follow that archetype. Parton's independence from her husband challenged the societal concept of a nuclear family.

Writers emasculated Dean and questioned his status as the breadwinner. Harrison described Carl Dean as a "reticent, stay-at-home" husband.[86] The term "stay-at-home" typically described women who took care of the household and family while the husband worked to provide for the family. This term does not accurately describe Dean because he held a job of his own and ran his own business. He wanted to be more than just Parton's husband; he wanted to make a name for himself too. Harrison delegitimized Dean's asphalt company and weakened his image because he lived a small-town life instead of the life of a celebrity's husband. Characterizing Dean as weak also meant that Parton's family did not, at least publicly, fit the typical mold of a strong patriarch and dependent wife.

Parton's marriage also challenged the nuclear family because of physical distance and financial independence. Parton owns two houses in addition to her home with her husband in Nashville: one in Bel-Air and one in New York's Central Park West.[87] Harrison wrote, "[when work allows] she is 'at home' in a twenty-three-room mansion that her husband" built near Nashville.[88] Harrison's choice to put "at home" in quotes showed that Harrison did not truly believe that the mansion is Parton's true home. Writers labeled her marriage as transgressive because Parton and her husband did not live with one another on a regular basis. The nuclear family needed two married parents living together under one roof. Parton and

Dean did not follow that standard by living separately most of the time. Parton and her husband did not live with one another, allowing for physical independence.

Parton and Dean's marriage involved an extreme amount of emotional independence. Parton stated, "what greater boredom can there be than when you're stuck in the face of someone you're supposed to love and obey?"[89] Society expected wives to obey and listen to their husbands, but Parton did not follow that expectation. She did not want to just obey her husband. Parton's marriage differed from the traditional Southern family because she did not consider herself subordinate to her husband and because they did not want to spend time together.

Parton might have favored her career over her family, and that uncertainty challenged the traditional image of a woman taking responsibility for the home first and then maybe having a job. Writer Karen Jaehne wrote that "it is work, not caprice, that governs her life (even more, one suspects, than the ties of affection and family bonding)."[90] The author suspected that Parton put more effort into her career than what she put into her family but could not know that for sure.[91] Southern society and the nuclear family model expected women to put the care of their households before any sort of career aspirations, and the journalist accused her of that because Parton traveled, lived, and worked without her husband. The simple assumption that Parton cared about her career more than her family did not support Southern womanhood.

Parton's lack of interest in having children did not align with nuclear family ideals. Harrison asked Parton about her family and potential children. Parton responded with, "my husband don't want children either; we're in perfect agreement."[92] When Parton did not seem interested in bearing her own children, Harrison noted, "perhaps because she mothered so many children [her nieces and nephews] for so long, she has no need and no wish, for children of her own."[93] Parton did not have an aching womb; she simply just did not want children. Parton did not feel that her duty as a woman included having children. Harrison tried to justify as to why Parton did not want children. Harrison's notation illustrated that society expected women to want and have children of their own. Parton did not want kids, which defied the societal norms of the nuclear family.

Parton's independence shined because she did not need society's approval on her marriage. Parton stated that "if people want to think I'm messin' around every night that's their business."[94] Parton did not deny extramarital affairs, but she said that she does not care what people think of her sexual actions. She did not care if people approved of her relationship. Mothers raised Southern women to care about how their peers view them.[95] This culture ingrained Southern women to please others and long for peer acceptance. Parton's lack of need for peer approval set her apart from other Southern women during this time.

Parton and her husband did not struggle with extramarital affairs even though they did not live with one another, which symbolized a nuclear household. In a conversation with a *Rolling Stone* author, Parton stated that "my husband likes the freedom as much as I do ... we're not afraid that one of us is gonna run off with somebody else."[96] Parton felt positive that her marriage would last.[97] She had no concern that her husband would cheat or have an affair with another person and visa versa.[98] Parton and Dean's trust in one another showed society an example of a healthy marriage.

Parton did not discourage advances from men other than her husband, which defied societal pressures to have a nuclear household. For example, Parton worked with country singer Merle Haggard during the late 1970s. Haggard told *People's Weekly* writer Dolly Carlisle that "he was smitten by the 'exceptional human being who lives underneath all that bunch of fluffy hair, fluttery eyelashes and super boobs.'"[99] Parton responded to Haggard's comments with the statement, "I didn't know whether to be embarrassed or flattered."[100] Parton's response did not shut down the flirtatious comment, but she also did not respond encouragingly. Southern society did not deem this flirtatious interaction as acceptable for married women because wives should not cause any trouble for their husbands. Parton's interactions with other men gave her husband reason to be upset and did not align with what a subordinate Southern woman should do.

Parton's marriage to Carl Dean did not align with the ideal nuclear family. Dean's asphalt paving company did not ensure his status as the dominant head of the household. Dean discouraged his wife's independence through a lack of public appearances. That discouragement did not hinder Parton from talking openly about her husband's feelings or private home matters. As Parton's career progressed, the two did not spend time together physically; Parton did not live with her husband on a regular basis. She and her husband did not want children, which challenged notions of women as child bearers. Her independence did not hinder the monogamy of her marriage. Parton's independence and disregard of the nuclear family challenged the society in place put forth by Southerners and feminists.

Sexual Expression

"It costs a lot of money to look this cheap!"[101]

Parton's openness about her sexuality challenged the Southern norms for white women and feminists. Parton wore clothes, shoes, makeup, and wigs that accentuated her body. One *Rolling Stone* author described Parton's external beauty: her "extraordinary body, alabaster skin and delicate features" in "skintight jeans and [a] ready-to-bust, low-cut sweater."[102] The writer also added that "the heels and wig add almost a foot" to her five-foot height."[103] Parton did not hide her hourglass figure; instead, she made sure to show her body off. Her tight clothes and low-cut tops made critics question her performance ability. Parton openly talked about her sexual desires and flirted, which increased the "dumb sexy blonde" stereotype that feminists advocated against. Parton's outward expression of her sexuality challenged the societal patriarchy.

Parton defied Southern norms by bringing progressive New York fashions down to the conservative South. Reporter Bruce Cook wrote about Parton's early career when she regularly performed at the Grand Ole Opry.[104] Cook stated that "the good ole boys nudged each other and snickered in recognition of her colossal shape." On the female side, Cook stated that "while the good ole girls may not have known much about New York fashions," they knew that Parton's clothes "were just a bit *declasse*."[105] Parton's clothing differed from Southern, conservative styles. Southern women did not dress sexually because they did not want to challenge their husbands' authority over them. Parton's immodest clothing pushed Southern society's understanding of sexually expressive women.

Parton's style caused critics to question her, which is why feminists did not approve of her sexual accentuation. A Ms magazine writer, Margo Jefferson, described how critics did not question Parton's talent, but instead questioned her appearance.[106] Jefferson quoted the questioning as "'but those clothes and wigs!' ... 'Do you think she knows how she looks?'"[107] Parton's critics did not approve of her appearance but did recognize her talent.[108] No matter how much talent Parton possessed, society wanted her to look and act a specific way. She dressed as an object of sexual desire, and the second-wave feminists discouraged this because this kind of behavior strengthened the "dumb sexy blonde" stereotype. Feminists believed that

that sexual stereotype made it hard for people to take Parton and other women seriously. Parton challenged norms put forth by feminists by her choice to accentuate her sexual features.

Parton's career ambitions convoluted the societal understanding of a woman who worked. Connie Berman of *Good Housekeeping* wrote when describing Parton, "and if in her towering wigs and outrageous outfits, she seems larger than life, so do her ambitions."[109] This quote demonstrated that society believed that women who accentuated their bodies could not have large goals. Women who flaunt their bodies are commonly assumed to be less ambitious than women who dress modestly. The fact that Parton dressed promiscuously and also wanted to be successful challenged social norms. Society only expected women as one or the other: immodest without goals or reserved and ambitious.

Both feminists and Southern society did not support Parton's flirtatious attitude. Harrison interviewed Parton and asked her why she touches people so much.[110] Parton responded to the questions with the statement: "Maybe some men think I'm a flirt, but if I'm a flirt, then I do flirt with everybody–men, women and children."[111] Harrison stated that "occasionally she [Parton] kneels at my feet; crouched before the sofa, she rests her hands on my knees, lightly caressing to emphasize a point. She likes to touch people."[112] Harrison's description sexualized a very innocent gesture: a slight touch on the knee. Subordinated Southern women would not have flirted with men other than their husbands, but Parton did engage in these activities. Feminists thought that the type of flirting that Parton engaged in led to the sexualization of women. Parton's flirtatious attitude fueled the sexualization of women and challenged her husband's dominant role.

Parton openly told people that she enjoyed sex, which Southern women usually steered away from. Although in the immediate wake of the sexual revolution of the 1960s, people openly talked about their sex lives more, but Southern culture did not embrace this sexual progression as fully because of women's subordinate role.[113] Parton stated, "I really like it, and I'm not ashamed to say it. I'm not gonna be hypocritical and say I just feel it now and then," in regard to sex ... "sex is an overwhelming emotion, haven't you noticed? Natural as breathing. I will say that if I feel the need to express any emotion, I'm gonna do it."[114] Parton openly described her sexual desires, which could have been troublesome for her husband. Parton's open expression about her sexual desires defied norms for Southern women.

Parton's actions led writers to compare her to other sex symbols. Harrison stated that Parton has "been compared to Mae West; she has also been compared to Marilyn Monroe."[115] Parton's status as a sex symbol came from characteristics and actions that she shared with West and Monroe: blonde hair, large breasts, and open sexual expression. Women are constantly compared to one another, which attested to the patriarchy that feminists tried to fight against. Parton's comparison to West and Monroe showed that her sexual expression added to what feminists tried to change.

Parton's sexual independence shined when she compared herself to a prostitute. Parton described herself as "a whore or a high-class prostitute, not even so much high-class, with the makeup and the bleached hair and the boobs and the tight-fittin' clothes and the high heels."[116] Parton knew that her persona made her seem like a woman who sold her body for sex.[117] Parton's description of herself shows that she knew how she seemed to the world and that she did not care how others thought of her. Traditional Southern women would not make statements like these in fear of their husband's retaliation, but Parton did not fear that. Parton's description of herself as a low-class prostitute showed her independence.

Parton's public nudity opposed societal notions for women. In an interview, Parton talked about the most outrageous thing she has ever done: publicly undressing.[118] Parton described when she went to dinner with friends and on the way back home completely undressed and walked on the road.[119] This act of public nudity showed that she felt confident enough to show her entire body. Southern women would not engage in actions such as this because sexual expression could be viewed as a threat against their husbands. Parton engaged in public nudity and showed her sexual confidence.

Parton's sexuality shined when she posed for the pornographic magazine: *Playboy*.[120] *Playboy* appealed to the sexual desires of men through soft pornographic magazines. The sole fact that Parton posed for *Playboy* threatened her status as a wife because of the level of promiscuity. Known for nudity and minimal clothing, *Playboy* clothed Parton in a black bodysuit and bunny accessories.[121] Her shoot differed from traditional magazine shoots because Parton dressed relatively reserved. *Playboy* also added a man in a full-body rabbit suit into the photo shoot, who stood behind Parton in the photographs in a "catcall ready" position.[122] This positioning increased sexualization because it made Parton an object of desire for the male rabbit and other men. This shoot, a great example of her nuanced persona, showed how she paved her own way but not to the point of ruining her career; she fulfilled the obligation for celebrities to be sexy and sell fantasy while also dressing relatively modestly. Parton's posing for *Playboy* defied societal norms for Southern women and other *Playboy* models.

Parton's openness about her sexuality challenged the Southern norms for white women and feminists. Parton's accentuation of her body and open sexual tendencies increased the "dumb sexy blonde" stereotype that feminists advocated against. Additionally, Parton's sexuality differed from Southern norms because women tried not to upset their husbands. Parton's expression of her sexuality challenged societal patriarchy.

Conclusion

Parton dually challenged and reinforced the patriarchy established by Southern society through her regional representation, her atypical family, and her open sexuality during the 1970s and 1980s. Parton used her fame and status to bring attention to the Smoky Mountains of rural Appalachia. Parton's marriage to Dean challenged and supported the nuclear family. Parton's openness about her sexuality challenged the Southern norms for white women and feminists. Parton's career aligned and also defied standards set by Southern society and second-wave feminists.

Parton spearheaded individualism throughout her career and inspired other women. Society expected Southern women to obey the patriarchy. Women did not try to increase their freedom for fear of retribution from their husbands. Parton's life showed society that a woman could be independent. Second-wave feminists wanted more equality but only fought for white middle-class women who acted respectfully. Parton showed that women can be individualistic and challenge feminine norms. Parton's reinforcement and challenge of Southern white womanhood paved the way for other women to do the same.

Notes

1. "Dolly Parton," *Rolling Stone*, December 11, 1980, 39–43.
2. "Dolly Parton," 39–43.
3. "Dolly Parton," 39–43.
4. "Dolly Parton," 39–43.
5. "Dolly Parton," 39–43.
6. "Dolly Parton," 39–43.
7. "Dolly Parton," 39–43.
8. Barbara Frit Harrison, "Other Dolly Parton," *McCall's* 108, no. 1–6 (February 1981): 56–118.
9. Harrison, "Other Dolly Parton," 56–118.
10. Harrison, "Other Dolly Parton," 56–118.
11. Harrison, "Other Dolly Parton," 56–118.
12. Harrison, "Other Dolly Parton," 56–118.
13. Harrison, "Other Dolly Parton," 56–118.
14. Harrison, "Other Dolly Parton," 56–118.
15. Harrison, "Other Dolly Parton," 56–118.
16. Harrison, "Other Dolly Parton," 56–118.
17. Harrison, "Other Dolly Parton," 56–118.
18. Harrison, "Other Dolly Parton," 56–118.
19. Graham Hoppe, "Icon and Identity: Dolly Parton's Hillbilly Appeal," *Southern Cultures* 23, no. 1 (2017): 49–62, www.jstor.org/stable/26391677.
20. Hoppe, "Icon and Identity," 49–62.
21. Nadine Hubbs, "'Jolene,' Genre, and the Everyday Homoerotics of Country Music: Dolly Parton's Loving Address of the Other Woman," *Women & Music* 19, (2015): 71–76, 211.
22. Pamela Wilson, "Mountains of Contradictions: Gender, Class, and Region in the Star Image of Dolly Parton," *The South Atlantic Quarterly* 94, no. 1–2 (January 1998): 109–134.
23. Hoppe, "Icon and Identity," 49–62.
24. Hoppe, "Icon and Identity," 49–62.
25. Hoppe, "Icon and Identity," 49–62.
26. Hoppe, "Icon and Identity," 49–62.
27. Hoppe, "Icon and Identity," 49–62.
28. Hoppe, "Icon and Identity," 49–62.
29. Hoppe, "Icon and Identity," 49–62.
30. Hubbs, "'Jolene,' Genre, and the Everyday Homoerotics of Country Music," 71–76.
31. Hubbs, "'Jolene,' Genre, and the Everyday Homoerotics of Country Music," 71–76.
32. Hubbs, "'Jolene,' Genre, and the Everyday Homoerotics of Country Music," 71–76.
33. Hubbs, "'Jolene,' Genre, and the Everyday Homoerotics of Country Music," 71–76.

34. Hubbs, "'Jolene,' Genre, and the Everyday Homoerotics of Country Music," 71–76.

35. Hubbs, "'Jolene,' Genre, and the Everyday Homoerotics of Country Music," 71–76.

36. Wilson, "Mountains of Contradictions," 109–134.

37. Wilson, "Mountains of Contradictions," 109–134.

38. Wilson, "Mountains of Contradictions," 109–134.

39. Wilson, "Mountains of Contradictions," 109–134.

40. Daphne V. Wyse, "To Better Serve and Sustain the South: How Nineteenth-Century Domestic Novelists Supported Southern Patriarchy Using the 'Cult of True Womanhood' and the Written Word" (master's thesis, Buffalo State College, 2012), https://digitalcommons.buffalostate.edu/cgi/viewcontent.cgi?article=1007&context=history_theses.

41. Cynthia A. Kierner, "Hospitality, Sociability, and Gender in the Southern Colonies," *Journal of Southern History* 62, no. 3 (1996): 449–480, http://doi.org/10.2307/2211499.

42. Florence King, *Southern Ladies and Gentlemen* (New York: St. Martin's Press, 1975).

43. Marilyn Schwartz, *The Southern Belle Primer: Or Why Princess Margaret Will Never Be a Kappa Kappa Gamma* (New York: Main Street Books, 1991).

44. Jane Sherron De Hart, "Second Wave Feminism(s) and the South," in *Women of the American South: A Multicultural Reader*, ed. Farnham (New York: New York University Press), 275–279.

45. De Hart, "Second Wave Feminism(s) and the South," 275–279.

46. *Encyclopaedia Britannica*, s.v. "Feminism: The Second Wave of Feminism," accessed March 5, 2020, https://www.britannica.com/topic/feminism.

47. *Encyclopaedia Britannica*, "Feminism: The Second Wave of Feminism."

48. *Encyclopaedia Britannica*, "Feminism: The Second Wave of Feminism."

49. *Encyclopaedia Britannica*, "Feminism: The Second Wave of Feminism."

50. *Encyclopaedia Britannica*, "Feminism: The Second Wave of Feminism."

51. *Encyclopaedia Britannica*, "Feminism: The Second Wave of Feminism."

52. Dolly Parton (@DollyParton), Twitter post, Jun 20, 2014, 11:48 a.m., https://twitter.com/DollyParton/status/480014214715944960.

53. Connie Berman, "Dolly Parton Scrapbook," *Good Housekeeping*, 1979, 140–143.

54. Harrison, "Other Dolly Parton," 56–118.

55. Bruce Cook, "Dolly Parton Goes Pop," *The New Leader* 61, no. 1–13 (1978): 29–30.

56. Frederic A. Birmingham, "Dolly Parton: A Basket of Orchids," *Saturday Evening Post*, September 1979, 66–69.

57. Cook, "Dolly Parton Goes Pop," 29–30.

58. "Dolly Parton," 39–43.

59. Berman, "Dolly Parton Scrapbook," 140–143.

60. Berman, "Dolly Parton Scrapbook," 140–143.

61. Harrison, "Other Dolly Parton," 56–118.

62. Harrison, "Other Dolly Parton," 56–118.

63. Birmingham, "Dolly Parton: A Basket of Orchids," 66–69.

64. Birmingham, "Dolly Parton: A Basket of Orchids," 66–69.

65. Harrison, "Other Dolly Parton," 56–118.

66. Harrison, "Other Dolly Parton," 56–118.

67. Harrison, "Other Dolly Parton," 56–118.

68. Harrison, "Other Dolly Parton," 56–118.

69. Karen Jaehne, "Parton's Such Sweet Sorrow: The Quotable Dolly," *Film Comment* 25, no. 5 (1989): 62–63, www.jstor.org/stable/43453456.

70. Jaehne, "Parton's Such Sweet Sorrow," 62–63.

71. Harrison, "Other Dolly Parton," 56–118.

72. Harrison, "Other Dolly Parton," 56–118.

73. Jaehne, "Parton's Such Sweet Sorrow," 62–63.

74. Jaehne, "Parton's Such Sweet Sorrow," 62–63.

75. Jaehne, "Parton's Such Sweet Sorrow," 62–63.

76. Jaehne, "Parton's Such Sweet Sorrow," 62–63.

77. Greg Hernandez, "Dolly Parton on Her Gay Following: 'I Think Everybody Should Be Allowed to Be Who They Are, and to Love Who They Love'," *Greg In Hollywood*, October 25, 2014, http://greginhollywood.com/dolly-parton-on-her-gay-following-i-think-everybody-should-be-allowed-to-be-who-they-are-and-to-love-who-they-love-107290.

78. Sarah Kettler, "Inside Dolly Parton's Private Marriage to Carl Dean," *Biography*, November 7, 2019, https://www.biography.com/news/dolly-parton-carl-dean-marriage-relationship-secretive; Jaehne, "Parton's Such Sweet Sorrow," 62–63.

79. Jaehne, "Parton's Such Sweet Sorrow," 62–63.

80. Harrison, "Other Dolly Parton," 56–118.

81. Harrison, "Other Dolly Parton," 56–118.

82. Jaehne, "Parton's Such Sweet Sorrow," 62–63.

83. Jaehne, "Parton's Such Sweet Sorrow," 62–63.

84. Harrison, "Other Dolly Parton," 56–118.

85. Harrison, "Other Dolly Parton," 56–118.

86. Harrison, "Other Dolly Parton," 56–118.

87. Harrison, "Other Dolly Parton," 56–118.

88. Harrison, "Other Dolly Parton," 56–118.

89. Harrison, "Other Dolly Parton," 56–118.

90. Jaehne, "Parton's Such Sweet Sorrow," 62–63.

91. Jaehne, "Parton's Such Sweet Sorrow," 62–63.

92. Harrison, "Other Dolly Parton," 56–118.

93. Harrison, "Other Dolly Parton," 56–118.

94. Harrison, "Other Dolly Parton," 56–118.

95. Schwartz, *The Southern Belle Primer*.

96. "Dolly Parton," 39–43.

97. "Dolly Parton," 39–43.

98. "Dolly Parton," 39–43.

99. Dolly Carlisle, "What are Merle Haggard's favorite memories? Not San Quentin, but His crush on Dolly Parton," *People Weekly*, November 23, 1981, 137–138.

100. Carlisle, "What are Merle Haggard's favorite memories?"

101. Dolly Parton (@DollyParton), Twitter post, July 13, 2011, 8:43 p.m., https://twitter.com/DollyParton/status/91306847855853568.

102. "Dolly Parton," 39–43.

103. "Dolly Parton," 39–43.

104. Cook, "Dolly Parton Goes Pop," 29–30.

105. Cook, "Dolly Parton Goes Pop," 29–30.

106. Margo Jefferson, "Dolly Parton: Bewigged, Bespangled ... and Proud," Ms 7, no. 1–6 (June 1979): 14–24, https://vt.hosts.atlas-sys.com/illiad/illiad.dll?Action=10&Form=75&Value=1521409.

107. Jefferson, "Dolly Parton: Bewigged, Bespangled."

108. Jefferson, "Dolly Parton: Bewigged, Bespangled."

109. Berman, "Dolly Parton Scrapbook," 140–143.

110. Harrison, "Other Dolly Parton," 56–118.

111. Harrison, "Other Dolly Parton," 56–118.

112. Harrison, "Other Dolly Parton," 56–118.

113. King, *The Florence King Reader*.

114. Harrison, "Other Dolly Parton," 56–118.

115. Harrison, "Other Dolly Parton," 56–118.

116. "Dolly Parton," 39–43.

117. "Dolly Parton," 39–43.

118. "Dolly Parton," 39–43.

119. "Dolly Parton," 39–43.

120. Tara McGinley, "That Time in 1978 When Dolly Parton Posed for Playboy with a Super Pervy-Looking Bunny," *Dangerous Minds*, April 4, 2016, https://dangerousminds.net/comments/that_time_in_1978_when_dolly_parton_posed_for_playboy_with_a_super_pervy-lo.

121. "Dolly Parton Playboy Cover," *Playboy*.

122. McGinley, "That Time in 1978 When Dolly Parton Posed for Playboy with a Super Pervy-Looking Bunny."

14. Keepin' It Movin': Appalachian Women's Resistance Through Music

KAT MCGOWAN

As a child, I remember making blackberry pies with my Nana, Joyce Gibbs, mesmerized by her rich, deep accent. Her beautiful working hands, always manicured, rolled out the pie dough onto a bed of porcelain flour. Her hands showed no traces of the factory work she performed for numerous years. Her hands showed no burns from touching scorching nylon, no callouses from the gardening work she loves doing so dearly, and her knees show no scars from growing up in the deep country woods. Gibbs never skipped a day doing her hair and makeup; her classic beauty is highlighted in her age.

In 2019 I sat down with Gibbs and recorded an interview about her experiences as a woman in Appalachia. She was married at age seventeen and had my mother at age eighteen. When my mom was twelve, Gibbs went through a divorce due to her husband's infidelity, which she described as an "isolating experience." I asked her if she considered herself a feminist, and she responded, "oh lord! No!" I laughed and asked her, "why not?" She told me that she just never thought about it. My Nana is an Appalachian woman through and through; she is a "pearl-clutching," God-loving woman from the Virginia and North Carolina border. In almost the same breath, when discussing some of the men in her life, she said, "men think we are their slaves, if you ever are dating a man who is drunk, violent, or cheats, you better run girl!" Gibbs and I bonded over a shared love of country music, and many of the songs I have chosen to discuss, in this chapter, were presented to me through Gibbs' remarkable life as a mother, wife, factory worker, and woman. In return, I dedicate this chapter to her, and all the women like her, to honor and give voice to their lives and experiences as unique and hardworking women.

For generations, Appalachian women have found solace in music. Appalachia has a long-standing revolutionary and political undercurrent, such as the musical protests against a series of mountain top removals in the 1980s and 1990s.[1] Many women found themselves unable to push back against their oppressions because of numerous factors including poverty, internalized sexism, and fear of becoming social pariahs.[2] Women, like Hazel Dickens, who wrote songs that directly address labor exploitation and feminism left a huge mark as the first frontwomen of the bluegrass and folk music scene.[3] Black women, who are often left out in discussions surrounding Appalachian music, also often used music as a poignant way to express identity, oppression, and emotion in a more direct and soulful way.[4] Music offered a form of acceptable resistance and gave many women a sense of catharsis, knowing that others could relate to the same things they experience.

The conversation surrounding Southern women is often oversimplified in that there is a lack of understanding of how these women saw and explored the world. Society used to value traditional roles, kept by men and women alike. Most people believed that women should maintain certain qualities of femininity and traditional gender roles of labor in the private sphere. However, many women simply desired to be respected for their jobs and acknowledged as an important part of the public sphere. Many of these women would likely not label themselves feminist, as they were often excluded and demonized by second-wave feminists on the basis of sexuality, race, and class.[5] Further, second-wave feminism was a middle-class phenomenon that mostly comprised of women who had free time. In the 1970s, there were many Southern feminist groups, such as the Atlanta Freedom for Movement Girls – Now organization.[6] However, most women instead focused on labor organization and demands, like at the Southern Women's Coal Miners Conference.[7]

Women play a huge and important role in country music, which I will be exploring in this chapter. Many historians have previously written about Appalachian women's resistance, as well as Appalachian music, but there are not very many writings on the two of these studies combined. This chapter will help bridge that gap by focusing specifically on musical impacts associated with passive and active resistance.

In this chapter, I will use songs and their lyrics to analyze their musical and social appeal. I will answer the following question: how did music serve as a form of resistance for women? To answer this question, I will look at song lyrics as well as the song's elements like rhythm, chords, dynamics, and cadence. I will also use magazine articles, music charts, interviews, labor conference notes, and records of popularity or dissent to paint a whole picture of Appalachian women's music from 1950 through 1980. I will argue that Appalachian women musicians and songwriters used music as a cathartic release from their everyday lived experiences, as well as a form of resistance from their oppressions; this music can be broken up into three categories: social justice, heartbreak ballads, and labor rights.

Social Issues and Music

Popular ideas surrounding Southern womanhood and country music starlets indicate that the public pictured these women as docile, dependent, and submissive.[8] However, when taking a deep dive into these women's lives, attitudes, and lyricism, a completely different and nuanced story is told. Women in country music pushed the envelope on what is appropriate to say and do, as well as making bold choices, with an appearance in fashion, all while balancing a positive public image.

"Harper Valley P.T.A." by Jeannie C. Riley is a perfect example of women expressing the frustration that they have with the strict social and cultural rules placed on them by their conservative communities. Riley released "Harper Valley P.T.A." in August 1968, and its "radical" message generated a sizable public reaction. The lyrics reveal a culture of judgment and the marginalization of women who do not follow strict social orders:

> I wanna tell you all the story 'bout
> A Harper Valley widowed wife
> Who had a teenage daughter
> Who attended Harper Valley Junior High
> Well, her daughter came home one afternoon
> And didn't even stop to play
> And she said, "mom, I got a note here from the Harper Valley P.T.A."
> Well, the note said, "Mrs. Johnson
> You're wearin' your dresses way too high
> It's reported you've been drinking
> And a-running 'round with men and goin' wild
> And we don't believe you oughta be a-bringin' up
> Your little girl this way"

And it was signed by the Secretary
Harper Valley P.T.A.[9]

These lyrics flesh out the type of judgment women experienced from other women, who they may or may not have regularly interacted with. While the lyrics discuss exclusion based on activities and appearance, they also reveal strict social codes women were expected to abide by, codes that were fueled by internalized sexism.

Apparent by its tremendous success, which would not be matched again until Dolly Parton's "9 to 5," "Harper Valley P.T.A." took the number one slot on the Billboard country and pop charts in September and October of 1968.[10] Many people related to the song, so much so that Dolly Parton covered the song in 1969.[11] Additionally, there was a sequel called "Return to Harper Valley" written and performed on Nashville Now in 1984,[12] later a film was made starring Barbara Eden in 1978,[13] and in 1981 "Harper Valley P.T.A." was made into a TV series.[14] The consistent revitalization of the song and its message demonstrates the popularity and excitement generated by the song's groundbreaking message.

This song is an explicit strike on internalized sexism in small Southern towns. The song constituted a "radical fight against the establishment"[15] in its message about women's freedom to express themselves the way they wanted to, including sporting mini-skirts and socializing with men. At the same time, it called out hypocritical messages about the scrutiny women faced in daily life.

Well, it happened that the P.T.A. was gonna meet
That very afternoon
And they were sure surprised
When Mrs. Johnson wore her miniskirt into the room
And as she walked up to the blackboard
I can still recall the words she had to say
She said, "I'd like to address this meeting of the Harper Valley P.T.A.
Well, there's Bobby Taylor sittin' there
And seven times he's asked me for a date
And Mrs. Taylor sure seems to use a lotta ice
Whenever he's away
And Mr. Baker can you tell us why

Your secretary had to leave this town?
And shouldn't widow Jones be told to keep
Her window shades all pulled completely down
Well, Mr. Harper couldn't be here
'Cause he stayed too long at Kelly's Bar again
And if you smell Shirley Thompson's breath
You'll find she's had a little nip of gin
And then you have the nerve to tell me
You think that as a mother I'm not fit
Well, this is just a little Peyton Place
And you're all Harper Valley hypocrites"
No, I wouldn't put you on because it really did
It happened just this way
The day my mama socked it to the Harper Valley P.T.A.
The day my mama socked it to the Harper Valley P.T.A.[16]

The song creates an image of a strong woman confronting her bullies in a way that society would not have deemed as socially acceptable for the time. Women were expected to give into restrictions on behavior and appearance. "Harper Valley P.T.A." does the opposite and instead uses the frustration many women had towards social standards as fuel to create a nationwide hit.

While the song skyrocketed Riley into stardom, it was met with some pushback. Riley received letters claiming that she was trying to ruin the reputation of the P.T.A. [17] In interviews, Tom C. Hall, the writer of the song, claims the song is about a true story from his childhood in Olive Hill, Kentucky. He said that his single mom was a "free spirit" who challenged his small town's social conventions. She too showed up at a P.T.A. meeting and berated the members for their "indiscretions" and hypocrisy. As a boy of nine or ten, Hall was impressed.[18]

It is important to note that Hall specifically wanted Riley to sing the song because of her bold outward appearance for the time. Riley often wore miniskirts, deviating away from the more traditional clothing associated with 1960s country music. However, Riley quickly defended her reputation in 1984 during a *Nashville Now* interview about "Harper Valley P.T.A." and its sequel, insisting that she is "right of center" when asked about her political leanings.[19] This is an example of the fine line women in country music had to walk, given their conservative-leaning audiences. In other words, Riley did not want to risk her fan base by associating with the left-wing.

Tanya Tucker's 1975 hit, "I Believe the South Is Gonna Rise Again" is another example of country music hosting a message for social change. The title of the song uses a Southern pride tagline[20] with racist implications derived from the fight to uphold American slavery during the Civil War. However, the song is instead used to send a hopeful message about the liberation of all Southern people. "I Believe the South Is Gonna Rise Again" is one of the first hit songs in the region written by a white person to explicitly address the American racial divide.

> Our neighbors in the big house called us redneck
> 'Cause we lived in a poor share-croppers shack
> The Jacksons down the road were poor like we were
> But our skin was white and theirs was black
> But I believe the south is gonna rise again
> But not the way we thought it would back then
> I mean everybody hand in hand
> I believe the south is gonna rise again.[21]

The lyrics specifically discuss race and class in the first stanza, immediately allowing the listener to understand the message of progress towards racial and economic equality. Tucker's song is groundbreaking in its explicit anti-racist message in the country genre.

Bobby Braddock, the songwriter behind "I Believe the South is Gonna Rise Again," sums up his views of racial tensions in the South: "things are both better and worse than I thought they would be. In many ways, there is a familiarity between Southern whites and blacks, far more intimate than the relationships between the races in other regions."[22] This is likely due to class solidarity that exists in the Appalachian region. He continues, "yet, there is an underlying prejudice so embedded that it will take more than a few laws and a generation to erase."[23] Braddock acknowledged the deep-rooted systemic racism that exists in the South. He gave an example of how these prejudices appear, "today, few self-respecting white Southerners will overtly display race prejudice when blacks are around, but many will still use the word, 'n****r' behind their backs."[24] Race-relations in the South are a nuanced topic, and racial tension is often revealed in the privacy of people's homes or only amongst like-minded racist individuals.

This interview shows that there was a group of white Southerners who understood the depth of racial tensions and an audience of supporters large enough to make this song a chart-topping hit.[25] This song shows a brave optimism in the discussion of class solidarity and hope for eventual equality in the South.

The South is an area of diverse political and social views and cannot be generalized. There are many different kinds of people with a variety of experiences that influence their outlook on the world. To this end, many women songwriters began battling against the conventions designed to hold them back and prevent them from expressing their views and opinions.

Ballads of Resistance and Heartbreak

While explicit messages about gender and race appear in country music, many women artists preferred to express emotions and issues they face in love and relationships through heartbreak ballads. These women often sang about the pain they experienced at the hands of disloyal or unsupportive partners. Their messages often involve infidelity, drinking, absent partners, disproportionate workloads, and even abuse. The songs offered artists a catharsis from these oppressive forces while allowing listeners to experience solidarity amongst the numerous women who face similar oppression. Heartbreak anthems helped women feel supported in their own heartbreak.

Women were not willing to take all the blame for problems such as post-war delinquency and problems faced in the home. The earliest recorded song in this chapter is "It Wasn't God Who Made Honky Tonk Angels," written by budding star Kitty Wells in 1952.[26] I chose to discuss this song because of the immense controversy surrounding the track. The song is a response to Hank Thompson's "The Wild Side of Life" (1952),[27] written about women who chose social life over marriage. During the post-war era, American divorce rates were at an all-time high. It was presumed that "drinking and delinquency" rose among women, and many Americans blamed this on women abandoning their place in the home.[28] Those sentiments are apparent in the song's lyrics:

I didn't know God made Honky Tonk angels
I might have known you'd never make a wife
You gave up the only one that ever loved you
And went back to the wild side of life
The glamor of the gay nightlife has lured you
To the places where the wine and liquor flow
Where you wait to be anybody's baby
And forget the truest love you'll ever know.[29]

"The Wild Side of Life" captures the anger many men had with women who broke away from the traditional roles prescribed to them. Wells wrote "It Wasn't God Who Made Honky Tonk Angels" as a direct response to Thompson's song. Her song is told from a woman's perspective, explicitly shifting the blame away from women and putting it in the hands of men who mistreat women to the point where they give up on love and go to the "honky tonks" for satisfaction:

As I sit here tonight, the jukebox playin'
The tune about the wild side of life
As I listen to the words you are sayin'
It brings memories when I was a trusting wife
It wasn't God who made honky tonk angels
As you said in the words of your song
Too many times married men
Think they're still single
That has caused many a good girl to go wrong.[30]

The opening lyrics of this song, as well as the first line of the chorus, directly call out Thompson's track. In addition, Wells uses the exact chord progression and tune of "The Wild Side of Life." There is no mistaking who this song is directed to. The song continues:

It's a shame that all the blame is on us women
It's not true that only you men feel the same
From the start
Most every heart that's ever broken
Was because there always was a man to blame.[31]

"It Wasn't God Who Made Honky Tonk Women" was subject to controversy and contradictions surrounding its success. Due to the explicit message of this song, two major staples of country music, NBC Radio as well as The Grand Ole Opry, banned it.[32] This was likely because men heavily controlled both platforms. Despite this ban, the song made the number one spot on the Billboard country charts and maintained this position for six weeks. Two main factors are attributed to the sustained success of the song, despite attempts to limit its growth: the fascination with the drama surrounding the song, and the closeted support of listeners, specifically women.

Wells later stated that she was not a feminist but a housewife and mother who wanted to tell her truth. Loretta Lynn spoke about the song stating, "I thought, 'Gee, here the women are starting to sing! I think with that song she touched in me what I was living and what I was going through and I knew there were a lot of women that lived like me.' I thought, 'Here's a woman telling our point of view in everyday life.'"[33] The song spoke to what many women experienced in their own lives and offered a sense of solidarity amongst Appalachian women.

Loretta Lynn also wrote a song that generated controversy with her 1975 hit, "The Pill."[34] This is another song spoken from a woman's perspective about the newly widespread availability of the birth control pill. The birth control pill itself received much of the blame for the sexual revolution in the 1960s and 1970s. Many people attributed the rise of the pill to the rise of sexual promiscuity, single motherhood, babies born out of wedlock, and loosened morals of the youth.[35] Loretta Lynn's song, in contrast, speaks to why so many women felt excited over the newfound freedom, control, and autonomy of their reproductive health:

> You wined me and dined me
> When I was your girl
> Promised if I'd be your wife
> You'd show me the world
> But all I've seen of this old world
> Is a bed and a doctor bill
> I'm tearin' down your brooder house
> 'Cause now I've got the pill
> All these years I've stayed at home
> While you had all your fun

And every year that's gone by
Another baby's come
There's a gonna be some changes made
Right here on nursery hill
You've set this chicken your last time
'Cause now I've got the pill.

Later in the song, Lynn reveals what she will do with her new freedom. She talks about how she plans on wearing "miniskirts, hot pants, and a few little fancy frills / yeah I'm makin' up for all those years since I've got the pill!"[36] This attitude revealed a newfound liberation for many women. They regained control of their bodily autonomy and had the freedom to control the direction of their futures.

While this song achieved success, the success multiplied over the years as the song grew in popularity. However, Lynn received a large amount of push back, including bans on the song from over sixty radio stations, from Tulsa to Boston.[37] A 1975 article in *People* magazine by Robert Windeler titled "Loretta Lynn's 'Pill' Is Hard for Some Fans to Swallow" explains that "through word of mouth and the FM underground 'The Pill' is selling fifteen thousand copies a week. For Loretta Lynn, the most honored woman in country music, it is her biggest hit ever."[38] The reaction "The Pill" faced was very similar to the one "It Wasn't God Who Made Honky Tonk Women" faced years earlier. When songs pushed the envelope farther than deemed appropriate, male-controlled radio stations suppressed them in an effort to prevent the spread of those ideas. Nevertheless, interest in these messages seemed to grow.

Loretta Lynn's discography is full of songs about blue-collar women and their struggles due to men, class, and family. Windeler claims, "The Pill is also a milestone in Loretta's career as the poet laureate of blue-collar women—those who marry young and get pregnant often. In the songs she writes and those that are written for her, Loretta speaks to these unliberated, work-worn American females, and this time she's pushing oral contraceptives."[39] Lynn is quoted saying that, "My mama's just sorry she didn't have the pill so she wouldn't have had eight of us to feed."[40] Speaking to the message of the track, Lynn explained that women, like her mother, would have benefited from birth control and would have had more expendable money to potentially escape from the cycle of poverty.

Lynn believes in accessible birth control and the right for women to control when to have children and how many they will have. She also pointed out the pill's ability to affect the behavior of men. The article further relays Lynn's defense of the song, "It's just a wife arguin' with her husband," she says, "The wife is sayin', 'You've kept me barefoot and pregnant all these years while you've been slippin' around. Now you straighten out or I'll start, now that I have the pill.'" Loretta was upset that her record riled people up: "Why," she reasoned, "it's a husband and wife, not two unmarried people, so that's not dirty." In addition, she spoke to her own experiences as a wife and mother, "if I'd had the pill back when I was havin' babies I'd have taken 'em like popcorn. The pill is good for people. I wouldn't trade my kids for anyone. But I wouldn't necessarily have had six and I sure would have spaced 'em better."[41] Loretta Lynn stands her ground on the issue and continues to support accessible birth control.[42]

While these two songs are explicit in their message, other popular songs spoke more subtly to the experiences Appalachian women faced with heartbreak and mistreatment. These songs did not receive the same pushback that "The Pill" and "It Wasn't God Who Made Honky Tonk Angels" did. However, "Crazy" by Patsy Cline and "Midnight Train To Georgia" by Gladys Knight and The Pips are great examples of successful heartbreak anthems.

While many songs discussed specific oppressions that women faced, others used ballads to express deep emotions surrounding heartbreak and relationships, especially failed relationships. "Crazy," recorded by Patsy Cline, was a 1961 hit song written by Willie Nelson.[43] The song is about a woman who felt like she was crazy for feeling heartbroken after her lover left her for another woman. This song appealed to many women who felt foolish or "crazy" after their husbands or boyfriends left for another woman:

> Crazy, I'm crazy for feeling so lonely
> I'm crazy, crazy for feeling so blue
> I knew you'd love me as long as you wanted
> And then someday you'd leave me for somebody new
> Worry, why do I let myself worry?
> Wondering what in the world did I do?
> Crazy for thinking that my love could hold you

I'm crazy for trying and crazy for crying
And I'm crazy for loving you.

Cline reportedly did not like singing vulnerable heartbreak ballads, but record producer Owen Bradley wanted her to continue to sing songs about mistreatment and heartbreak. These types of songs sold the most copies because women could relate to them.[44] The immense popularity of heartbreak ballads amongst women demonstrates some common experiences women lived through.

The musical arrangement of "Crazy" was complicated and used chord progressions outside of the typical country progressions of the time. Paul Kingsbury, a music historian at the Country Music Hall of Fame and Museum, explains, "instead of the usual three or four chords that were just major chords and sevenths, he was writing 'Crazy' with jazzy minor sevenths, major sevenths, minors. If you count the chords, there are about seven chords in 'Crazy,' very different for a country song at the time."[45] These elements made "Crazy" a genre-bending hit that had a solemn and heartbroken sound, so much so that it served as a pivotal turning point for country heartbreak ballads in the future.[46]

"Midnight Train To Georgia" by Gladys Knight and The Pips is different from other songs in this chapter, as it is not a part of the country genre but instead soul. Buddah Records released the song in 1973, and it became a huge national hit, eventually winning a Grammy.[47] The song is about a woman who migrated to Georgia after her partner's dreams failed to come into fruition in Los Angeles.

He's leavin' (leavin')
On that midnight train to Georgia
(Leavin' on the midnight train)
Yeah, said he's goin' back
(Goin' back to find)
To a simpler place in time
(Whenever he takes that ride) oh yes he is
(Guess who's gonna be right by his side)
And I'll be with him (I know you will)
On that midnight train to Georgia
(Leavin' on the midnight train to Georgia)

I'd rather live in his world (live in his world)
Than live without him in mine.[48]

For black American women, the song resonated with a long tradition of migration. According to writer Lindsay Johnson, "while many women in the early decades of the century waited at home for their wandering men, women moved with their families to Northern cities in hopes of economic betterment during the Great Migration following World War I." She continues:

> These decades of black migration reveal complex patterns of out-migration from the South, often in cyclical waves as portions of an extended family moved north or west and back again, though with an overall trend towards moving out of the South. It was not until the 1970s that the South experienced a net increase of African Americans as migration patterns reversed. Black families began to move back to the South, typically joining extended family members still residing there.[49]

Johnson's analysis of "Midnight Train to Georgia" suggests that to understand the song completely, a listener needs to understand the history of migration of black women intersected with gender dynamics. While Jim Weatherly, the writer of the song, based it off of a conversation he had with Farrah Faucet about Lee Majors' "Midnight Flight to Houston,"[50] Gladys Knight wanted to change the location and means of transportation to better fit her experiences as a black woman.[51] Johnson explains:

> The history of 'Midnight Train' is unusual; originally conceived as a country-western song, it was recorded first on acoustic guitar with white male vocals, then by Cissy Houston as an R&B song with strong country-western elements (such as a harmonica playing 'Tara's Theme' from Gone With the Wind), and then recorded again by Gladys Knight in an entirely R&B version.[52]

The evolution of this song created a more authentic track for Gladys Knight and The Pips, which made the message more meaningful.

Gender dynamics are very prevalent in "Midnight Train to Georgia." The speaker of the song picked up her life and moved for her partner because his dreams did not work out. The track catch line at the end of the chorus, "I'd rather live in his world, than be without him in mine,"[53] reveals a complex obligation for women to put their dreams aside for the comfort of the man they are with. This obligation was and often still is deeply felt by women, making it a popular crossover hit.

Southern women employed several different tactics to achieve the goals for each of their individual songs. Whether they used explicit and direct lyrics or appealed mostly to emotion, they all used musical expression to relate to their audiences. Listeners likely felt a deep resonance with these songs as they discuss common experiences women face in the realm of control over their bodies, infidelity, heartbreak, and migration. These songs linked the audiences to the performers and created a feeling of solidarity and catharsis for many women experiencing similar circumstances.

Resistance to Labor Exploitation

Appalachia has a very rich labor history, with a long record of class struggle and fights for labor rights. It is also the birthplace of the American labor union.[54] With this long history of revolutionary labor identity, it makes sense that labor would come up as a popular topic in country music. Southern society often expected women to play dual roles: laborers in the private and public sphere. This is because as there were, and still are, high rates of poverty in the Appalachian region. Due to this phenomenon, women performed varying types of labor such as secretarial work, housework, child-rearing, domestic services outside the home, as well as jobs like coal mining and office work.

The song "9 to 5" by Dolly Parton appealed to Appalachia's frustration with labor exploitation, and as a result, achieved climbing success following its release in 1980.[55] The track was the first song since "Harper Valley P.T.A." to achieve the number one spot on the country and pop charts.[56] Parton wrote the song while on the set of the movie, 9 to 5, starring herself, Lily Tomlin, and Jane Fonda.[57] The song itself is an explicit complaint about how the workforce exploits their female employees' labor. It discusses office workers who go to work early each day just to be ignored and "put money in the boss man's pocket."[58] The song captures the office worker's alienation as she is used as a tool for someone else's profit, never receiving credit, promotions, or raises:

> Workin' 9 to 5, what a way to make a livin'
> Barely gettin' by, it's all takin' and no givin'
> They just use your mind and they never give you credit
> It's enough to drive you crazy if you let it
> 9 to 5, for service and devotion
> You would think that I would deserve a fat promotion
> Want to move ahead but the boss won't seem to let me
> I swear sometimes that man is out to get me!
> They let you dream just to watch 'em shatter
> You're just a step on the boss-man's ladder
> But you got dreams he'll never take away
> You're in the same boat with a lotta your friends
> Waitin' for the day your ship'll come in
> An' the tide's gonna turn and it's all gonna roll your way.

The song "9 to 5" is an anthem for the average American worker. Parton validated people's frustrations with the workplace while simultaneously cementing her status as a working-class idol. "9 to 5" inspired workers to demand change in their workplaces. Karen Nussbaum, who was a labor leader and activist, remembers her experiences as an office worker in the 1970s. She recalls, "it was the kind of job where you were just not seen ... You were just part of the wallpaper ... I remember sitting at my desk one day and a student came in—I worked at a university—and looked me dead in the eye and said, 'Isn't anybody here?' It was those kinds of things that just got under your skin a lot."[59] Nussbaum and a group of coworkers created an organization called "9 to 5" to support women in the workforce.[60] This organization shows that the song had a deep resonance with people in the workforce and turned into a rallying call for frustration with the workforce.

While "9 to 5" resonated with many workers nationwide, it also reflected a rich culture of women-led labor activism in Appalachia, which often appeared in music from the region. More "underground" songs like "The Rebel Girl" by Hazel Dickens appealed to a more specific audience than songs like "9 to 5." In "The Rebel Girl," Dickens spoke to working-class laborers in the Appalachian region and gave working-class women the attention they deserved in an empowering way. Dickens also sang about working-class women in comparison to what was the ideal picture of womanhood:

> There are women of many descriptions
> In this cruel world, as everyone knows.
> Some are living in beautiful mansions,
> And are wearing the finest of clothes.
> There's the blue blooded queen or the princess,
> Who have charms made of diamonds and pearls
> But the only and thoroughbred lady
> Is the Rebel Girl.[61]

In a society that expected women to be housewives in the private sphere, this message was incredibly empowering to the women who had to work in order to feed themselves and their families. Not only does Dickens say it is okay to be a part of the working class, but she also exclaims that it is an ideal experience of womanhood, a message not often heard in popular culture at the time.

Dickens continued her message of class solidarity in the next chorus and verse. She declared working women as the "strength of this world" due to their contributions to the labor force and dedication to their class. This was a very empowering message to women who felt underappreciated in the realm of labor:

> She's a Rebel Girl, a Rebel Girl!
> She's the working class, the strength of this world.
> From Maine to Georgia you'll see
> Her fighting for you and for me.
> Yes, she's there by your side with her courage and pride.
> She's unequaled anywhere.
> And, I'm proud to fight for freedom
> With a Rebel Girl.
> Though her hands may be hardened from labor
> And her dress may not be very fine
> But a heart in her bosom is beating
> That is true to her class and her kind.
> And the bosses know that they can't change her
> She'd die to defend the worker's world.

And the only and thoroughbred lady
Is the Rebel Girl.[62]

This song appreciates hard-working women in a way that was uncommon in popular media. The "rebel girl" in this song is beautiful and valuable for all of the things she is: a worker, a woman, and a rebel.

Historian Kelly Landers analyzed Dickens' life of activism and leadership for working-class people, especially working-class women. Landers writes, "she may never have sought a position of power, and would never admit to her own influence, but Hazel Dickens has proven herself to be a great leader."[63] Part of Dickens' appeal is that she was not a figure of authority and was unalienable to the working class because she herself was a member of that class and presented herself in that way. Landers writes, "she is an example of a leader who gained power through her actions and her character, rather than by virtue of a title. Her leadership depended on soft power, and others followed her of their own volition."[64]

Dickens provided hope and solidarity to working-class women using the folk genre. Landers writes:

> Art forms, like folk music, that revere tradition, tend to reinforce traditional roles and expectations in social settings as well as artistic settings. Musicians are expected to preserve conventions while living in a modem world and must struggle to reconcile maintaining tradition while incorporating progress. So, women involved in folk music are typically expected to adhere to certain gender norms as well.[65]

Dickens is a great example of a nuanced relationship with femininity that was present in Appalachia at the time. Women valued traditional ideas of womanhood while also maintaining a level of transgression against these ideals. Dickens wanted the public to value women's labor as equal to men's labor. These ideas are more common in some of her other songs like, "Mama's Hand."[66] Dickens represented the working-class Appalachian woman, one that embodied femininity, strength, and class advocacy.

Conclusion

Women in the Appalachian region faced all kinds of hardships, and many used music as a cathartic release of the tensions they faced from these challenges. Women used music to own their independence in a world where society expected them to be docile, submissive, and subservient. Listening to this music is empowering, even today. Whether it was to rebel against the restrictive social standards of presentation and behavior or to appeal to the commonalities of heartbreak that frequented broken and abusive relationships, these musicians used their music as an art of expression and resistance. They used their understanding of the world they occupied and wrote what they knew to be true.

Appalachian women cannot be painted with a broad stroke. Experiences among these women vary greatly depending on race, sexuality, career, and class. In writing this paper, I aim to speak on common experiences with understanding and compassion. Too often, women are labeled without any sophisticated reasoning; therefore, I hope that this essay instead adds depth to these women and their experiences.

To my loving Nana, who I am sure will be reading this: I hope this chapter speaks to you and makes you feel heard. I hope that you drive down Highway 220 in your Ford pickup truck with the windows down and feel the power of the songs you shared with me. Lastly, I hope this small gift to you compares to all the life lessons and understanding that you have given me.

Notes

1. Travis D. Stimeling, "Music, Place, and Identity in the Central Appalachian Mountaintop Removal Mining Debate," *American Music* 30, no. 1 (2012): 2.
2. Catherine Keron, "Establishing Female Resistance as Tradition in Country Music: Towards a More Refined Discourse" (electronic thesis, Western University, 2016), 132, https://ir.lib.uwo.ca/etd/3970.
3. Smithsonian Folkways Recordings, "Remembering Hazel Dickens | Smithsonian Folkways Magazine," accessed March 31, 2020.
4. Fred J. Hay, "Black Musicians in Appalachia: An Introduction to Affrilachian Music," *Black Music Research Journal* 23, no. 1 (2003): 7.
5. Wini Breines, "What's Love Got to Do with It? White Women, Black Women, and Feminism in the Movement Years," *Signs* 27, no. 4 (2002): 1095–1133.

6. "Freedom for Movement Girls—Now," Women's Liberation Movement Print Culture, Duke Digital Repository, accessed April 16, 2020, https://repository.duke.edu/dc/wlmpc/wlmms01027.

7. "Field Audio Tape of Viola Cleveland Discussing Women In the Mines," Appalshop Archive, accessed April 16, 2020, https://www.appalshoparchive.org/Detail/objects/8796

8. Jimmie N. Rogers, "Images of Women as Depicted in the Messages of Loretta Lynn," *Studies in Popular Culture* 5 (1982): 42-49, www.jstor.org/stable/45018089.

9. Jeannie C. Riley, vocalist, "Harper Valley P.T.A.," recorded 1968, track 1 of *Harper Valley P.T.A.*, Plantation Records.

10. Billboard, "Rewinding the Country Charts: In 1968, Jeannie C. Riley's 'Harper Valley P.T.A.' Didn't Skirt Social Issues," September 28, 2016.

11. Dolly Parton, vocalist, "Harper Valley P.T.A.," recorded 1969, track 5 of *In The Good Old Days (When Times Were Bad)*, RCA Records.

12. Nashville Now, "Jeannie C. Riley ~ Interview/'Return To Harper Valley'," YouTube video, January 24, 2016, https://www.youtube.com/watch?v=-gylPHxafsc.

13. *Harper Valley P.T.A.*, film directed by Richard Bennet (April Fools Productions, 1978).

14. *Harper Valley P.T.A.*, TV series directed by Sherwood Schwarts (NBC Studios, 1981).

15. Nashville Now, "Jeannie C. Riley."

16. Riley, "Harper Valley P.T.A."

17. Nashville Now, "Jeannie C. Riley."

18. Elizabeth Blair, "50 Years Of Sockin' It To The P.T.A.," accessed April 16, 2020, https://www.npr.org/2018/09/18/648848244/50-years-of-sockin-it-to-the-p-t-a.

19. Nashville Now, "Jeannie C. Riley."

20. Tanya Tucker, "I Believe The South Is Gonna Rise Again," recorded 1975, Track 7 of *Tanya Tucker/Super Hits*.

21. Tucker, "I Believe The South Is Gonna Rise Again."

22. Chris Willman, *Rednecks & Bluenecks: The Politics of Country Music* (New York: New Press, 2005), 179.

23. Willman, *Rednecks & Bluenecks*, 179.

24. Willman, *Rednecks & Bluenecks*, 179.

25. Billboard, "Tanya Tucker," accessed April 16, 2020, www.billboard.com/music/tanya-tucker/chart-history/CSI/song/364041.

26. Kitty Wells, "It Wasn't God Who Made Honky Tonk Angels," recorded 1952, single in *It Wasn't God Who Made Honky Tonk Angels*, Decca Records.

27. Mary Bufwack, "Kitty Wells: Don't Blame The 'Honky-Tonk'," NPR.org, accessed April 10, 2020.

28. Bufwack, "Kitty Wells."

29. Hank Thompson, "The Wild Side Of Life," recorded, 1952, single, *The Wild Side of Life*, Capitol Records.

30. Wells, "It Wasn't God Who Made Honky Tonk Angels."

31. Wells, "It Wasn't God Who Made Honky Tonk Angels."

32. Bufwack, "Kitty Wells."

33. Loretta Lynn quoted in Pecknold, Diane, and Kristine M. McCusker, *A Boy Named Sue: Gender and Country Music*. (Univ. Press of Mississippi, 2010), 48.

34. Loretta Lynn, "The Pill," recorded 1975, single, *The Pill*, MCA Records.

35. Case Western Reserve University, "History of Contraception- Oral Contraceptive Pill," accessed April 10, 2020, https://case.edu/affil/skuyhistcontraception/online-2012/pill.html.

36. Lynn, "The Pill."

37. PEOPLE.com, "Loretta Lynn's 'Pill' Is Hard for Some Fans to Swallow," accessed April 10, 2020.

38. PEOPLE.com, "Loretta Lynn's 'Pill.'"

39. PEOPLE.com, "Loretta Lynn's 'Pill.'"

40. PEOPLE.com, "Loretta Lynn's 'Pill.'"

41. PEOPLE.com, "Loretta Lynn's 'Pill.'"

42. American Masters, "Loretta Lynn's Feminism and Her Banned Song 'The Pill,'" March 2, 2016.

43. Patsy Cline, "Crazy," recorded 1975, track 7 of *Showcase*, Decca.

44. Linda Wertheimer, "Patsy Cline's 'Crazy' Changed The Sound Of Country Music," NPR, accessed April 11, 2020, https://www.npr.org/2000/09/04/1081575/crazy.

45. Wertheimer, "Patsy Cline's 'Crazy' Changed The Sound Of Country Music."

46. Wertheimer, "Patsy Cline's 'Crazy' Changed The Sound Of Country Music."

47. GRAMMY.com, "Gladys Knight Performs 'Midnight Train To Georgia,'" January 17, 2020.

48. Gladys Knight and The Pips, "Midnight Train To Georgia," recorded 1973, track 1 on *Imagination*, Buddah Records.

49. Lindsay Johnson, "Brooklyn College | 'I'll Be With Him on the Midnight Train to Georgia': The Traveling Woman in 1920s Blues and 1970s R&B," accessed April 11, 2020.

50. Marc Myers, "Anatomy of a Song: 'Midnight Train to Georgia,'" *Wall Street Journal*, August 8, 2013, Life and Style.

51. CBC Radio, "The Problem With This Song: Midnight Train to Georgia | CBC Radio," CBC, July 15, 2016.

52. Johnson, "Brooklyn College | 'I'll Be With Him on the Midnight Train to Georgia,'" 2020.

53. Gladys Knight and The Pips, "Midnight Train To Georgia."

54. Huber, "Red Necks and Red Bandanas: Appalachian Coal Miners and the Coloring of Union Identity, 1912-1936," 195–210.

55. Dolly Parton, "9 to 5," recorded November 3, 1980, track 1 on *9 to 5 and Odd Jobs*, RCA Records.

56. Gary Trust, "Dolly Parton Worked '9 to 5' to No. 1 on the Hot 100: Rewinding the Charts, 1981," Billboard, February 21, 2019.

57. Trust, "Dolly Parton Worked '9 to 5' to No. 1 on the Hot 100."

58. Parton, "9 to 5."

59. Lynn Neary, "A Cup Of Ambition And Endurance: '9 To 5' Unites Workers Across Decades," NPR.org, accessed April 14, 2020.

60. Neary, "A Cup Of Ambition And Endurance."

61. Hazel Dickens, vocalist, "The Rebel Girl," by Joe Hill, recorded 1990, track 14 on *Don't Mourn, Organize: Songs of Labor.*

62. Dickens, "The Rebel Girl."

63. Kelly Landers, "Freedom's Disciple: The Life, Music, and Impact of Hazel Dickens," n.d., 13.

64. Landers, "Freedom's Disciple," 13.

65. Landers, "Freedom's Disciple," 110.

66. Landers, "Freedom's Disciple," 116.

Notes on Contributors

Alicia Aucoin is a History major at Virginia Tech graduating in the spring of 2020. Alicia's areas of interest include twentieth-century history as well as European history and world politics. Inspiration for this project grew out of her interest in post-World War II American society. After graduation, Alicia plans to pursue a career in either national security or foreign relations.

Gillian Barth is a History and English double major at Virginia Tech with a minor in American Studies, graduating in the spring of 2021. Gillian contributes to the *Virginia Tech Undergraduate Historical Review* as a student editor and is also an ambassador for the College of Liberal Arts and Human Sciences. Her interests lie in the intersection of history and literature, which can be studied in her publication "The Wrath of Kern County: Banning The Grapes of Wrath in the Summer of 1939." Gillian is equally passionate about women's history and her chapter in this volume reflects her newfound interest in how northern and southern women dealt with the absence of their husbands, fathers, and brothers during the Civil War.

Grace Barth is a History and Political Science double major at Virginia Tech. Grace's favorite areas of study are vast, from the history of the Middle East to the history of rock 'n' roll. Inspiration for this project grew out of her interest in analyzing feminism in the media. Her interest in *The Mary Tyler Moore Show* and second-wave feminism is attributed to her mother, who loved watching *The Mary Tyler Moore Show* growing up.

Helen Hickman is a History and Political Science major at Virginia Tech graduating with the class of 2020. Her areas of interest include women's history, environmental history, and political communication. The inspiration for her chapter in this book came from a lecture from Dr. Kiechle's American Environmental History class as well as her mother, who like Lillian Gilbreth, managed to have both a family and a career. Helen hopes that her chapter inspires others to learn more about Gilbreth and her fascinating yet often overlooked life. Following graduation, Helen plans to earn a law degree and pursue a career as an attorney.

Savannah Lawhorne is a History major with a minor in Psychology at Virginia Tech. While Savannah agrees that all areas of history hold their own fascinations, she is particularly interested in modern warfare and German history. Savannah often analyzes research with a psychological approach, leading to her interest in World War II and a realization that although many people research the Holocaust, few talk about the important role women played in fighting the Nazis. Savannah plans to carry on her love of history by pursuing a career in public history.

Kat McGowan is a History major at Virginia Tech graduating with the class of 2020. Kat's areas of interest are fashion history, women's history, music history, and social and economic movements. The inspiration for her chapter in this book is attributed to the interesting and beautiful lives of the women in her life, specifically her family residing in the South. Kat plans to attend graduate school and become a teacher to pass on her love of history to the next generation of scholars.

Caroline McLean is a double major in History and International Studies with a minor in Spanish at Virginia Tech and will graduate in the spring of 2021. Caroline's area of interest is social history, as she is fascinated with studying history from the bottom up. However, this project grew out of her interest in the study of little-known historical events.

Marian Mollin is an Associate Professor of History at Virginia Tech. Her research explores the connections between gender, protest, activism, and culture, with a focus on the history of American social movements and the religious left. Dr. Mollin is the author of *Radical Pacifism in Modern America: Egalitarianism and Protest* (2006), a co-editor of *The Religious Left in Modern America: Doorkeepers of a Radical Faith* (2018), and the author of numerous journal articles and book chapters as well as her current book in progress, *The Power of Faith: Understanding the Life and Death of Sister Ita Ford*. An award-winning teacher, Dr. Mollin leads classes on US women's and gender history, sexuality in American history, the history of the 1960s, and various courses designed to help students develop skills in historical research, writing, and analysis.

Madison Sheehan is a double major in English and History at Virginia Tech graduating in the spring of 2020. Madison's research interests are literature and American history. Her chapter was inspired by her love of baseball, and her research led to her discovery of the women of the All-American Girls Professional Baseball League. Madison plans to pursue a master's degree in secondary English education at Virginia Tech.

Elizabeth Sholtis is a History and Professional and Technical Writing major at Virginia Tech, graduating in the spring of 2021. Elizabeth's areas of interest are women's history, as well as the history of alcohol, which both combine in her paper "Shaking Things Up: The Influence of Women on the American Cocktail." However, the inspiration for her chapter came from Elizabeth's favorite TV show, *The Marvelous Mrs. Maisel*. Elizabeth is excited to be pursuing a field study in editorial design in the fall of 2020.

Trenton Spilman is a double major in History and Creative Writing at Virginia Tech graduating in the spring of 2020. Trenton grew up with a fascination for creative writing and reading fiction. This project grew out of his interest in fiction, the history of popular culture, and women's history. Trenton will be pursuing a career in publication, specifically writing fiction.

Bethany Stewart is a History major at Virginia Tech with minors in Leadership and Social Change. Bethany serves as a student editor for the *Virginia Tech Undergraduate Historical Review* and as a recruitment ambassador for the College of Liberal Arts and Human Sciences. Her interest in her research stemmed from numerous family visits to Pigeon Forge and Gatlinburg, Tennessee: Dolly Parton's hometown. Bethany hopes to pursue a career in the public history field after graduating in 2021.

Alyssa Thompson is a History major at Virginia Tech graduating in the spring of 2020. Alyssa's areas of interest include African American history, civil rights, and criminal law. Alyssa will attend the University of Richmond's School of Law in the fall of 2020. Alyssa plans on becoming a criminal defense attorney that focuses on cases involving violations of civil rights, so that she can use her knowledge gained through her history degree.

Liv Wisnewski is a History and Theatre major at Virginia Tech graduating with the class of 2021. Liv's areas of interest are entertainment and fashion history, particularly that of theatrical costumes. Inspiration for this project stemmed from her interest in historical celebrity culture, especially in Alice Roosevelt's personal brand of misbehavior. Following the completion of her bachelor's degree, Liv intends to earn her master's degree and pursue a career in museum collections.

Olivia Wood is a double major in History and Classical Studies at Virginia Tech graduating with the class of 2021. Olivia's areas of study include Greek and Roman history as well as the Latin and Greek languages. This project spiked her newfound interest in women's history and Olivia was able to develop her chapter, "Seeing Eleanor: The First Lady of the World," based on this new passion. Olivia plans to purse a career in social science and foreign language education.

Photo Credits

Front cover photo:

Col. Sherrell, Supt. of Public Buildings and Grounds, has issued an order that bathing suits at the Washington bathing beach must not be over six inches above the knee. Photograph. Washington D.C, 1922. From Library of Congress Prints and Photographs Division. https://www.loc.gov/item/90708909/. (accessed June, 2020)

Back cover top photo:

14-yr, old striker, Fola La Follette, and Rose Livingston. Photograph. Bain News Service, 1913. From Library of Congress: Bain News Service Photograph Collection. https://lccn.loc.gov/2014692415 (accessed June, 2020)

Made in the USA
Middletown, DE
04 June 2021